COOPERATIVE CLASSROOM MANAGEMENT

Robert L. Williams
The University of Tennessee

Kamala Anandam
Bethune-Cookman College

Charles E. Merrill Publishing Company
A Bell & Howell Company
Columbus, Ohio

233082

Published by
Charles E. Merrill Publishing Company
A Bell & Howell Company
Columbus, Ohio 43216

International Standard Book Number: 0-675-08961-1

Library of Congress Catalog Card Number: 73-75329

2 3 4 5 6 7 8–78 77 76 75 74

Printed in the United States of America

Prologue

The publication of a new book dealing with classroom behavior modification may not, at first, appear to merit a full-scale celebration. Some small ripple of gratification, yes, but not unrestrained euphoria. Why not become ecstatic at the mere thought of a new book in classroom behavior management? An honest answer is that the market is now being flooded with such books. Although many of these books are excellent, educators appear to be becoming somewhat satiated with all this talk about behavior modification.

We have the urge to say that though our book also deals with classroom management, it is a totally unique document. Knowing that you would categorically reject such a preposterous claim, we will simply say that the book deals with some of the more important ethical, social, and academic considerations underlying classroom management. Our sensitivity to these issues has primarily evolved from interaction with students. On many occasions, our students have asked impertinent, embarrassing, and nasty questions about the acceptability and long-range utility of classroom management procedures. We have not found suitable answers for most of these questions in other behavior modification texts. Naturally, this text answers all of these questions. (Would you believe "a few"?)

Our book has a transcending theme—cooperation. Behavior modification has too frequently been viewed as a unidirectional process. The teacher controls the student, the counselor desensitizes the client, and the parent disciplines the child. We wish to interpret behavior management in a somewhat different light; that is, as an arrangement in which everyone, particularly the child, has an input into the behavior change process. Classroom management entails collaboration between the teacher, the principal, the counselor, the parent, and most especially the child. No one plays God. The person whose behavior is being modified, as well as those who are affected by his behavior, is always given the option of identifying changes he wishes to make in his behavior and the optimal means of achieving those changes.

Enough of this beating around the bush. Specifically, the book is divided into seven major chapters. Chapter I deals with ethical, philosophical, and pragmatic objections to classroom behavior management. We wager that this chapter will treat even those impossible questions you've been raising about behavior modification. Chapter II focuses on classroom contingency contracting, particularly as it is applied to groups of students at the junior and senior high school levels. Chapter

III provides a behavioral analysis of the sociological dimensions of classroom management. Emphasized are teacher sincerity, positive student affect, peer reinforcement, peer tutoring, and peer modeling. Chapter IV is for the student who is ridiculously serious about classroom behavior management. It describes major observational schemes and research designs used in the study of classroom behavior. Chapter V explains specific contributions that helping agents such as principals, counselors, and parents can make to the classroom environment. Chapter VI appraises the impact of operant procedures on study behavior, academic achievement, and creativity. Receiving special emphasis are individualized learning packages and performance contracting. Chapter VII is reserved for dreams and speculations. It explores the possibility of using classroom management procedures to improve the general state of society. Areas discussed are race relations, sexual stereotypes, drug abuse, population control, and international conflicts. Now how could you possibly close the book on issues as titillating and relevant as these?

We would like to acknowledge our professors at George Peabody College and The University of Tennessee, for launching us on the journey into the professional "unknown"; our families and friends here in the U.S. and in India, for allowing us to pursue our task of discovering the "unknown"; our students at The University of Tennessee and Maryville College, for causing us always to question what we claim to "know"; and the numerous students and teachers in the public schools of Tennessee, for helping us empirically expand the limits of our "knowledge."

RLW
KA

Contents

Chapter 1

DECLARATIONS OF CONSCIENCE

An Examination of Major Objections to Classroom Management

Questions of right and wrong are always with us. The areas of man's greatest scientific attainment—such as nuclear physics, neurology, and genetics—are full of complex ethical questions. The possibility of being able to control man's behavior through systematic environmental manipulation has also raised some excruciating ethical problems. In fact, the most serious objections to classroom management are clearly of an ethical nature. As Baer (1971) has recently pointed out, the principal question underlying behavior modification is not "Can we?" but "Should we?"

Why should behavior modifiers be concerned about the ethical and philosophical objections to classroom management? Why shed tears over the malicious attacks to which we are subjected? We still have much for which to be thankful. We present papers, publish articles, write books, consult with school systems, our kids still play with us, and our husbands and wives still love us. But in spite of the literally hundreds of research studies demonstrating the efficacy of behavior modification techniques, behavior modifiers have failed to make a grass-roots impact on public education in America. In some locales, we are hard-put to find a single teacher who can serve as an adequate role model for other teachers.

What accounts for this distressing state of affairs? Are teachers too intellectually obtuse to understand the methodology of behavior modification? Are behavior modifiers too inarticulate to explain operant

1

methods clearly? We believe the major breakdown has come on ethical and philosophical grounds. Unresolved ethical questions about behavior modification have prevented many teachers from using operant strategies in their classroom. What is even more demoralizing is that often ethical objections prevent teachers from even understanding the methodology of behavior modification. If we behavior modifiers expect to have a pervasive impact on American education, we must deal far more adequately with ethical and philosophical objections to classroom management.

We strongly suspect that *you* have some unanswered ethical questions about classroom behavior modification. You're not going to listen to all the positive things we have to tell you about classroom management until we deal with those objections. We shall attempt to respond to your objections clearly and candidly, although we don't pretend to be able to answer all such questions. While operant theory provides many useful techniques for changing student behavior, it is not education's Holy Grail.

Objections to classroom behavior management usually fall into five areas: (1) assumptions concerning the responsibility for human behavior; (2) emphasis on overt behavior as opposed to internal, phenomenological events; (3) techniques used in studying and modifying human behavior; (4) effects of operant procedures on children's attitudes and mental health; and (5) behavior modifiers as persons. Within each of these areas, we shall try to answer the specific questions that you might ask.

Who's Responsible for What We Are?

People have always been concerned about fixing responsibility for what happens to them. We like to give credit for success and assign blame for failure. As a rule, we are inclined to take the credit for our "good" behaviors and blame others for our "bad" behaviors. Skinner (1971) equates this proclivity for giving and taking credit with the concept of "human dignity." An analysis of who is ultimately responsible for human thoughts, feelings, and behavior is not an inconsequential undertaking. Our conclusions about final responsibility can fundamentally affect the way we treat people. In thinking about the issue before us, our minds (excuse the terminology) are immediately flooded with questions. Does the ultimate control of the individual lie outside the individual? Do we assume some measure of control over our own destinies or does personal control always elude us? Can we legitimately give a person credit for his good behavior or blame him for his bad behavior? In an academic setting, how much responsibility should students assume in defining the objectives and procedures of classroom behavior management? Who really determines how a student behaves in the classroom, the student or his teacher? We could continue asking these provocative questions, but you're probably getting anxious to hear some answers.

Isn't classroom behavior modification based on the premise that we can control people's behavior? Most proponents of behavior modification do believe that all behavior is caused and lawful. They attribute causation to both hereditary and environmental factors. These lines of causation obviously interact; i.e., hereditary endowment affects the way a person responds to a particular set of environmental stimuli. For example, a child with XYY chromosomes may respond much more aggressively to a given environment than a child with XY chromosomes. Behaviorists have generally assumed that the ultimate causes of human behavior are external to the individual. A person certainly doesn't determine his genetic endowment, his prenatal environment, or even his early postnatal environment. It has been suggested that at some point a child begins to *act upon* his environment instead of simply *reacting to* it. But what determines the way a person acts upon his environment? Is it not his genetic makeup, his previous environmental experiences, and the reward and punishment contingencies within his present environment? Does a person acting upon his environment ever transcend genetic and environmental causation? Behavior modifiers think not.

The assumption that behavior is determined by genetic and environmental variables does not necessarily imply that behavior modification is a unidirectional process. Behavior modification is actually a reciprocal process in which the individual both controls and is controlled. As a matter of fact, we seldom modify anyone's behavior without his modifying our behavior (see Figure 1). The way a person responds to our approval dictates whether we will continue to approve him or respond in some other way. In the classroom, teacher and students continuously alter each other's behavior. Several researchers have demonstrated that positive student behavior produces an increase in the rate of teacher approval (Berberich, 1971; Graubard, Rosenberg, and Miller, 1971; Klein, 1971; Sherman, 1971). This increase in teacher approval would undoubtedly serve to increase desirable student behaviors even more. According to Patterson and Reid (1970), we reinforce someone else to about the same extent he reinforces us.

Consequently, an increase in positive reinforcement from either teacher or students is likely to produce an increase in positive reinforcement from the other party.

"Boy, have I got this guy conditioned! Every time I press the bar
down he drops in a piece of food."

FIGURE 1

Another point of view never hurts

From *Jester* magazine. As adapted in *Learning,* Sarnoff A. Mednick, © 1964, Prentice-Hall, Inc.

Despite the omnipresence of control, we are frequently unaware of how we are controlling or being controlled. Processes such as the forming of friendships, falling in love, and developing tastes for certain foods may proceed without our being able to describe precisely why they are occurring. It might make you feel better to know that proponents of behavior modification are not exempt from some measure of ignorance about behavioral contingencies. Even the "wisest" of behavior modifiers doesn't know how to completely control the behavior of another person. He knows how to modify a multitude of human behaviors, but what he doesn't know about behavior modification is undoubtedly far greater than what he does know.

Do behavior modifiers actually claim that people don't make decisions? The concept of "making decisions" is fundamental to Western culture. We feel particularly human when we talk about freedom of choice and personal responsibility for our actions. Consequently, most behavior modifiers would have to admit that the concept of will is a very reinforcing concept. In the same breath, they would affirm that it is a reinforcing *fiction* which has no place in the scientific study of behavior. The will is a mentalistic construct that tells us nothing about relationships between behavior and environmental or genetic factors. There is simply no way to scientifically corroborate the presence of personal volition.

Though the concept of will appears to be a scientific liability, most human beings choose (whoops!) are conditioned to believe that they make decisions. We have even heard rumors to the effect that some behavior modifiers fantasize about decision making. Most people in the Western culture find believing in personal control more reinforcing than believing in external control. "Controlling" is a very reinforcing concept; "being controlled" is not quite so tantalizing. A major reason people are threatened by behavior modification is not that they object to using operant techniques in modifying others' behavior; instead they fear that these techniques will be used in modifying *their* behavior. If you're concerned about this, be comforted by the fact that a thorough study of behavior management principles decreases the probability that these techniques can surreptitiously be used against you. It is also quite possible to apply operant principles in the management of your own behavior. Procedures which have proven useful in self-management of behavior are changing setting events (e.g., altering the situation in which the inappropriate behavior is likely to occur), recording the target behavior, removing existing reinforcers for undesirable behaviors, making high priority activities contingent upon specified behavioral changes, and administering aversive stimulation following undesired behaviors (Duncan, 1969; Goldiamond, 1965).

In sum, a study of behavior modification can allow you to exercise a greater measure of control over your own life. It can allow you to maximize your reinforcing experiences and minimize aversive experiences. We are not saying that you will actually be making decisions, but it will certainly seem as if you are. Stated differently, your neurological processes will allow you to behave in ways which are to your benefit. Determinists would assume that the nature of these processes is very much a function of your genetic and environmental history. So ultimately the causes of your behavior would still be external. Sorry about that!

Has external determination of behavior been empirically proven? No, but don't get confused; we are not contradicting ourselves. Our discussion has focused on assumptions. We assume that ultimately all behavior is externally determined. We can empirically demonstrate a sequence of events, e.g., B follows A; we cannot empirically demonstrate that B is caused by A. Causation is an inference we make from empirical observations. You may answer that if external determination of human behavior is just an assumption, we have as much right to assume that man makes decisions as to assume that his behavior is determined by external phenomena; we can assume that man has something within him (e.g., will or volition) which allows him to transcend genetic and environmental variables. However, such an assumption would make it difficult to explain why we study human behavior scientifically. Scientific investigation is based on the premise that the phenomena under study are inherently orderly and measurable. The will doesn't quite meet these criteria. Each of us must decide if he believes that science is worthwhile, that is, if he believes that everything has order, or if he believes that some phenomena are inherently inexplicable.

Aren't we just as responsible for another's behavior when we manipulate that behavior environmentally as when we alter it biochemically? First, the possibility of modifying man's behavior via drugs, electrical stimulation of the brain, and destruction of neural tissue has been rather conclusively established (Krech, 1968; "Probing the brain," 1971). It may be possible to biochemically alter some of the most significant features about man, such as his ability to learn, his drive states, his emotional reactions, and his moral behaviors. Does environmental manipulation present the same kind of ethical concerns as biochemical intervention? Yes, but perhaps to a lesser degree. Whether behavior is changed environmentally or biochemically, the ultimate source of control is external to the person. Physiological psychology has demonstrated that environmental manipulation produces definite physiological changes within the organism (e.g., alteration in RNA structure, production of neurotransmitters, greater weight of cerebral cortex, and increased thickness of the cortex). What is the difference between inducing these physiological changes environmentally and inducing them biochemically? The major differences are in the extent, rate, certainty, and irreversibility of the change.

At present it appears that more extensive changes in man can be produced biochemically than environmentally. A few surgical incisions and/or the right kind of medication and we practically have a new person. The evidence is quite conclusive that some children's emotional reactions and academic performance can be dramatically altered through biochemical procedures. While changes in these areas may be achieved to some degree through environmental stimulation, the rate of change is usually much slower than through biochemical manipulation. The certainty of the change also seems greater with biochemical modification. Once the drug takes effect, the behavior automatically changes. In environmental manipulation, the child may become aware of the contingencies and refuse to cooperate. The child may also modify the environmental contingencies by his responses to them. Biochemical intervention is potentially more of a unidirectional process, in which we do something to alter the child's behavior without his doing very much to change our behavior. The possible irreversibility of a change is perhaps the most frightening aspect of any type of behavior control. There are few environmentally produced changes which cannot be reversed, but removal of neural tissue or the application of certain drugs may be a one way street.

There is currently a controversy in the professional literature concerning biochemical modification of children's classroom behavior. Stimulants such as amphetamines and methylphenidate (Ritalin) have been administered to hyperkinetic children, those who exhibit excessive random activity, have a short attention span, and/or are diagnosed as having minimal brain damage. Regrettably, most of the studies which have attempted to appraise the effectiveness of these stimulants have been poorly done, as shown in Sulzbacher's (1972) comprehensive review of the medication literature from 1937–1971. Of the 753 studies identified by Sulzbacher, less than 4 percent could be considered well controlled. A well controlled medication study is one which (1) employs placebos or double-blind procedures (neither the person who administers the drug nor the one who appraises the child's behavior knows which medication the child is receiving), and (2) utilizes direct measures of behavior (as opposed to subjective ratings by teachers, parents, and physicians). Approximately one-half of the adequately controlled studies produced significant results.

The major benefits of neurological stimulants appear to be increased ability to focus behavior, less disruptive activity, better peer relations, and improved self-esteem. Contrary to much popular opinion, these drugs do *not* make children lethargic, do *not* produce devastating side effects, and do *not* foster long-term drug dependency.[1] We see no ethical reason why medication should not be employed in instances where it produces definite improvement in behavior. However, medica-

---

[1] The entire November 1971 issue of the *Journal of Learning Disabilities* is devoted to a discussion of the use of medication with hyperkinetic children.

tion should not be used as a substitute for environmental control or as a tool for inducing acquiesence to educational mediocrities. As a general rule, drugs should be used only under the supervision of trained professionals and with the full consent of the child and his parents. Every attempt should be made to transfer the source of behavioral control from the medication to environmental contingencies.

If all human behavior is externally determined, can we hold anyone responsible for his own behavior? This is one of those nasty questions that is always asked. The usual implication is that if all behavior is ultimately determined by external factors, then no one is personally responsible for the way he behaves. That being the case, should we give a person credit for good behavior or condemn him for bad behavior? Behavior modifiers can accept praise and blame as techniques of modifying behavior but not as techniques of meting out moral justice. In other words, we might punish a criminal if that were effective in modifying his behavior or the behavior of others. We would not punish a criminal to make him pay his moral debt to society. Paradoxically, behavior modifiers sometimes employ moral or ethical concepts in modifying behavior. To illustrate, we might attempt to modify a person's behavior by appealing to his sense of ethical responsibility. Obviously, the use of external controls is inconsistent with the concept of personal responsibility.

It sounds as if behavior modifiers don't really believe that people are personally and ethically responsible for their behavior, yet in many instances act as if people are responsible. We must personally confess to being beset with certain ethical tendencies. We feel, for instance, that the way you treat people may have serious ethical ramifications. We believe that humanitarian behaviors are ethically right and that belligerent, abusive behaviors are ethically wrong. Yet we understand how we have been conditioned by family and society to hold these ethical views. We also readily admit that persons who are reared in other kinds of environments are likely to take actions and hold ethical views which are repugnant to our own. We are simply unable to reconcile some of our own conflicts about personal responsibility versus external determinism. Scientifically, we must contend that ultimately all behavior is externally determined. Personally, we find it much more reinforcing to believe that we have some measure of personal responsibility for our actions. We have simply been conditioned by our culture to hold views which are inconsistent with what we scientifically believe to be correct. We suspect that other behavior modifiers share our ambivalence on this point.

Who is actually responsible for a child's success or failure in the classroom? This question has agonizing implications. If a child behaves disruptively at school, makes little progress in his academic work, and in general fails to accomplish anything significant, who is to blame? It is deflating for the teacher to admit that *he* is responsible, that he erred in his objectives, his instructional activities, and his reinforcement procedures. It is more palatable to place the blame on the child and say that he is unmotivated, stupid, and mean. Yet if you seriously consider such factors as the child's home life, his community milieu, and his peer group, you can readily identify variables which have contributed to his behavior at school. So who is responsible, the child or his environment? If you lean toward the latter, then we must admit that the teacher is a part of that environment. Certainly the child's broken home, his ghetto surroundings, and his delinquent peers contribute greatly to his behavior at school. Nevertheless, we contend that the way you respond to him and to his classmates is the major determinant of his success or failure within the classroom.

To accept primary responsibility for your students' behavior is a sobering proposition. Yet acceptance of such responsibility may be fundamental to improving some students' behavior. As long as you blame the child or others for his failure, you may perceive little possibility of helping him. But once you admit that you may be contributing to his failure, you can legitimately ask, "What can *I* do to help him succeed?" This is where behavior modification comes in. By attending to appropriate behavior, by formulating clearly defined behavioral objectives, by altering instructional activities, and by initiating contingency contract procedures, you may be able to modify the behaviors of even the most disruptive students. We have frequently observed that a child who behaves very disruptively in one class may respond beautifully in another class. Obviously, there are variables within the two classroom environments which are producing very different behaviors. Most probably, one teacher is assuming responsibility for modifying the child's behavior and the other teacher is not.

Acceptance of responsibility for students' behavior means that you can also take some credit for their success. In fact, some students can succeed only if you exercise extreme care in the management of their learning environment. A study by Sidman and Stoddard (1966) demonstrates the dramatic changes that can occur in a person's behavior when his environment is carefully programmed. These researchers worked with a forty-year-old microcephalic idiot whose mental age was thought to be about eighteen months. Here was a person assumed to be incapable of learning much of anything. Yet by meticulous programming of his environment, the experimenters taught him to discriminate between geometric shapes at a level which would approximate our own ability to differentiate between these shapes. In addition, he was trained to use a pencil appropriately and to trace letters. His intellectual accomplishments during the year of the study exceeded all such accomplishments for the first forty years of his life. His behavior changed because somebody assumed the responsibility for changing it.

We do not mean to imply that acceptance of responsibility for students' behavior obligates you to produce a high level of achievement from each student. Most teachers have neither the time nor the skill to formulate the kinds of programs that some students need to achieve spectacular success. There may also be limitations imposed by genetic endowment and previous environmental experiences which no amount of programming could transcend. But you can teach students to emit appropriate social behaviors and you can help them improve their academic skills, even though no one can say how much improvement is possible.

Despite our very logical arguments, you may be unwilling to accept responsibility for the success or failure of your students. Your contention may be that students in your classroom are free to become whatever they will. If you make this assertion, you are deceiving yourself. In most learning environments the teacher makes decisions about what behaviors are to be learned, the goals, the classroom conduct, the grades, and the presentation of content. Do such decisions not affect student behaviors? The teacher inevitably modifies student behavior, either accidentally or deliberately. He may be oblivious to the effect a particular method of instruction has on the learner's behavior, but that does not negate the reality of that effect. All teachers modify student behavior even though they may deny it or be unaware of it.

Who should decide how children ought to behave in the classroom? If the teacher is primarily responsible for students' academic success, should he not also be the one who decides how children ought to behave in the classroom? We have traditionally behaved as if the teacher should decide. That being the case, a teacher armed with a repertoire of operant techniques would be an extremely powerful person. He would know how to get students to do essentially what he wanted them to do. Some contend that the teacher's training and experience makes him a better judge of what is appropriate for a child than the child could be for himself. The teacher is thus cast in the role of deciding what is desirable social conduct, what are relevant academic goals, and what should be done to achieve these objectives.

Others argue just as vociferously that no one can know as much about a student's needs as the student himself. Reasoning from this premise, you would assume that the child is in the best position to judge what would be beneficial to him.

We advocate a compromise between a teacher-dominated and a student-dominated classroom. The teacher and the students should pool information in order to formulate contingencies which are the most acceptable to all concerned. This approach, frequently referred to as *contingency contracting*, entails participation from both teacher and students in the identification of classroom objectives and defensible techniques for achieving those objectives. Contracts may be worked out on either an individual or group basis.[2] With this approach the teacher not only seeks input from students, but attempts to establish agreement as to how the classroom should be managed. No one's rights are abrogated. Teacher and students jointly decide upon objectives and the best procedures for reaching those objectives. The probable effect of student involvement in the determination of classroom contingencies is the enhancement of academic productivity (Alschuler, 1969; Lovitt and Curtiss, 1969).

Who has the responsibility of deciding whether systematic behavior modification techniques will be used in the classroom? It's obvious that the teacher typically makes the final judgment as to what techniques will be used in his classroom. But when behavior management specialists train a teacher to use reinforcement procedures, they certainly increase the likelihood that he will employ these procedures in his teaching. So indirectly the behavior mod experts are responsible for the application of operant strategies in the public schools. That's a responsibility that should not be taken lightly. Although one might assume that nothing but good could come from the use of reinforcement techniques, these methods can be used to induce conformity, to teach behaviors with adverse ethical connotations, and to teach academic trivia. Teachers are undoubtedly doing these things already; systematic behavior modification could simply make them more efficient in doing so (see Figure 2). The fact that a majority of teachers are quite illiterate in operant approaches may be to students' advantage. Unless teachers are committed to helping students reach objectives which are important to the students, it is unwise to train these teachers in the methodology of classroom management. However, assessing a teacher's commitment to this principle could be very

---

[2] An excellent delineation of different types of individual contracts is provided in C. L. Thompson and W. A. Poppen, *For Those Who Care: Ways of Relating to Youth.* Columbus, Ohio: Charles E. Merrill Publishing Co., 1972.

Ten forty-three.
In exactly TWO MIN-
UTES I'll ring the
FIRST BELL and
they'll all
stand still!

So I'll SCREAM at 'em
and take their NAMES
and give them FIVE
DETENTIONS AND
EXTRA HOMEWORK!
NEXT time they
won't move after the
first bell!

Because when they've
learned not to question
the FIRST BELL, they'll
learn not to question their
TEXTS! Their TEACHERS!
Their COURSES!
EXAMINATIONS!

All, that is, except your potential
DEVIATE! Your fledgling REBEL!
Your incipient BOAT ROCKER!
THEY'LL try to move all right!
THEY'LL have to learn the HARD
way not to move!

They'll grow up to accept
TAXES! HOUSING
DEVELOPMENTS!
INSURANCE! WAR!
MEN ON THE MOON!
LIQUOR! LAWS!
POLITICAL SPEECHES!
PARKING METERS!
TELEVISION!
FUNERALS!

Non-movement
after the
first bell
is the
backbone
of Western
Civilization!

FIGURE 2

And all this was accomplished without positive reinforcement subjective. We could ask him what his commitment is, administer a test which ostensibly measures his feelings about student involvement, or actually observe the extent to which he involves students in classroom planning.

Since we have more than enough teachers and prospective teachers who need training in operant methodology, where should behavior modification specialists focus their efforts? In the past, we have primarily worked with teachers who were faced with serious behavior problems in their classes. As a result, we have served a remedial or patchwork function in American education. We have also increased the chances of the conventional education system's surviving a bit longer. Perhaps what we should do is let the patient expire. If such a day should come, then we could start from scratch in building an educational environment full of positive reinforcement experiences. However, concern for teachers and students who need help now will prohibit our waiting for the day of deliverance. That being the case, why not invest most of our efforts in academic situations where we can effect long-term changes in instructional and administrative procedures?

Summary Statements

Let's see if we have in mind the major principles discussed in this first section. The issues discussed are such that they sometimes elicit the wildest of interpretations. So before you go out thinking that Williams and Anandam said such and such, let us take one last chance to clarify what we were attempting to say.

1. In the final analysis, all behavior is determined by external events, i.e., by hereditary and environmental variables.
2. Though human beings do not actually make decisions (i.e., transcend hereditary or environmental causation), they can use behavior modification procedures to maximize their rewards and minimize their punishments.
3. The proposition that all behavior is ultimately determined by external events is an assumption, not an empirical fact.
4. One has every right to assume that human beings have volition, though this assumption seems to be inconsistent with the scientific study of behavior.
5. One is controlling behavior no less through environmental manipulation than through biochemical intervention. However, behavior change may be more rapid, extensive, and permanent in the case of physiological manipulation.
6. From a scientific viewpoint, we cannot hold anyone morally re-

sponsible for his own behavior. From a personal viewpoint we do hold people ethically accountable for their behavior.

7. The teacher should accept a great measure of responsibility for a child's success or failure in the classroom. In so doing, the teacher may be able to help a child whom he would otherwise assume to be stupid and incorrigible.
8. Students and teacher should cooperatively determine classroom objectives and procedures for reaching those objectives.
9. Unless teachers are committed to student involvement, we question the propriety of training them in classroom behavior management.

What Shall We Study: Behavior, Thoughts, or Feelings?

Although most behavior modifiers subscribe to both determinism and behaviorism, the two viewpoints are not inseparable. Freud, for example, was very much a determinist but not a behaviorist. The focus of his study was largely upon conscious and unconscious psychic phenomena. He used the patient's behavior (mainly verbal responses) simply to reconstruct the person's internal world. Behavior modifiers, on the other hand, usually stop with a study of the subject's behavior. Their insistence upon analyzing behavior rather than internal, mentalistic events has incurred the wrath of many educators and psychologists, particularly those who are phenomenologists. A primary contention of phenomenologists is that human experience can best be understood from an internal frame of reference. Behaviorists are accused of ignoring the most important subject matter of human existence—thoughts and feelings. As a consequence, we are said to present a one-sided, superficial view of man. An even more serious indictment is that refusal to deal with internal phenomena is tantamount to ignoring the major determinants of human behavior. In other words, one must know something of what's happening inside a person to be able to understand why that person behaves as he does.

Since you may already be familiar with the statements of leading phenomenologists on man's internal experiences, it is more important that we focus now on the behavior modifier's perceptions of man's inner world. In looking inward, we (the authors) do not propose to speak for the entire behaviorist camp. In fact, some of our declarations will probably be viewed by other behavior modifiers as blasphemous, heretical, and treasonable. This section tells what *we* believe about the experiences which occur within a person. We've been given no mandate to speak in behalf of any international association of behavior modifiers.

Doesn't behavior modification theory deny the existence of feelings? No! From our own personal experiences, we are sure that even behavior modifiers have feelings. We experience anger, sadness, loneliness, anxiety, joy, love, all the feelings that other people experience. Behavior modifiers have even been known to speak openly of the existence and importance of feelings. Yet, their scientific study still focuses on behavior rather than internal events, because they feel that only when things are stated behaviorally can they be assessed objectively.

Assessing the effectiveness of your teaching will undoubtedly be of paramount concern to you. A teacher may aspire to create in his students such lofty attitudes as a love for truth, an appreciation of art, a respect for democracy, and even a positive outlook on life. But how could he determine if these objectives had been attained? Defining what you want from students via constructs that refer exclusively to affective and cognitive processes precludes the possibility of assessment. You can assess whether a student is able to identify five outstanding paintings, enumerate three criteria for judging the quality of a painting, and has attended any recent art exhibits. You cannot directly measure whether he possesses an internal appreciation of art.

Some people feel that even though we cannot look inside a person to determine the nature of his thoughts and feelings, we can identify behaviors which are highly correlated with these internal processes. Unfortunately, we can never be sure how closely behaviors correspond to internal phenomena. We have a pretty good idea as to how accurately our own behavior represents our thoughts and feelings, but we cannot make the same judgments about others. Despite this limitation, it may still be worthwhile to make some educated guesses about what is happening inside the person. For example, we feel that it is far better to try to get some idea about a person's perception of self-worth via behavioral measures (e.g., test scores, behavior in groups) than to ignore this variable completely. We are sympathetic toward attempts to provide behavioral correlates of dimensions such as self-esteem, self-control, anxiety level, and creative thinking. These internal phenomena are important in and of themselves.

Is it important to study the etiology of feelings and thoughts? Since feelings and thoughts cannot be measured directly, it is difficult to determine empirically how they develop. But feelings and thoughts are genuinely important, and it is vital that we attempt to find out how they evolve. External rewards and punishments seem to be powerful contributors to feelings and attitudes. Most everyone feels euphoric when he receives approval from a significant other or distraught when he is chastised by someone important to him. Most of us approve ourselves for the kinds of behavior for which we receive approval from others. To illustrate, in a class in which we had trained the teacher to approve appropriate behavior openly, a student named Michael White finished taking his turn reading orally to the class. When the teacher did not immediately issue approval for Mike's contribution, as she had frequently done in the preceding weeks, he said aloud to himself, "Michael White, that's really good reading." Most of us engage in such self-approval, though perhaps a bit more subtly and covertly than Mike.

While it is often assumed that changes in behavior follow changes in self-esteem, the sequence of events may be just the opposite. Sopina (1971) has shown that adolescents' self-concepts improve in areas where their behaviors improve. Wahler and Pollio (1968) found that modifying a child's deviant behavior via social approval led to improvement in the child's self-perceptions. It follows, therefore, that the logical way to improve self-esteem is to arrange contingencies for improving behavior. Deibert and Harmon (1970) give a classic demonstration of what we're saying. A small group of male students in an undergraduate psychology course adopted as their class project the changing of the personality of a shy, reticent, wallflowerish girl. They began by taking her out on dates and being very attentive to her. Though the prospect of dating her was not awe-inspiring, they made sure that her weekends were booked solid for several weeks in succession. Little happened on the initial dates; she said little and did little. But after a few dates, she began to dress and wear her hair more provocatively. She also began to talk and laugh and loosen up in some rather reinforcing ways. By the end of the course her behavior had changed so profoundly that these students kept right on dating her. What really changed about this girl? Her overt behavior certainly changed, but we bet some pretty important self-perceptions also changed. Before you get too upset about the tactics used by these students, let us say that the purpose of this example is not to show methodology, but to point out that self-esteem may change as a result of changes in behavior.

We believe that many internal perceptions other than self-esteem can be altered by external contingencies. Our phenomenological perception of others is one such dimension. Cormier (1970) has shown that students who are the recipients of considerable teacher approval come to describe their teachers in a more positive way. Sherman (1971) found that when students behave more appropriately, teachers also describe them in more positive terms. Our attitude toward another person may largely be a function of the amount and type of reinforcement we have received from that person. Other internal phenomena such as divergent or creative thinking may also be affected by a person's reinforcement history. (Chapter VI will discuss this possibility in depth.) Even self-control is not entirely independent of external control. People generally select norms from some reference group. The so-called inner-directed person may really be quite dependent on the actual or fantasized approval of a few individuals. In conclusion, (1) it is important to investigate the etiology of internal phenomena, and (2) there is no better way to account for these phenomena than through examining the person's reward and punishment history.

Does refusal to deal directly with internal phenomena mean that we are disregarding a major source of behavioral causes? This is almost the question of whether an S–R or S–O–R model generates the more complete explanation of human behavior (S = stimulus; O = organism; and R = response). No one denies that stimuli cannot produce responses without first being assimilated by the organism. Remove the contributions of afferent, central, and efferent nerve fibers and you have neither perception nor behavior. Actually, the most immediate causes of a behavior are the electrochemical messages that are transmitted from the central nervous system to the muscles and glands. Physiological psychologists contend that there cannot be a comprehensive explanation of human behavior until we are able to describe in minuscule fashion how the nervous system mediates perception and behavior.

Before you accuse us of being hopelessly confused, permit us to clarify a couple of points. We are not equating phenomenology and neurology. The two approaches are similar only in that they investigate events that ostensibly occur within the skin. They are different in that neurologists study actual physiological events (internal behaviors, if you wish), whereas phenomenologists study internal processes (such as feeling and thinking) which cannot be subjected to direct measurement or observation. We know about phenomenological processes only through our perceptions of what is occurring within us and what other people say is occurring within them. While you can philosophize about phenomenological processes to your heart's content, we have not yet developed scientifically respectable methods for studying these processes. In contrast, neurological events may be studied with considerable scientific precision.

We want to reaffirm that we are not opposed to studying events that occur within the individual. We do oppose using internal phenomena which cannot be measured or verified through public observation as explanations for human behavior. We may subjectively believe that a certain kind of feeling produces a particular kind of behavior. For example, when people feel depressed, they may talk less. If we conjecture that Johnny is not talking because he feels depressed, have we explained his behavior? Or must we identify those X, Y, Z events which have caused him to be depressed and, in turn, to not talk? If we find that certain kinds of teacher comments (e.g., ridicule, sarcasm) are followed by reduced talking, do we embellish our explanation of Johnny's behavior by affirming that the teacher's comments caused him to become depressed? As long as we can systematically relate Johnny's behavior to things which are happening in his environment, we do not need to refer to feelings and thoughts as explanations for that behavior. We can simply say that Johnny is not talking because his teacher ridicules him and is sarcastic when he talks.

Summary Statements

You could legitimately conclude that we believe the following about the study of thoughts, feelings, and behavior. Illegitimately you could formulate somewhat more colorful possibilities.

1. Many behaviorists (including us) do not deny the existence of feelings and thoughts.
2. Internal phenomena such as feelings and thoughts are important in their own right.
3. Since feelings and thoughts cannot be studied directly, it is permissable to use self-report, personality tests, and overt behavior to get some idea about what is happening inside a student.
4. Inasmuch as thoughts and feelings cannot be measured or verified through public observation, they should not be used as scientific explanations for behavior.

How Shall We Approach the Study and Modification of Human Behavior?

Even though a person may accept deterministic and behavioristic positions, he must still deal with the acceptability of specific procedures for studying and modifying human behavior. Many people accept the premise that environmental factors profoundly affect man's behavior but object to some of the procedures used by behavior modifiers in studying and manipulating those factors. In other words, a specific research or behavior management strategy may be considered unethical, whereas another may be viewed as completely acceptable. Our

objective at this point is to deal with specific research and methodological strategies which are most frequently questioned on ethical
grounds.

Don't operant researchers treat people like lower animals? Terms such
as "respondent conditioning," "operant conditioning," "extinction,"
"partial reinforcement," and "stimulus generalization," which are frequently used by behaviorists in explaining human behavior, probably
sound very reminiscent of the animal studies which you encounter in
introductory psychology. We must confess that many of the basic
principles of behavior modification were derived from experimentation
with laboratory animals. Psychologists often use animals in experimentation because of the degree to which they can control the animals'
environment and thus precisely identify the factors responsible for
changes in the animals' behavior. Animal experimentation has allowed
psychologists to delineate simple conditioning procedures which could
then be tested in more complex environments. Most of the respondent
and operant principles which have emerged from the laboratory have
since been corroborated with humans in applied settings. Variables
such as reinforcement schedule, delay of reinforcement, and amount
of reinforcement affect human behavior in much the same way as they
affect animal behavior. Therefore, disciples of behavior modification do
believe that many environmental changes affect the behavior of men
and animals in a somewhat similar fashion.

This discussion should not be construed as meaning that behavior
modifiers make no distinction between human and animal behavior.
Man's behavior is much more complex in nature than that of animals.
Language is perhaps the behavior which most dramatically sets man
apart from lower animals. Because of language, we are able to describe
environmental contingencies to human subjects and markedly short-cut
the process of behavior change. Behavior modifiers would also agree
that man's nervous system is considerably more complex (primarily in
the cortical areas) than that of other animals. Because of the complexity of the nervous system, man is capable of manifesting many
behaviors which animals could never be trained to do. For example,
though some animals have demonstrated an ability to deal conceptually
with their environment, humans are undoubtedly capable of much
higher levels of conceptual reasoning than are animals. We must hasten
to point out that animals also exhibit certain behaviors that probably
could not be produced in man. The superiority of man's behavior is
usually established in his own environment. While a monkey's behavior
might seem rather nonfunctional in downtown New York, we might

appear equally inept in the monkey's natural habitat. (On second thought, maybe a monkey *could* do about as well as the rest of us in downtown New York.)

Is anything really accomplished by conducting short-term behavior management studies? Behavior modifiers have achieved quite a reputation for producing quick and notable changes in human behavior. The literature is full of studies in which long-standing behavioral problems were brought under control in a matter of days. Non-believers quite legitimately question the permanency of these "cures." Why is it that most behavior modification studies do not deal with the long-term effects of operant procedures? The reinforcement contingencies acting upon researchers may partially account for the brevity of these studies. Frequently the researcher is under pressure to get his work into print as quickly as possible. In this respect, a one-month study has some obvious advantages over a twelve-month study. A second, and perhaps more important, contingency is the pressure of producing positive results. If a two weeks' application of a treatment condition has produced dramatic improvement in behavior, why risk an attenuated treatment effect by extending the study over a twelve-month period? In our own research, we have seen beautiful initial changes in behavior begin to dissipate after several weeks of treatment application. Many studies might have similar results if the researchers were to extend their treatments over a period of several months.

For practical as well as ethical reasons, we believe the time is past due to conduct long-range behavior management studies. It is doubtful that we can solve the world's problems with treatment conditions whose long-term effectiveness has not been unequivocally established. Short-term studies are fine to get some initial ideas about the potency of treatments. But once the effectiveness of an operant strategy has been confirmed in several short-term studies, we desperately need to determine what the impact of that treatment would be over a period of several months or years.

What happens to teacher and student behavior after a behavior modification study has been completed? Like the previous question, this one is concerned with the long-range effects of behavior modification. The question now is what happens to the teacher and students once the experimenter formally terminates his research study. Does the teacher continue using the operant procedure specified in the study or does he revert to his old way of doing things? If the teacher reverts to old procedures, do the students also revert to their baseline behaviors?

Since few studies have done this kind of follow-up, we can do little more than speculate about the nature of post-treatment behaviors.

In our own research, we have found that slightly less than 50 percent of the teachers who assist us in studies continue using the treatment procedures once the research is finished. Teachers may stop using the experimental procedures for a number of reasons: (1) the major external source of reinforcement for utilizing the procedures is removed once the experimenter leaves; (2) reinforcement contingencies within the school (i.e., what the principal and other teachers approve) may discourage continuation of treatment procedures; (3) the application of the experimental procedures during the study may have required so many special arrangements (e.g., observers in the room, extensive record keeping, feedback sessions with the experimenter) that the treatment conditions acquire aversive connotations; (4) the teacher may have ethical objections to the treatment procedures; (5) without assistance from the experimenter, the teacher may begin to misapply the treatment and, consequently, get poor results; or (6) the teacher may simply be unwilling to expend the effort the treatment conditions require. As we will note in Chapter V, principals and counselors have the potential for eliminating most of these local barriers to classroom behavior management.

The second part of the question relates to the long-term impact of operant procedures on student behavior. If the improvement in social or academic behavior disappears twenty-four hours after a study is completed, we might wonder about the propriety of applying the procedures in the first place. Again, there is a paucity of research data dealing with this point. An investigation by Hewett, Taylor, and Artuso (1969) indicated that students actually exhibited a higher level of task attention after a token economy system had been terminated than while the system was in effect. O'Leary and Becker (1967) have also provided follow-up data indicating that gains in appropriate behavior under a token system may carry over to the following school year when the token system is no longer in effect. The most extended follow-up to date is a study conducted by Nedelman and Sulzbacher (1972). They charted the progress of an initially autistic child over a ten-year period. Extensive use of shaping and reinforcement procedures allowed the child to eventually enter a regular classroom situation and function at grade level in most subject areas, even after the initial shaping and reinforcement program ended.

The question of permanence of behavioral change is obviously an important one. The challenge to behavior modifiers is not only to assess the long-term effectiveness of operant methodology but to isolate those factors which will contribute to the permanency of appropriate behaviors. Some of these factors have tentatively been suggested by O'Leary and Drabman (1971) in a very fine review of classroom token reinforcement programs. Their major point is that we should use our specialized treatments to produce behaviors which would naturally elicit other types of reinforcement (e.g., social approval, better grades) once the experimental procedures have been withdrawn.

Is it defensible to modify a child's behavior without his being aware of what you're doing to modify that behavior? In animal research, we seldom concern ourselves with whether the subjects are aware of the reward and punishment contingencies. Many psychologists have dealt with humans in a similar manner, i.e., they have not been concerned with whether the subjects knew what was being done to change their behaviors. Several researchers have shown that it is possible to alter certain behaviors without the individual's being told or being able to verbalize the contingencies used in modifying those responses (Hirsch, 1957; Philbrick and Postman, 1955; Sassenrath, 1962). But in a great many instances, individuals become aware of these contingencies. What happens then? The conditioning process would probably be accelerated if the subject considered the payoff for emitting the behavior a highly reinforcing consequence. However, if he were resistant to the idea of being manipulated, knowledge of contingencies might impede the conditioning process.

The major ethical concern underlying awareness of contingencies is that an individual cannot exercise control over his own behaviors if he is unaware of what is being done to modify those behaviors. We see no reason to be surreptitious in the application of behavior management procedures in the classroom. The teacher can be quite candid in indicating that he is going to reward students for appropriate behaviors and minimize attention to their inappropriate behaviors. Numerous researchers have shown that instructions regarding reinforcement contingencies significantly enhance acquisition of responses (Finkler, 1971; Herman and Tramontana, 1971; Kanfer and Marston, 1962; Spence, 1966). It is our conviction that teachers should spend considerable time helping children to become aware of the contingencies controlling their own behavior and to identify modes of behavior which would produce more positively reinforcing consequences.

Is it right to award credits for nonacademic behaviors? If you're at all familiar with the types of contingency contracts being used in public education, you know that credit is sometimes awarded for such behaviors as bringing paper and pencil to class, having appropriate materials, and refraining from disruptive behavior. This credit (usually in the form of points and tokens) may affect the child's grade, his access to free-time activities, and his tangible payoffs. Is it defensible to base these rewards on anything other than the child's academic achievement?

It is less than startling to note that certain social behaviors affect academic achievement. Whether a child brings paper, pencil, and appropriate books to class and whether he behaves disruptively in class may decisively affect his academic progress. The best way to be sure that these social behaviors are in order is to deal with them directly, i.e., provide immediate reinforcement for them. This reinforcement is usually accomplished by awarding tokens which can later be cashed in for back-up reinforcers such as tangibles, free time, and grades. The beauty of this arrangement is that you indirectly facilitate academic achievement by directly reinforcing appropriate social behaviors.

Above and beyond the obvious relationship between social and academic behaviors, what is objectionable about officially rewarding desirable social responses? We have historically given students passing grades for "trying" and have not been averse to promoting students to keep them with their chronological age groups. Specifying credit for particular social behaviors simply provides an objective means of affirming that a child is trying. Wouldn't most teachers assume that the child who always brings paper, pencil, and appropriate books to class, who always turns in assignments, and who refrains from disruptive behavior is trying hard? If so, what is ethically reprehensible about rewarding him for his efforts? (However, in situations where students are already achievement-oriented, it would be unnecessary and perhaps even offensive to reward them for nonacademic behaviors).

Isn't the giving of tangible rewards equivalent to bribing children? Bribery is the provision of a tangible payoff for *inappropriate, dishonest,* or *illegal* behavior. The objective of bribery is to corrupt the recipient. Learning to read, to solve math problems, to write, and to speak another language can hardly be considered dishonest, illegal, or corrupt accomplishments. Receiving a tangible reward for honest academic performance is no more a bribe than receiving a salary for an honest day's work.

The contingent use of tangible rewards has proven to be a powerful technique for increasing academic performance, particularly among children from impoverished economic backgrounds. Many of these children have few, if any, educational materials in their homes and have encountered frequent failure at school. Consequently, these

students may come to your classroom completely turned off to traditional educational procedures. Employment of tangible rewards for
appropriate academic behavior is a significant way of developing
academic skills when such rewards as grades, teacher praise, and
acquisition of ideas do not prove to be very reinforcing. Once an academic skill such as reading begins to be developed, it is likely that the
payoff from the skill itself will assume greater prominence. It is more
probable that a child will experience the inherent benefits of reading
if he is taught to read proficiently via tangible rewards than if he fails
to learn to read because of the impotence of traditional academic
procedures.

Though tangible payoffs are probably the most universally reinforcing consequences that we can employ in the classroom, they can be
used atrociously. One teacher reported that her use of candy just
wasn't improving the behavior of her students. Upon observation of
her classroom operations, the consultant discovered that she never
offered candy until the children started being disruptive—at which
time she would promise them candy if they would be good. By promis-
ing candy only when children behaved inappropriately she was inadvertently reinforcing bad behavior. When children have to behave
badly to produce the promise of a tangible payoff, they are essentially
being bribed.

*Are behavior modifiers opposed to the use of punishment in the class-
room?* A classic study by Skinner (1938) was interpreted by many
psychologists as demonstrating that aversive stimulation has only a
temporary suppressive effect on behavior. What the study actually
demonstrated was that a mild form of punishment given under certain
circumstances only temporarily reduces a behavior. Since then many
psychologists have felt that a reinforcement–extinction combination
would be a much more effective and permanent means of producing
behavioral change than would punishment. In attempting to weaken
inappropriate responses, behavior modifiers have reinforced behaviors
which are incompatible with the inappropriate responses, withheld
reinforcement for the inappropriate behaviors (extinction), removed
the child from the situation in which his inappropriate behaviors were
being reinforced (time out), and subtracted reinforcement privileges
whenever inappropriate behaviors were emitted (response cost). In
dealing with undesirable behaviors, they have made very little use of
punishing techniques such as striking a child or verbally chastizing
him. Although several studies (Birnbrauer, 1968; Lovaas, Schaeffer,
and Simmons, 1965; Lovaas and Simmons, 1969; Risley, 1968) have
shown shock to be effective in reducing disruptive behaviors of

severely disturbed and retarded youngsters, the utility of physical punishment in regular classroom settings has not yet been demonstrated. Behavior modifiers are also quick to point out that adverse side effects (e.g., counter-aggression, social withdrawal, and anxiety reactions) may occur when aversive stimuli are used to reduce a behavior. We must admit, though, that in these cited shock studies no bad side effects were reported.

We suspect that the antipathy of behavior modifiers toward physical and verbal punishment is a function of more than the 1938 Skinner study or the possible adverse side effects of punishment. Many proponents of behavior modification are personally repulsed by the use of punishment. In their opposition to punishment, behavior modifiers are subscribing to a concept of freedom that most of us cherish—that is, freedom from coercive or aversive control. It is paradoxical that especially since Skinner's recent book *Beyond Freedom and Dignity* (1971), behavior modifiers have been viewed as opponents of freedom. Just another of those sad cases where gracious, honest, and mature people are unfairly maligned by unthinking critics.

Isn't it wrong to penalize the whole group because of the behavior of one child? Though behavior modifiers have a pronounced antipathy toward corporal punishment and social ridicule, they are not above removing reward privileges for inappropriate behavior. In fact, some utilize an arrangement (group contingent reinforcement) under which each child stands to gain or lose from the behavior of other children. Under group contingent reinforcement, child X might be performing extremely well but still miss out on the group reward because of child Y's goofing off. Although group contingent rewards can be used very effectively in the classroom (see Chapter II, p. 63), they can also be used very unethically. We believe that it would be indefensible to put all rewards on a group contingent basis. Rewards such as grades, teacher approval, and special privileges should be primarily contingent on each individual's behavior. Secondly, group contingencies should not be used in conjunction with established privileges, e.g., going to the restroom, going to lunch, taking previously specified recess time. While it is probably inappropriate to withhold these privileges under any circumstances, most especially they should not be withheld from one child because of the behavior of another child. Group contingent reinforcement should not jeopardize any standard privilege; instead, it should relate entirely to new prerogatives.

Now that we have pointed out the limitations of group contingent reinforcement, let us briefly discuss its virtues. Some of the most potent reward activities are designed for groups, for instance, playing group games, informal socializing within the group. Since these group activities usually entail lots of movement and talking, it would be difficult for some students to continue studying while others were engaging in the group activities. Hence, you would probably want your class to participate in these activities on an all-or-none basis. It follows that the class as a whole should participate in the activities only if everyone in the class has earned the right to participate.

This arrangement does not solve the problem of students' losing reward privileges because of the behavior of other students. Group contingent reward makes every child's behavior vitally important to the group, but this is similar to many other common activities. If the quarterback fumbles the ball on the one-yard line, the whole team suffers. Many work situations demand that everyone execute his responsibility correctly. One person's ineptitude can impair the productivity of the whole group. Social situations can be jeopardized by the awkward behavior of one individual. As the world becomes more populous, our interdependencies will undoubtedly increase. Group contingent rewards can help children to assume the responsibility of working for the benefit of the group as well as for his own benefit.

Group contingent rewards are often attacked on the basis of how they affect interpersonal relationships within the group. In particular, punitive peer pressure is often brought to bear upon the offending student. Several researchers (Schmidt and Ulrich, 1969; Wilson, 1971; Wilson, 1972) have anecdotally reported cases of nasty facial expressions, threatening gestures, and abusive language toward the nonproductive or disruptive student. Wilson (1972) noted that one child initially appeared to be unaffected by the teacher's group contingencies. However, during a later implementation of the treatment his behavior abruptly improved. A behind-the-scenes investigation revealed that some of the child's classmates had conducted a little T-group session with him out on the playground. They had essentially told him that unless he shaped up in the classroom they were going to beat the . . . . out of him. We do not consider peer pressure against the offending student necessarily to be bad. It would, of course, be very undesirable for the teacher to set group standards which were beyond the attainment of some students. This would most probably occur when the contingencies relate to academic achievement rather than social behavior. It would make the offending child the object of group scorn and would leave him without recourse for changing his status.

There is also a type of intragroup effect that emerges from group contingent reinforcement which is unquestionably positive. Group contingencies sometimes produce a special type of camaraderie which is evidenced in group members' helping one another. For example,

Bronfenbrenner's (1970) study of Russian classrooms and Hamblin, Hathaway, and Wodarski's (1971) study of inner-city children have indicated that under group contingencies the more precocious students may assume the role of tutors for the slower students. (More about that in Chapter III.)

Don't behavior modifiers favor a mechanized, impersonal, and dehumanizing classroom environment? Advocates of behavior modification have often endorsed the use of automated instruction in the academic milieu. In fact, programmed instruction represents one of the major contributions of operant conditioning theory to public education. We personally like the idea of using the computer to design instructional programs for individual students, to take each student through programs step-by-step, to provide lots of success feedback to the student, and to answer questions posed by the student. Subject matter which is basically factual in nature can potentially be taught more efficiently by a machine than by a person.

Our affinity for educational technology does not blind us to the realization that certain skills can be developed only through human interaction. Machines can teach principles of behavior but the application of these principles in solving man's social problems awaits the human touch. We must also depend upon man for the development of new principles. A machine can teach us what is known, but we need man to extend what is known.

We do not envision an academic environment in which a child spends the entire day with a teaching machine or computer. Since there is some indication that extended exposure to CAI (computer-assisted instruction) can lead to a decrement in social skills (Sears and Feldman, 1968), we recommend that considerable time be reserved for interpersonal experiences. Such occasions would allow you to use role modeling and social reinforcement to teach appropriate social behaviors. We believe that utilizing machines to teach basic facts could actually give the teacher and students more time to devote to the development of practical and humanitarian skills.

Summary Statements

In this section we have attempted to appraise the acceptability of specific strategies used in the study and modification of human behavior.

1. Although behavior modifiers believe that the basic principles of operant conditioning which have been derived from laboratory research with animals can be applied to man, they readily admit

that man's behavior is considerably more complex than that of lower animals.

2. Even though operant procedures have proven highly effective in producing quick and dramatic changes in behavior, their long-term effectiveness has not been securely established, because most behavior modification studies are of short duration and fail to examine what happens to teachers and students after the studies are terminated.

3. In modifying a child's behavior, you should inform him of the contingencies or let him participate in the formulation of the contingencies.

4. It is appropriate to award credit for nonacademic behaviors whenever the absence of these behaviors is clearly interfering with academic progress.

5. Since academic achievement would not be considered corrupt, dishonest, or illegal, behavior modifiers do not consider tangible rewards for academic achievement to be bribes.

6. In dealing with inappropriate behaviors, behavior modifiers prefer nonreinforcement procedures such as extinction, time out, and response cost to the use of punishment.

7. Group contingent rewards are ethically defensible if they relate to new privileges and do not impose standards which are beyond the attainment of some students.

8. While behavior modifiers favor the use of machines to transmit knowledge, they recognize that human interaction is important in the extension of knowledge and application of knowledge to social problems.

How Does Behavior Modification Affect Children?

As a consequence of your moving to a different locale, your child is about to enroll in a new school. Being a concerned parent, you are naturally quite anxious to know something about the educational program of that school. The first thing you learn is that the school makes extensive use of behavior modification procedures. You now envision an atmosphere of contingent social approval, success experiences, contingency contracts, tangible payoffs, and free-time activities. How would you feel about your child's attending that school? Slightly uneasy? You would undoubtably have little anxiety about the school's ability to increase appropriate behavior. However, you might be afraid that the immediate changes in your child's behavior would be accomplished at the expense of his future emotional well-being. You might be worried that undesirable attitudes toward himself and others would evolve from his experiences in an operantly controlled environment.

If you should learn that some of the child's teachers would be using positive reinforcement techniques while others would not, what kinds of concerns would you have? A major consideration would probably be the child's immediate emotional health. Wouldn't a school environment which is half positive reinforcement and half something else precipitate confusion and conflict in a child? Because of this possibility, some educators contend that the individual teacher should make no attempt to reinforce appropriate behavior systematically. There's no way we can accept that conclusion.

Can children get so much positive reinforcement at school that it's difficult for them to adjust to the world outside the classroom? The likelihood of a child's experiencing a completely positive atmosphere at school is about .000001. But if the child should primarily experience positive reinforcement (e.g., success, approval, free time) at school, would that make it more difficult for him to tolerate all the aversive experiences that occur in the world outside the classroom? Asked another way, do children learn to tolerate painful stimuli in the extra-school environment by being subjected to aversive stimuli in the classroom environment? Perhaps some degree of habituation to aversive stimuli does occur. Because of the failure and disapproval experienced in the classroom, the student may tolerate such disappointments a bit more easily in the world outside the classroom.

In spite of the possibility of habituation, we feel there is more to be lost than gained by using aversive stimuli in the classroom. The child who is most likely to experience positive reinforcement outside the classroom is the child who has experienced positive reinforcement in the classroom. If positive reinforcement is the most effective procedure to use in teaching academic skills and building self-respect, it should also maximize the child's likelihood of success outside the classroom. We are assuming that academic skills and positive self-regard will increase the amount of approval and success that a child will eventually experience outside of school. And it is hard for us to see how being beaten, ridiculed, and failed at school would increase his chances of success outside the formal academic environment.

Won't the long-range effects of tangible reinforcement be to make children dependent upon material rewards? As we have unequivocally noted, tangible rewards for appropriate behavior need not be construed as bribes. Nonetheless, some people fear that extensive use of tangibles in school would create materialistic dependencies. Eventually a child would do his assignments, tell the truth, and act decently only if he were tangibly rewarded. Meichenbaum, Bowers, and Ross (1968) found that, following a period of tangible reinforcement for certain appropriate behaviors, institutionalized girls refused to emit other appropriate behaviors until promised a tangible payoff. Deci (1972) found that college students decreased their affinity for a specified activity following tangible reinforcement for engaging in that activity. In contrast, the students (particularly the males) were more inclined to work on the activity following verbal reinforcement. These studies certainly suggest the possibility of dependency upon tangibles.

Some of the most perplexing problems of our society are a function of our emphasis on material rewards. It is distressing when people are willing to work hard and treat their fellow man decently only when tangible benefits are involved. So we must make a concerted attempt not to perpetuate or perhaps even accentuate this material emphasis through our systems of reward in school. Common sense dictates that we not use tangibles when other kinds of rewards, e.g., knowledge of success, social approval, and free-time activities, would be highly reinforcing. If we have to use tangibles to develop certain skills, we must make provisions for systematically transferring control of these behaviors to other types of reinforcers. Gradually switching to partial schedules of tangible reinforcement, pairing other potential reinforcers (e.g., approval, knowledge of success) with tangible payoffs, and developing academic skills which will generate other kinds of reinforcement should facilitate this transfer. Studies by Hewett, Taylor, and Artuso (1969), O'Leary and Becker (1967), and Prince (1967) indicate that such transfer is attainable.

Won't reinforcing one child in the class be perceived as favoritism by the other children? Teachers are rightfully concerned about the amount of time they spend exclusively with one child. Many operant studies deal with the behavior of a single child and entail a vast expenditure of time for record keeping and administering treatment procedures. When reading such a study, the teacher naturally wonders how other students would react if he attempted to utilize the suggested procedure with only *one* child. We must admit that any behavior modification strategy which provides lots of reinforcement for one child while minimizing reinforcement for other children will legitimately be construed as favoritism.

Luckily, the basic principles of reinforcement which work with one student also work with other students. Contingent attention to appropriate behavior, for example, has been demonstrated to be effective with a wide range of children. That being the case, the teacher need not approve one child to the exclusion of other children. We favor a classroom atmosphere in which the teacher intermittently approves each child for behaving appropriately. With this kind of arrangement, each child's behaviors can be positively affected by direct teacher approval and by his seeing other children approved for appropriate behaviors. Another technique which can be applied to the class as a whole is contingency contracting. An effective contract provides a number of different options to students. Students under the same contractual arrangement might be pursuing very different activities. Nevertheless, each student has essentially the same rights and privileges as any other student. Since most of the operant procedures which will be discussed in this book can be applied to the class as a whole, they need not create problems of favoritism.

Let's assume that Roger is a highly disruptive child in your class and that modifying his behavior does require spending appreciably more time with him, at least for a while, than with most other children. The building of new behaviors often requires continuous reinforcement and successive approximations, both of which make heavy demands upon the teacher's time. Keep in mind that if this student is highly disruptive, you are probably already spending an excessive amount of time with him. Exhortations, threats, and public floggings take time too, you know. How many times a day do you have to say, "Roger, turn around," "this is the tenth time I've asked you to be quiet," "get back to work," "leave Suzie's dress alone," "if I have to ask you one more time . . ."? So which is more palatable, to spend a great deal of time positively reinforcing Roger or a great deal of time chastising him? A child who is disruptive not only monopolizes your time, but the time of other students. Therefore, reducing his disruptive behavior means that other children can devote more time to their lesson activities. However you look at it, other children stand to gain by your using sufficient positive reinforcement to reduce the disruptive behavior of this student. Otherwise, admonitions and threats continue to make heavy demands on your time and probably cause the disruptive behavior to get worse.

Won't it be confusing to children to be reinforced in one class and not in another? Be assured that children are reinforced for some type of behavior in all classes, yet what they are reinforced for and how they are reinforced can be quite different from class to class. In one class, students receive attention for lesson-related activities whereas in another they receive attention for disruptive behaviors. In one class, students are reinforced via positive payoffs and in another by reducing negative consequences. So the question you really want to ask is what happens when the contingencies and types of reinforcement differ from class to class.

We have found the behavior of students to be quite situation-specific; that is, when the contingencies of reinforcement change, the behavior also changes (Kuypers, Becker, and O'Leary, 1968; Meichenbaum, Bowers, and Ross, 1968; O'Leary et al., 1969). If the payoff in classroom A is for lesson-related behavior and the payoff in B for disruptive behavior, we could expect the child to do his lessons in A and behave disruptively in B. However, situation-specific behavior does not necessarily remain situation-isolated. A student who is reinforced in room A for appropriate behavior may generalize that reaction to room B. As a result, teacher B may begin responding more positively to the student. Such approval would then serve to strengthen appropriate behavior in situation B. So behavior changes in one situation may precipitate chain reactions which eventually affect behavior in many situations.

Probably the best way of increasing generalization across situations is to upgrade a child's academic skills. If a child's reading skills are upgraded in classroom A, it is likely that his academic productivity would increase in classroom B. With the improvement in academic performance should come an increase in teacher approval and other positive benefits. This kind of generalizing across situations has been clearly substantiated by Walker, Mattson, and Buckley (1969). However, despite the possibility of situational generalization, behavior which is *not* eventually reinforced in a particular situation will not persist in that situation.

You may be wondering if it would really be to a student's advantage to receive a high rate of positive reinforcement in your class only to be castigated in the next class. If the student is going to be chided in the next class, it is all the more imperative that he receives lots of positive reinforcement in your class. School is not such that teachers consistently approve students for the same kinds of behavior. But if appropriate behaviors are important, then positive reinforcement must be available for these behaviors in at least some classroom situations. Furthermore, a highly reinforcing experience in your class may allow the child to psychologically tune out a highly aversive experience in the next class.

Will modifying one behavior exhibited by a child have any effect on his other behaviors? Does decreasing one inappropriate behavior indirectly weaken other inappropriate behaviors? Does strengthening one appropriate response produce increments in other appropriate responses? What we're talking about is the concept of response class (or response generalization), i.e., a set of behaviors that covary. According to this concept, all the behaviors in a response class would be affected by the manipulation of any one behavior in the group. If a teacher could modify several behaviors in different response classes, he might indirectly alter a wide range of student responses without specifically focusing on all those responses. Also, some responses like stuttering could be very difficult to treat directly but modifiable by changing other behaviors in the same response class (Wahler et al., 1970).

Several research studies have confirmed the reality of the response class phenomenon. In their work with retarded children, Lovaas and Simmons (1969) indicated that whining, avoiding adults, and self-destructive behaviors seemed to be members of a single response class. Sajwaj and his associates (Sajwaj et al., 1970) reduced a preschool retarded child's excessive talking to his teacher by having the teacher ignore that behavior. The decline in the target behavior was accompanied by changes in five other nonmanipulated responses, including talking to other children and engaging in cooperative play. Buell et al. (1968) have also demonstrated that nonmanipulated behaviors (including verbalization, cooperative play, and baby-talk) can be altered by treating one target behavior.

Although these studies indicate that the response class paradigm is applicable to the behavior of young children, we have little direct evidence of its applicability at older age levels. In fact, practically no research has been done on this issue at the junior high level or beyond. The evidence from young children, however, indicates that generalization across behaviors is usually positive. You can rest easy.

Are behavior modification techniques as effective with high school and college age students as with elementary students? The implication of this question is that students may eventually outgrow behavior modification. Although the literature includes many accounts of behavior modification at the preschool and primary age levels, relatively few studies have been conducted with high school and college age students. One of the major techniques used with young children is contingent social attention. We wonder if adolescents would be equally amenable to teacher attention and approval. We could identify only one study in which the effectiveness of teacher approval with adolescents was directly contrasted with its effectiveness at the elementary level. This not-too-recent study by Hurlock (1924) demonstrated that approval was slightly more effective with older children (eighth graders) and reproof with younger children (third graders) in raising intelligence test scores. We could at least conclude from Hurlock's study that approval appears to have considerable potential with older students.

Several current studies substantiate the effectiveness of teacher approval with older students. When the findings of these studies are compared with the results of investigations using preschool and primary age children, it seems that teacher approval is equally effective across age levels. One study (McAllister et al., 1969) assessed the effects of teacher approval and disapproval on the talking out and turning around behaviors of low track eleventh and twelfth grade English students. The approval was directed toward the class as a whole and always specified what was being approved (i.e., not talking out, not turning around). Disapproval was directed toward specific students and specific behaviors (talking out, turning around). The combination of approval and disapproval was highly effective in reducing the target behaviors. Another study (Cormier, 1970) found that contingent teacher praise and attention was much more effective than baseline conditions in controlling the classroom behaviors of disadvantaged adolescents. Noncontingent approval was also more effective than baseline conditions, though not as effective as contingent approval.

Another procedure that has been widely used with young children is tangible reinforcement (primarily candy and trinkets). Rewards of this type have also been extensively used with adolescents in institutionalized and specialized settings (Clark, Lachowicz, and Wolf, 1968; Meichenbaum, Bowers, and Ross, 1968; Schwitzebel and Kolb, 1964; Staats and Butterfield, 1965; Staats et al., 1967). Application in regular secondary classroom settings has been limited. Glynn (1970) used a series of prizes related to the history and geography content being studied to reinforce the academic achievement of ninth grade girls. The students performed significantly better under a self-determined reward system and an experimenter-determined system than under a chance-determined system and no reward system. At the college level, Siegel, Lenske, and Broen (1969) employed monetary payoffs to reduce speech disfluences (repetition of words or interjection of unwarranted sounds between words) of college students with no unusual speech problems.

A type of behavior management system that has probably been used more extensively with adolescents than with elementary age children is contingency contracting. Typically, in contingency contracting privileges and grades are used to reward appropriate student behaviors. MacDonald, Gallimore, and MacDonald (1970) employed privileges controlled by parents, relatives, peers, and pool hall proprietors to get chronic junior high age nonattenders back in school on a regular basis.

Several of our own research studies have assessed the effectiveness of contingency contracting on the classroom behavior of junior and senior high school students (Anandam and Williams, 1971; Arwood, Long, and Williams, 1972; Sapp, 1971; Williams and Anandam, 1972; Williams, Long, and Yoakley, 1972). Contracting has consistently been effective in helping adolescents attain higher rates of study, appropriate social behaviors, and better grades.

Contingency management has also been used successfully at the college and graduate level (Johnston and Pennypacker, 1971; Keller, 1968; Lloyd and Knutzen, 1969; Lloyd, 1971; Malott, 1968; McMichael and Corey, 1969; Myers, 1970). In most of these programs, students earn points for a variety of activities, and grades are then based on the number of points earned. In appraising the use of contingency management with college and graduate students, we have concluded that the following factors contribute most to the success of such a system: (1) Grading standards (i.e., number of points necessary for a particular grade) are specified at the beginning of the course. (2) Number of points that a student can earn for engaging in a particular activity is specified at the beginning of the term. (3) Students are provided enough activities from which to choose that they can eliminate 25 to 50 percent of them without jeopardizing their chances for an A. Students are also allowed to suggest activities not on the instructor's list, in which case the instructor individually negotiates with the student as to the acceptability of the activity and the amount of credit to be earned for that activity. (4) Students are awarded direct credit for everything the instructor deems vital in the course. For example, the instructor doesn't assume that students will read course materials just for their personal edification. Instead, students are granted credit for preparing written or oral reviews on the designated materials. (5) Deadlines are established as to when activities can be engaged in for credit. Our advice is to clear the books every term. We believe in the concept of self-pacing but we try to arrange setting events and reinforcement contingencies so that any student can complete the course during the term. (6) If a comprehensive exam is used in the course, it is administered at least three times during the quarter or semester—at the beginning, near the middle, and at the end. The beginning exam gives the student some idea of his baseline knowledge in the course and indicates specific directions for study. The midterm exam tells the student how well he is doing before it's too late to correct deficiencies. The final exam serves as an index of how far the student has advanced during the term. We recommend using the same exam or equivalent forms so the student can make direct comparisons between his initial, mid, and final examination scores. (7) Students are given the option of operating under an arrangement other than a point system. The idea of earning points is repugnant to the personal ethics of some students. These students will probably do much better and take more kindly to your course if they are granted the prerogative of suggesting an alternative means of evaluation. As will be seen in the next chapter, many of the ideas just suggested can also be applied with a high degree of success at the junior high and secondary levels.

In summary, we have to admit that the number of behavior modification studies conducted at the high school and college level is considerably smaller than the number at the elementary level. Nevertheless, those which have been conducted with high school and college age students have consistently demonstrated that such procedures as teacher approval, tangible payoffs, and contingency contracting can be highly effective with older students.[3]

Are behavior modification techniques as effective with advantaged students as with disadvantaged? Students used in many behavior management studies are from economically disadvantaged backgrounds. Several studies suggest that tangible payoffs may be more effective with these students than with the advantaged (Douvan, 1956; Terrell, Durkin, and Wiesley, 1959). Conversely, other research indicates that teacher approval may be more reinforcing to advantaged students than to disadvantaged (Zigler, 1962). We readily admit that setting events (in this case instructional activities) and reinforcement procedures may need to be quite different for advantaged and disadvantaged students. However, this does not mean that one group is more amenable to behavior modification than the other.

The only procedure that we (the authors) have systematically compared in advantaged and disadvantaged settings is contingency contracting. We have appraised its effectiveness in severely disadvantaged inner-city settings, suburban middle-class schools, and upper-class private schools. Three major findings have come from these studies: (1) baseline levels of appropriate behavior are much lower for disadvantaged students than for advantaged—25 percent in inner-city settings, 60 percent in suburban middle-class schools, and 70 percent in private schools; (2) the increment in appropriate behavior produced by contracting is much greater in disadvantaged than advantaged settings —50 percent in inner-city schools, 25 percent in suburban schools, and 10 to 15 percent in private schools; (3) the level of appropriate behavior under contracting is fairly similar in the three settings—75

---

[3] Several applications of operant procedures with adolescents are described in J. D. Long and R. L. Williams (eds.), *Classroom Management with Adolescents.* New York: MSS Educational Publishing Company, Inc., 1973.

percent in the inner city, 80 to 85 percent in suburbia, and 80 to 85 percent in private schools.

Thus the conventional operant procedures (e.g., contingent teacher approval, tangible payoffs, and contingency contracts) have a more dramatic impact on the classroom behaviors of disadvantaged students than those of advantaged. If the baseline level of appropriate behavior is already about 70 percent, one obviously has less room for improvement than if the baseline is 25 percent. However, even with students who are already behaving appropriately and achieving at a high level, there is something to be gained by applying behavior modification techniques.

Summary Statements

By now you've learned that just when we seem to be on the brink of utter confusion, we come forth with our summary statements. We dare not think what life would be like without a few summary statements now and then.

1. Experiencing a high degree of positive reinforcement at school should make it easier for the child to adjust to the world outside of school, because positive reinforcement leads to increases in self-esteem and achievement, which in turn enhance the child's ability to cope with the external world.
2. Unless some attempt is made to transfer behavioral control from tangible reinforcement to social reinforcement and knowledge of progress, students may become dependent on tangibles. This transfer can be effected by shifting to intermittent schedules of tangible reinforcement and by pairing social and knowledge-of-progress stimuli with tangible payoffs.
3. Positive reinforcement procedures should be applied to all the students in a class. Otherwise, some students may perceive the teacher as exhibiting favoritism.
4. Children's behavior seems largely to be situation-specific; i.e., they behave in line with local contingencies. If appropriate behavior is being reinforced in one class but ignored in another, students will behave accordingly.
5. Some behaviors seem to be interrelated (response class). Modifying one behavior in a response class will indirectly lead to changes in other behaviors.
6. Conventional operant procedures, for instance, teacher approval, knowledge of progress, tangible payoffs, and contingency contracting, appear to be as effective with high school and college age students as with elementary.

7. The behavior of advantaged students can be altered through behavior modification procedures. Because of initially high baselines
of appropriate behavior, the degree of improvement will not be as
substantial as with disadvantaged students.

What Are Behavior Modifiers Really Like?

It is hard to divorce your attitude toward a philosophy from your
personal contact with those who espouse that philosophy. Resistance
to behavior modification may be more a function of direct interaction
with self-proclaimed behavior modifiers than of an extensive analysis
of behavior modification theory, research, and practice. If behavior
modifiers overlook that fact, they are pretty myopic. If they were perceived as warm, sincere, and tolerant individuals, there is little doubt
that their philosophy would receive a fairer hearing. We are distressed
that educational programs designed to develop specialists in behavior
modification often focus almost exclusively on teaching the methodology rather than producing individuals whose personal qualities are
such that people will listen to what they have to say.

Are behavior modifiers mechanical, superficial people? The fact that
behavior modifiers deliberately and systematically approve certain
kinds of behavior while withholding approval for other types is interpreted by some as meaning they are superficial people. Behavior that
is deliberate instead of spontaneous is viewed as mechanical and
artificial. We will quickly admit that a systematic application of reinforcement principles will not allow you to be totally spontaneous in
your reactions to students. There may be times when you want to shout
at them but will refrain because you know that shouting would only
compound the problem. To be an effective behavior modifier, you will
have to discipline yourself to look for appropriate behaviors and attend
to those behaviors when they occur. You may even have to think about
specific ways of attending to such behaviors.

It is probably true that most of us would like to operate completely
spontaneously, yet we fear that total spontaneity would frequently lead
to catastrophic results. How many of us are secure enough to let
everyone know exactly how we feel toward them, right on the spot?
Be honest with yourself—what would be the consequences of making
your thoughts and feelings known completely spontaneously? We
are implying that you already exercise a great deal of deliberate,
conscious control over your behavior. If your objective is to help
people learn more appropriate modes of behavior, what is wrong with

consciously attempting to respond to them in a fashion that would help them behave more appropriately? To make you feel better about the issue of spontaneity, we have personally found that after a person disciplines himself to emit the right behaviors he can later emit those behaviors rather spontaneously. We mean that he no longer has to ask himself, "Now, how should I respond to that behavior?" He automatically comes forth with an appropriate response. Spontaneity in a behavior seems to develop primarily from that behavior's being consistently reinforced. Approval comments, for example, usually result in considerable reinforcement for the approver. Over time, such reinforcement may cause approval to be issued quite automatically.

The issue of sincerity is probably far more critical than that of spontaneity. Some have gotten the idea that behavior modifiers go around artificially praising people. We are all turned off by back slapping, buttering up, brown nosing, and white mouthing. From both a practical and ethical perspective we believe that sincerity is useful. Artificial praise is not only ethically unacceptable to us; we feel that it also catches up with you in a practical sense. That is, people discover that you are insincere, and your praise becomes aversive. It is, of course, possible that a person can be quite sincere in his approval and yet be construed as being insincere. For that reason, we will give extensive attention to cues that people use in judging the sincerity of another's approval in a later section of the book.

Behavior modification does not entail the fabrication of approval in order to accomplish behavioral change. It does entail looking for appropriate behaviors and giving people credit for manifesting those behaviors. Behavior modification philosophically emphasizes the efficacy of recognizing what is good about people.

Why are behavior modifiers so incorrigibly arrogant? Proponents of behavior modification have never been known for their humility. We somehow leave the impression that we believe our viewpoint is the only defensible way of looking at human beings. Lines such as "If you like truth, you'll love behaviorism," "Omnipotence teamed with humility," or, in lay terminology, "We're right but we're humble," succinctly convey the spirit of behavior modification (*Behaviorally Speaking,* June, 1971, p. 10).

Why do people think behaviorists are so intolerably arrogant? For one reason, behaviorists are intolerant of imprecise terminology, i.e., they define their concepts in observable, measurable terms and are quick to attack others for not doing the same. Secondly, behavior modifiers speak with unrestrained confidence about the efficacy of their methodology. This confidence is a function of the multitudinous studies which have demonstrated the potency of operant procedures and of their own experiences in applying operant procedures in the classroom. Precise language and workable methods are unfortunately not sufficient to convert the world to behavior modification. It's enough to make you cry!

Behavior modification specialists need to examine much more critically how they train teachers to use operant procedures. We should be bright enough to recognize that we must work with teachers in essentially the same manner we expect them to work with children. If we are intolerant and aversive with teachers, it is likely they will be intolerant and aversive with children. To illustrate, in a meeting with a group of administrators, one robust-looking principal declared early in the session that he was supremely committed to using reinforcement procedures in the classroom. However, he went on to describe the difficulties he had had in getting one of his teachers to use these reinforcement approaches. In spite of his efforts to train the teacher, the teacher had continued to bring behavior problems to him. The principal proceeded to relate to the group how he had finally laid down the law to this teacher and told him either to shape up or else. After recounting his experiences with the teacher, almost in the next breath, he leaned back in his chair and said, "I'll tell you, I really believe in this positive approach." He apparently saw no inconsistency between the way he was dealing with this teacher and the way he was asking the teacher to deal with his students.

Behavior modification specialists should give serious attention to their own reinforcement value when working with teachers. If we become personally aversive to teachers, they won't buy our methodology. And if we become personally reinforcing to them, they will be much more inclined to try the methods we recommend. One essentially becomes reinforcing by using reinforcement. Our approval is perhaps the most reinforcing payoff that we have to offer teachers. To use lots of approval sincerely with some teachers means that we must be willing to start at a very rudimentary level and shape their behaviors toward a higher level of teaching proficiency. In other words, we must begin by reinforcing behaviors that only remotely resemble desirable teaching procedures. We must also be willing to deal with whatever problems teachers perceive as most important. We have found that teachers are initially inclined to identify problems which may seem rather superficial to us. Yet if we ignore these problems, we convey disrespect for their opinions and also leave the impression that we are not going to be useful resource persons. So if the teacher identifies Sally's twiddling her thumbs as his major problem, we must first deal with thumb twiddling.

Teachers are also inclined to describe their problems in nonbehavioral terminology. They talk about attitudes, motivation, and feelings. It is, of course, easy to put them down on this point, but this would probably be done at the expense of making ourselves aversive to them. Why not recognize the legitimacy of their concerns and try to help them behaviorize their ideas of a "bad attitude," "low motivation," etc.? The sky is not going to fall if we exercise a little tolerance toward nonbehavioral descriptions of classroom events.

Many teachers have serious ethical reservations about classroom behavior management procedures. These reservations are often treated rather flippantly by behavior modification specialists. We often imply that questions of ethics are not really worth discussing. How many times have you heard behavior modifiers emphatically pronounce ethical objections to be dead issues? It is a mistake not to recognize the legitimacy of ethical reservations and deal with them as thoroughly and honestly as we can. We will have much more to say later on about procedures for training teachers in operant methodology, but suffice it now to say that we are often viewed as arrogant and dogmatic because we don't practice what we preach.

Do behaviorists and phenomenologists really behave differently? Behaviorists and phenomenologists have historically stood in opposition to each other. Yet, our earlier discussion of feelings and our emphasis on sincerity may have sounded quite phenomenological to you. Heaven help us, but it seems that the chasm between behaviorists and phenomenologists is lessening. Though behaviorists may be somewhat more systematic in approving what they consider to be desirable behavior, we have found individuals from both schools of thought to be quite humane and positive in their treatment of people. It would certainly be unfair to say that one group behaves in a more humanistic fashion than the other.

You would perhaps note some differences in the classroom operations of a behaviorist and a phenomenologist. We suspect the behaviorist would provide more structure than the phenomenologist. The behaviorist would be more likely to have established behavioral objectives for his students and to be using some type of formally delineated reward and penalty system, such as contingency contracting. The behaviorist would also use many external payoffs, whereas the phenomenologist would likely emphasize intrinsic rewards.

Summary Statements

It may be rather difficult to formulate valid conclusions about ourselves, but we shall make every attempt to be objective.

1. Behavior modifiers are charming, intelligent, and inspiring individuals. (Disregard this conclusion; it was just a slip of the pen.)
2. Although behavior modifiers attempt to respond to behavior in a systematic fashion, this is not to say they respond mechanically and artificially. Most behavior modifiers are concerned about the sincerity of approval and exhibit their approval in what seems to be a spontaneous fashion.
3. Because of the many research studies confirming the efficacy of operant procedures, behavior modifiers are very confident about their methodology. This confidence is often perceived by others as arrogance.
4. Behavior modifiers and phenomenologists both can be humane people. They differ primarily in their proclivity for structure and external rewards.

Finis

After our exhaustive discussion of the ethical and philosophical dimensions of classroom management, we might hope that your ethical reservations would have entirely disappeared. However, since that's not the case even with us, we doubt if it is with you. A more realistic hope is that you have a clearer perception of what the ethical issues are and some of the pros and cons associated with those issues. May we address ourselves to one final question.

What does behavior modification prove about the ultimate nature of man? Nothing. It demonstrates that a great deal of behavior can be modified by careful manipulation of environmental contingencies. It does not ultimately prove whether man has volition or is solely responsive to genetic and environmental variables. It does not prove whether man is or is not personally responsible for his own behavior. It does not prove whether man is exclusively a material being or has a spiritual dimension. It does not prove whether man is a product of chance or of some divine intelligence. These are very important questions for which behavior modification presently has no answers.

Chapter II

GETTING IT ALL TOGETHER
The Role of Contingency Contracting in Classroom Management

One of the first and foremost tasks in teaching is getting organized. We have seen teachers produce an extremely high level of appropriate behavior in the classroom simply by virtue of good organization; that is, providing a logical sequence of activities and proceeding from one activity to the next with minimal delay between activities. On the other hand, we have seen teachers fail miserably in their attempts to control student behavior primarily because of poor organization. Now at this point, you're probably saying, "Don't give me those platitudes about the virtues of organization; I want some specifics as to how to get organized." No sooner said than done.

The development of a contingency contract system represents one of the best ways to organize classroom proceedings. We're *not* claiming that all effective teachers use contingency contracting or that contingency contracting represents the sole means of organizing a class. All that we are saying is that it would be highly reinforcing to us if you would read this chapter and consider contingency contracting as one possibility for organizing classroom happenings.

Developing a Contingency Contract System

Our most auspicious intentions often go awry because we simply don't know where to begin in actualizing those intentions. We may have an

43

over-all goal in mind but possess only the vaguest of notions as to specific steps to take in reaching that goal. In designing a contingency contract for a class of average size, what things must be done to get the contract operational? What specific responsibilities should students assume? These are the types of questions that we wish to examine in this first section.

What exactly is a contingency contract? A contract is basically an agreement between the teacher and students as to how the classroom will be managed. The word *contingency* implies that certain consequences will be dependent upon specified student behaviors. Contingency contracts usually provide three major types of information: (1) specification of appropriate student behaviors; (2) specification of inappropriate student behaviors; and (3) description of consequences for both appropriate and inappropriate behaviors. We'll reserve the details of each type of information for a bit later in the chapter.

What's the difference between a behavior contract and a behavior proclamation? A primary objective in developing a behavior management plan is to identify consequences for behavior which would have the most facilitative effect on student performance. We shall refer to the person who determines these consequences as the *contingency manager.* It is he who defines the circumstances under which reward and punishment shall be given. If the teacher acts as the sole contingency manager, the behavior management plan is called a behavior *proclamation.* In this case, the students are not involved in either the development or the endorsement of the plan. If the students help to develop the plan and are then given the option of ratifying or rejecting it, the plan is called a behavior *contract.*

Which is better, a contract or proclamation? We have compared the effectiveness of proclamations and contracts in several junior and senior high school settings. When both approaches provide frequent rewards for positive student behaviors, there appears to be minimal differences in their effectiveness. We first compared the two approaches in an inner-city high school class characterized by a very low baseline of appropriate behaviors. In this setting, both contracting and proclamation raised the level of desirable behavior some fifty percentage points above baseline (Sapp, 1971). In two other high schools—one public (predominately middle-class) and one private (middle- and upper-class)—contracting produced small but consistently higher rates of appropriate behavior than did proclamation (Arwood, Long, and Williams, 1972; Williams, Long, and Yoakley, 1972). It appears then that the more economically and educationally advantaged the student, the more important is participation in the development and endorsement of a behavior management plan. This conclusion seems to emerge despite the fact that the students often suggest essentially the same contingencies as do teachers. Due to lack of research data, we do not yet know what the relative merits of proclamation and contracting would be with younger children or children in special classes (e.g., classes for the emotionally disturbed and educable mentally retarded). We suspect that it might be easier for these students to comprehend the mechanics of a proclamation than those of a contract.

A major variable affecting the workability of either system is the amount and type of reinforcement which it provides. A teacher might devise a proclamation that would present more intriguing reward possibilities than a system the students would develop. However, it is more likely that a behavior management plan developed with student participation will include contingencies acceptable to students than one developed without their participation. In evaluating behavior contracts presently being used by other teachers, you should be on the alert for imposters. Teachers are calling things "contracts" which allow neither for student involvement nor positive payoffs for appropriate student behavior. For that reason, some of your students may have acquired rather negative impressions of contracts by the time they reach your class. That being the case, it will be your task to convince them that your contracting plan is basically a systematic way of rewarding appropriate behaviors and accomplishments.

How should students participate in the development of a contingency contract? A first step is to elicit their input concerning what they perceive as appropriate and inappropriate student behaviors and acceptable consequences for those behaviors. With young children, you might initially explain that you need their help in developing a good classroom. The discussion could be initiated by your asking, "What are some things that you boys and girls could do to make this a really fine class?" After fielding responses to this question, you might then ask, "What are some things that students should not do while at school, some things that would keep us from having a good classroom?" A third question should be directed toward identifying reinforcing activities. You could explain to your students, "When boys and girls do good work, they are sometimes given special privileges. They get to do things which are lots of fun. What kind of special things would you like to do as a reward for your good work at school?" After each question, the students' responses could be recorded on the board and evaluated by the class as a whole.

With older students, you could simply administer a brief questionnaire asking them to list behaviors they consider appropriate, behaviors they consider inappropriate, and activities they would like to engage in if they had free time during the class. The students should be instructed to list a specified number of responses for each item. You could then tabulate the most frequently given responses to each item and use these as the basis of your contract.

Having obtained input from students, you are now in a position to formulate a tentative draft of the contract. Since a contract is an agreement between at least two parties (in this case you and your students), we could expect input from each party. Although a classroom contingency contract should reflect as fully as possible the students' recommendations, your ideas need not be completely subjugated to their opinions. Students may make recommendations which are a violation of school regulations or which are personally distasteful to you. For example, smoking pot might be listed as a high priority activity by many students. But if the school has a regulation prohibiting this behavior, you could hardly accept it as a reinforcing activity. So the tentative draft of the contract should reflect both student and teacher input. It should include only those things which you feel you could comfortably accept if the contract were implemented.

How you at this point explain the contracting system to students is a crucial determinant of its success. If you begin by emphasizing the consequences of inappropriate behavior, the students will probably get the idea that the contract is restrictive in nature and is to be used against them. If you indicate that the purpose of contracting is to reward good behavior and that the contract under consideration includes many of their own recommendations, it is more likely that they will perceive contracting as a worthwhile venture. It should be explained to students that contracting allows both them and the teacher to know what to expect from each other and increases opportunities for them to learn. In short, the whole objective of contracting is to make the classroom a more palatable situation for both teacher and students.

One purpose for discussing the tentative draft of the contract with your students is to allow them to question the inclusion or exclusion of certain items and make additional suggestions concerning the composition of the contract. Following this additional student input, you should prepare the final draft of the behavior contract. The contract should then be presented to the students for their formal ratification. Since the contract is an agreement between you and your students, both parties should sign each copy of the contract. Your signature indicates that you will judge student behavior by the standards set forth in the contract and will provide the consequences for student behavior which the contract specifies. If you are careless in the application of the contract, the students will come to regard the idea of contracting as ludicrous. For example, one teacher whom we ostensibly trained to use a contract system agreed to let students read comics and play with certain games when they met specified academic criteria. To protect his comic books and games from theft, the teacher started locking them in a nearby closet whenever he left his classroom. That sounded like a commonsense thing to do, but when the students were frequently unable to use these materials because the teacher had forgotten the key to his closet, we were somewhat less impressed with his common sense. Subsequently, the students in his class voted to discontinue the contract. The student's signature, on the other hand, means that he is willing to be evaluated according to the terms of the contract, i.e., he will receive points, free-time privileges, grades, tangible payoffs, and so on according to the criteria set forth in the contract.

Although contracting should be presented to your students as an attractive system of managing the classroom, no pressure should be exerted to get them to endorse the system. No threats are to be issued regarding those students who may not choose to sign the contract. Remember, your system is not really a contract if students are forced to ratify it. Students should be just as free to not sign as to sign. Usually less than 5 percent of students offer any overt resistance to endorsing a properly developed contingency contract.

How do you deal with students who choose not to sign the contract? First, you should explain to these students that they will be under the same regulations as before the contracting period. If the contract is introduced at the beginning of the year, you will need to spell out the specific contingencies, e.g., turning in homework every day, taking weekly examinations, that will apply to students not under the contract. Furthermore, only those students under contract should have access to the reinforcers, e.g., points, daily grades, free-time activities, which are available under the terms of the contract.

Since the contract is largely based on student input and designed for the students' benefit, why would a student not want to operate under the contract system? A private conference with the student may reveal that he has had some bad experiences with so-called contracts, that he has misunderstood some of the basic contingencies in the contract, or that he finds particular facets of the contract threatening. For example, he may feel that the contract is going to be excessively rigid, whereas in reality a contract can give students considerable freedom to pursue their own interests at their own pace. A confidential conversation with the student may give you a chance to dispell some of his misgivings. The confused or anxious student may also wish to see how other students fare under the contract before he makes his decision. It is quite permissible to allow reluctant students to sign the contract several days after its implementation, which would give them a chance to see the payoffs that other students derive under the contract system.

We've been slaving away trying to answer questions, so it's time for you to answer some questions. While we go for coffee, respond to the following questions. If you can answer all of them, take a break; otherwise, reread the first part of the chapter.

1. The term *contingency* in contingency contract system means that under a contract
   (a) Everything is a chance happening,
   (b) Certain reward and punishment events are conditional,
   (c) Students can get away with most anything,
   (d) The teacher acquiesces to student opinions.
2. Which of the following behavior management plans can most legitimately be identified as a behavior contract?
   (a) Teacher and students both provide input into the plan and both voluntarily ratify it,
   (b) The teacher determines the consequences of appropriate and inappropriate student behaviors,
   (c) Students assist in formulating the contingencies, but do not formally ratify the plan,
   (d) The teacher determines the contingencies, but students are given the option of ratifying or rejecting the plan.
3. Research on proclamations and contracts indicates that
   (a) There is no difference in the effectiveness of the two,
   (b) Disadvantaged students tend to do better under a contracting system than under a proclamation,
   (c) Both systems can be quite effective when they emphasize rewards for desirable behavior,
   (d) Advantaged students seem to be turned off by the idea of contracting.
4. Which of the following bits of information would a classroom behavior contract most likely *not* include?
   (a) Specification of appropriate student behaviors,
   (b) Specification of inappropriate student behaviors,
   (c) Description of consequences for both appropriate and inappropriate behaviors,
   (d) Delineation of school regulations concerning the use of drugs.

5. In formulating the contingencies to be included in a behavior contract, the teacher should
   (a) Include all student suggestions,
   (b) Include the student suggestions which he can comfortably accept,
   (c) Thank students for their suggestions, but disregard these suggestions in the actual formulation of contingencies,
   (d) Ask one or two of his favorite students to map out the contingencies.
6. If a student refuses to sign a contract, the teacher should
   (a) Tell him to shape up or ship out,
   (b) Indicate that he will probably make very poor grades if he doesn't accept the contract,
   (c) Give the student a chance to express his misgivings about the contract privately,
   (d) Make no attempt to find out why the student prefers not to operate under the contract.

We bet that you had no difficulty in answering these questions. Confusion about any of the questions should easily be eliminated by rereading the appropriate parts of the first section. If this procedure doesn't help you, you've got big problems!

Applying the Contract to Student Behaviors

We hope that you now not only have some notion of what contracting is all about but are feeling better about the prospect of actually using contracting. It's encouraging to see people who are willing to consider a new point of view and to do so with such a high degree of objectivity. With this sense of rapport, let us proceed to consider exactly how contracting can be used in changing behavior. The essence of behavior modification is the strengthening of certain behaviors and the weakening of others. Therefore, it might be appropriate at this time to identify behaviors you would want to increase and those you would want to decrease via contracting. The next task would then be to describe how to use the rewards and punishments available under a contract system to produce the desired changes in behavior.

What types of behavior should be formally rewarded under a behavior contract system? There are certain behaviors which are requisite to academic productivity in the classroom. We refer to such behaviors in Table 1 (see pp. 51-53) as "being prepared for class." This category includes behaviors such as attending class, coming to class on time, and having appropriate materials. As mundane as these behaviors might appear, without them it is extremely difficult for a teacher to accomplish very much academically. Though it's hard to believe, many classes are plagued by students' coming to class late and not bringing appropriate materials. In such cases, the teacher may spend much of the period just attempting to get started with the lesson. The point is that behaviors in the "being prepared for class" category cannot always be taken for granted. For some students these behaviors must be directly rewarded if they are to occur frequently.

The most important behaviors to increase are those which indicate academic productivity. Many times students don't accomplish very much because they don't know what's expected of them, often because the teacher has poorly defined academic objectives or has not communicated his objectives to the students. You should specify in your behavior management plan the academic products expected from your students.

The junior high school geography teacher who used the contract in Table 1 employed three means of assessing her students' academic progress: (1) daily checkups or homework, (2) daily learning activities, and (3) weekly examinations. The daily checkup was a five-minute quiz dealing with the work covered in class the preceding day. It was always given and checked at the beginning of a class period. The teacher felt that the checkup served as a bridge between work done on consecutive days and got each class period off to a serious start. Typically, students were allowed two minutes of review time at the beginning of the period just before the checkup was administered. Immediately following the checkup, the students exchanged papers and graded each other's work. The whole process of reviewing, taking the checkup, and grading the checkup generally required no more than ten minutes.

There were several possibilities for the daily learning activity. Usually the teacher would introduce new material through lecture, discussion, films, or film strips and then have the students make some type of written response to the material. The written reaction often involved answering either factual or opinion questions based on the material. However, group projects or class discussions were sometimes used in lieu of individual written assignments. If no written product was required, the teacher assigned credit on the basis of the student's contribution to the group project or class discussions. Unfortunately, this tended to be a rather subjective evaluation. About the only objective criterion that she used in determining a student's contribution to class discussion was the number of questions which the student asked or answered during that discussion. In the case of written assignments, the teacher applied essentially the same evaluative criteria to the work of all students, i.e., different students received the same amount of credit for answering a question correctly or giving their opinion on an issue.

TABLE 1

Junior High School Behavior Contract

I. *Being prepared for class*

Consequence

1. Attending class (checked fifteen minutes after bell).

For attending—earn 1 point
For not attending—0 point

2. Being on time (checked immediately after bell rings).

For being on time—earn 2 points
For not being on time—lose 2 points

3. Bringing paper and pencil.

For bringing these items—earn 2 points
Failure to bring either item—lose 2 points

4. Bringing appropriate books.

For bringing books—earn 2 points
Failure to bring books—lose 2 points

II. *Working in class*

1. Taking the daily checkup (five minute checkup at the beginning of class period). The checkup will be based on the previous day's lesson. Homework may be substituted for checkup.

Each checkup is worth up to 5 points. Student will lose 1 point each time he is observed looking on someone else's paper or the book.

2. Finishing the daily learning activity. This may be class discussion, a group activity, seeing a film, reading, or written work.

Each learning activity is worth up to 10 points.

3. Unit exam (given each Friday, made up of material from the daily checkups and learning activities).

The unit exam will be worth up to 30 points. Student will lose 1 point each time he is observed looking on someone else's paper or the book.

III. *Negative behaviors*

1. Hitting another student — Lose 2 points
2. Throwing objects — Lose 2 points
3. Loud talking or laughing — Lose 2 points
4. Getting out of your seat without permission — Lose 2 points
5. Chewing gum without permission — Lose 2 points

TABLE 1 (continued)

6. Eating without permission   Lose 2 points
7. Talking while the teacher is   Lose 2 points
   giving instructions
8. Using dirty words or signs   Lose 2 points
9. Looking out of the windows   Lose 2 points

After a student has been penalized three times (losing 6 points) during a class period, he will be sent to the assistant principal for the rest of the period. If a student receives ten penalties (losing 20 points) in class during a week, a letter will be sent to his parents (or guardians) describing the student's misbehavior.

IV. *Grades*

Your grades will be determined by the number of points you achieve. You will be graded each day. On Monday through Thursday, 22 points give you an $A+$, 17–21 an A, 12–16 a B, and 7–11 a C. Friday will be test day. You will receive a letter grade for the Friday test as follows: 30 points give you an $A+$, 25–29 an A, 20–24 a B, 15–19 a C, 10–14 a D, and less than 10 an F. You will also be given a grade each week. The weekly grade will be an average of your grades Monday thru Thursday and your grade on the Friday test. The grade you will receive for the nine weeks will be an average of the weekly grades. The semester grade will be an average of the nine weeks' grades.

V. *Privileges*

In addition to grades, certain privileges (honors activities) will be based on the points you earn. If you finish the daily learning activity and had earned at least 17 points on the previous class period, or at least 25 points on the Friday test, you may have the rest of the period as free time. During this free time you may do any one of the following honors activities:

1. Read comics.
2. Read magazines.
3. Read books.
4. Play games provided.
5. Draw.

Since some of your classmates will still be working on their learning activity while you are enjoying an honors activity, it is important that you be very quiet while you are engaging in the honors activity. Talking or any other loud noise during the activity will warrant revoking the free time for that day and deducting 2 points from your total. If you are not eligible for an honors activity, you may remain in your seat and work quietly with your own materials.

VI. *Daily Procedure*

If you are given written work for the daily learning activity and you feel you have completed it, you may turn in your work to your teacher

TABLE 1 (*continued*)

and engage in an honors activity, provided you are eligible according to the previous day's total. If you like, you may get the teacher's help to see if your work is correct before turning it in.

If you are given group work or other kinds of learning activities, the teacher will let you know when your work is completed. Generally, she will make an announcement about ten minutes prior to the end of the class period.

I, _____, agree to abide by the conditions and consequences specified in this contract and agree to take the grade decided according to my own behavior and performance on tests.

_____

Student

I, as your teacher, agree to help you with your tasks and award grades and privileges according to the specifications of this contract.

_____

Teacher

We have also used contingency contracting in conjunction with programmed instruction. Credit was awarded for three types of academic products: comprehension checks based on the programmed materials, unit tests based on the comprehension checks, and assignments done outside of class. After completing a specific number of frames in the programmed material, the student took a comprehension check on material included in those frames. The number of points a student achieved for each comprehension check was based on the percentage of correct answers. For example, a student getting 100 percent correct answers was awarded six points; a student getting 90 to 99 percent correct responses, five points, etc. After completing a specified number of comprehension checks, the student took a unit examination based on those checks. Again, credit was awarded in relationship to percentage of correct responses. The students paced themselves through the programmed materials, comprehension checks, and unit tests. The teacher simply made the comprehension checks and units tests available as each student finished the appropriate amount of material.

It is impossible at this point to specify all the academic products that teachers in various settings might expect of their students. Suffice it to say that specification of these products is essential to effective teaching. For example, if you teach first graders to read, how will you assess their reading progress? One simple index might be the number of words which they could pronounce correctly from designated materials. Another dimension might be the student's ability to answer questions about what he had read. Whatever content area you teach, you must identify the academic products which will manifest progress in that area. Products can be short-term (e.g., one class period) or long-term (e.g., one semester), individual or group, the same for all students or different from student to student. A contract can be suited to whatever kinds of behaviors and products you and your students deem desirable.

How can a contract be used to decrease disruptive behaviors? This question reflects the concern of many teachers. Inability to control disruptive student behaviors is a major source of teacher unhappiness and a principal reason why people drop out of the teaching profession. A semester of shouting, threatening, and pleading with students does wonders for your personality. It may be such a therapeutic experience that you wind up hating teaching, your students, and yourself. We are reminded of the principal who after several years of battling with students would conclude every school day by affirming that it was the *worst* day he had ever experienced. God help us if such a deplorable fate befalls you.

Before we answer the question, may we speculate as to why disruptive behaviors are of such paramount concern to teachers? First, some of these behaviors are personally irritating. Being hit in the posterior with an eraser, being called a "god damn son of a bitch," having students talk and laugh while you're trying to give instructions, or having students make obscene gestures when you ask them to do something just doesn't make you feel very appreciated. Beyond the personal irritation, teachers are practical enough to recognize that disruptive behavior may nullify most of their attempts to foster academic productivity. Disruptive behaviors keep not only the disruptive student but other students from attending to lesson-related activities.

Now back to the question of how a contracting system can help to curb disruptive behaviors. One approach used in contracting is to make no reference to disruptive behaviors, since the mere identification of them might make them more attractive to students. A quite different strategy calls for the listing of disruptive behaviors and the specifying of penalties for them. In this case, the student would lose credit whenever he exhibited one of the designated disruptive behaviors. Our experience indicates that penalizing students for inappropriate behaviors ordinarily leads to a faster reduction of these behaviors than simply ignoring them. This conclusion would be correct only if the backup consequences, e.g., good grades, free-time activities, tangible payoffs, are highly reinforcing to your students. If not, the gaining or losing of credit toward these consequences will have little effect on their actions.

There are some definite hazards involved in enumerating negative behaviors and corresponding penalties in your behavior management plan. One questionable strategy is trying to list all the inappropriate behaviors that might conceivably occur. A long list of negative behaviors gives the impression that the plan is restrictive and may challenge some students to find ways of being disruptive that are not on your list. A better approach is to keep the list of negative behaviors very short and include only those activities which interfere with the academic performance of other students. In fact, the wisest course of action may be just to list "disturbing others" as the only negative behavior and then provide several examples of what that might include, for instance, talking while the teacher is giving instructions, throwing objects, hitting other students.

Another mistake initially made in listing negative behaviors is not setting an upper limit on the number of penalty points a student can lose and remain in the class. The contract shown in Table 1 stipulated that when a student lost 6 points in a class period he would be sent to the assistant principal's office. If a student incurred ten penalties (-20 points) during the course of a week, a note was sent to his parents or guardians explaining the student's misbehavior. These limits were included at the suggestion of students. Before the limits were set, a few students had severely tested the behavior management plan by emitting an excessive amount of disruptive behavior. These instances led to students being penalized as many as fifteen times during one class period. After the limits were introduced, not one student exceeded them. If you do not have limits, some students may on occasion find getting penalized a reinforcing experience. These penalties may provide the same kind of reinforcing attention as do verbal reprimands for inappropriate behaviors. Also, a student may cease to care how many points he loses after incurring several penalties. One warning—if you limit the number of penalties a student can incur, the consequences of exceeding the limits must be nonreinforcing or highly aversive to students. We can envision situations in which being sent to the principal's office or having a note sent home to the parents would be quite reinforcing. You will need your students' assistance in identifying backup consequences which they regard as truly nonreinforcing or aversive.

We have observed that some students seem to respond to repeated penalties highly emotionally. Because of their anger, they may be more concerned about getting back at the teacher than earning a good grade or free-time privileges. In this case, allowing students the prerogative of an overt emotional reaction following a penalty may be sound strategy. Common reactions to penalties include, "He hit me first," "Everybody else has been doing it," "I don't care if you penalize me," "Punish me again; I don't care." A few students even respond to penalties with profanity. If you can, you should simply ignore the emotional outburst. If you penalize the student for his emotional reaction you will most likely only evoke another emotional reaction. You can also minimize emotional outbursts from the students by administering penalties in a business-like, nonemotional fashion, as "Bill loses two points for hitting Suzie," "Jimmy loses a point for talking while I'm trying to give instructions."

Specifically, what types of immediate consequences should be used to strengthen appropriate and weaken inappropriate behaviors? A crucial component in effective behavior management systems is the use of immediate consequences for behavior. The major sources of reinforcement for appropriate behavior in a traditional academic setting are grades and free-time privileges. However, neither of these can be used as immediate consequences for appropriate behavior. What is needed is some type of credit which could be given or taken away immediately following a behavior. This credit could later be used as the basis for grades and free-time activities. In contingency management systems, these immediate consequences are often administered via intermediate reinforcers called *tokens*. The most commonly used tokens are points and material objects such as poker chips. Tokens are given after behaviors to be strengthened and taken away after behaviors to be weakened. Tokens can later be cashed in for backup rewards such as grades, free-time activities, and tangible payoffs. With younger children it may be better to use material objects for tokens since they provide a concrete reward. A disadvantage of material tokens is that they require more time to dispense than do points and may be lost, stolen, or counterfeited. If you penalize students for inappropriate behavior, you might also incur more difficulty in taking away material items than in subtracting points. Consequently, we recommend the use of a point system for students who are advanced enough to understand the numerical concepts involved in administering that system.

What types of backup rewards make a point system effective? Surprisingly, there is some evidence that a point system without backup rewards would be quite effective in increasing appropriate student behaviors (Jens and Shores, 1969; Jessee, 1971; Sulzer, 1966; Sulzer et al., 1971). It may be that points provide immediate, systematic feedback which is highly reinforcing in its own right for some students. We have found that among severely disadvantaged students, points alone do not produce nearly the degree of appropriate behavior as do points leading to free time (Long, 1972a). However, in the same study, points produced a considerably higher level of appropriate behavior than baseline conditions. Despite the reinforcement value of points themselves, they can become even more reinforcing if they lead to highly desired payoffs. Three payoffs which are potentially quite reinforcing are free time, grades, and tangible items.

The free time concept is based on an approach called the Premack principle. Premack (1959) proposed that a preferred activity (e.g., drawing, reading comic books, looking at magazines, playing cards, engaging in informal conversation) could be used to strengthen a less preferred activity (e.g., doing an English assignment, working arithmetic problems) by making the preferred activity contingent upon the less preferred. Free-time privileges are thus used to strengthen appropriate academic behavior. We have discovered that students who were doing little or no work in the classroom began working very hard when free-time activities were made contingent on completing a specified amount of work. In fact, students may double or triple their rate of working when free time is used this way (Salzberg, 1972).

For the concept of free time to work the student must find at least one of the free-time options reinforcing. How do you identify the kind of activities that would be reinforcing to your students? If you use a contracting system, you will undoubtedly ask your students to suggest things they would like to do during free time. However, students' verbal report of what they want to do may not always agree with what they actually do (Atkins and Williams, 1972). You may think of some very good options which students, because of lack of familiarity with those activities, would not mention. For example, there is some indication that the study of Russian could be used as a highly reinforcing activity for disadvantaged students (Homme, 1966; Kaufman, 1972), yet very few students would initially list the study of Russian as a high priority activity. In the same vein, Packard (1970) found that using a private study booth, using a class typewriter, and serving as a teacher assistant were highly reinforcing activities for his third, fifth, and sixth grade students. The best strategy is to provide students a wide array of free time activities from which to choose, because what is reinforcing to one student may be neutral or aversive to another. Among possibilities for individual student use are art materials, comic books, magazines, picture books, puzzles, word games, and radios or record players with ear plugs. When everybody has earned free time, group activities such as talking, card games, dancing, paper football, and group games become possibilities.

Perhaps the most commonly used backup consequences in contingency contract systems are grades. Table 1 indicates that student grades can be tied directly to the points students earn. In considering the feasibility of using grades as backup consequences, let us first make clear that we are not endorsing the practice of giving grades. We have no evidence that grades *per se* enhance the potency of a point system. In fact, because of the negative associations that grades have acquired, they may even decrease the effectiveness of a point system (Jessee, 1971). You could probably have a highly effective point system without using grades as backup consequences; and in fact, we strongly advocate a nongraded system in which students work toward the attainment of specific objectives and no grades are given.

Since it is not likely that you will always be privileged to work in a truly individualized, nongraded program, perhaps we should give some more attention to a conventional, graded system. If the administrative arrangement in your school requires the awarding of grades, then it's better to base these grades on specific academic and social criteria (such as would usually be delineated in a contract) than to leave grading standards nebulous and unspecified. We do have some data to indicate that grades improve when they are based on contractual criteria (Williams and Anandam, 1972). That being the case, grades should acquire a more positive connotation when used in conjunction with a contracting system. Also, if points and/or free time are initially more reinforcing than grades, they might be made contingent upon grades. Under this system, a student might have to make an A on an assignment to earn 15 points and/or free time. In the long run, such contingencies should increase the reinforcement value of good grades.

Another type of backup reward, and one which is often unavailable in conventional academic settings, is a tangible payoff. There is little doubt that tangible rewards such as money, edibles, and trinkets can be highly effective in increasing appropriate behaviors (Birnbrauer et al., 1965; Higgins, 1967; Terrell, Durkin and Wiesley, 1959; Wolf, Giles and Hall, 1968). If you are fortunate enough to work in a setting where tangible rewards are accessible, how can you best use them to modify student behaviors? To avoid creating student dependency on tangible payoffs, you must make some attempt to systematically phase out the tangibles and transfer their reinforcement value to other stimuli. We believe this objective can partially be accomplished by gradually switching the tangible payoffs from continuous to intermittent schedules. At the outset, a child might be getting a tangible payoff every few minutes. Later on he might get tangible rewards only once a week or once a month. Consistently pairing other events such as praise, points, and good grades with tangible rewards should also increase the reinforcement value of the abstract rewards and make students less dependent upon tangibles.

Are you ready to answer some more questions? We've got to be sure you're still with us.

1. Regarding behaviors to be rewarded under a contract system, Williams and Anandam suggest that
   (a) Only those behaviors which indicate academic productivity be rewarded,
   (b) All students must be directly rewarded for coming to class on time and bringing appropriate materials if these behaviors are to occur consistently,
   (c) Teachers should reward only long-term academic products,
   (d) Whatever behaviors and academic products that teachers and students deem desirable be rewarded.

2. In dealing with disruptive behaviors, a teacher should
   (a) Penalize the student as many times as he behaves disruptively,
   (b) Set an upper limit on the number of penalties a child can receive and remain in class,
   (c) Penalize students when they get emotional about penalties previously received,
   (d) Tell students how ashamed he is of their disruptive behavior.

3. The authors' analysis of the relative advantages of points and material objects as tokens indicates that
   (a) Material objects are superior for all age levels,
   (b) A point system should be used when students are able to understand the numerical concepts involved in administering the point system,
   (c) Points should be used for appropriate behaviors and material objects for inappropriate behaviors,
   (d) Material objects take less time to dispense than do points.

4. Research regarding points and backup rewards has shown that
   (a) Points without backup rewards can be quite effective in increasing appropriate student behaviors,
   (b) Grades are the most powerful backup consequences,
   (c) Free time usually becomes ineffective after a few days,
   (d) Tangible rewards are effective only for disadvantaged students.

5. The reinforcement value of good grades may be increased by
   (a) Giving more low grades,
   (b) Making free time contingent upon good grades,
   (c) Making good grades contingent upon tangible payoffs,
   (d) Concealing the criteria for good grades.
6. With regard to the use of tangible payoffs as backup rewards, the authors suggest that
   (a) Tangibles should be systematically phased out as the major backup rewards,
   (b) Other types of rewards (e.g., praise, good grades) should be paired with tangible payoffs,
   (c) Tangible payoffs should gradually be switched from continuous to intermittent schedules,
   (d) All of the above.

We trust that you had no major problems with these questions. Perhaps at this point it would be appropriate to address ourselves to some of the logistical details involved in administering a contingency contract system.

Practical Details of Successful Contracting

By now you know the steps to take in setting up a contract, the purpose of contracting, types of behaviors to strengthen or weaken under a contract, and the kinds of reinforcers needed to accomplish the desired behavior changes. We have obviously dealt with some very important issues; yet we both know that there are unresolved details which could make your experience in contracting something less than ecstasy. What are the day-to-day difficulties that you might encounter in administering a contract system? Will you still have sufficient time left for teaching after implementing the terms of a contract? Will students get tired of a contract after a few weeks? What kind of evaluation of your system is fundamental to its long-range success?

How can one teacher possibly do all the record keeping involved in a contingency contract system? All this talk about awarding and subtracting points might elicit fears of interminable record keeping. Relax. Record keeping is not nearly the problem you might initially suspect. Typically it takes less than five minutes per hour of class time to keep records up to date. Most of the behaviors in the "being prepared for class" category (for example, having paper, pencil, and appropriate materials) can be checked at the beginning of the period when the roll is taken. In evaluating academic products, you can enlist the aid of your students by asking them to score their own or each other's work. The task of actually recording points can also be shared by students. We usually let one student each day serve as recorder. (This responsibility appears to be highly reinforcing for most students; perhaps it gives them a sense of power over the class.) The task of keeping records is sufficiently reinforcing in some classes to warrant its use as a free-time privilege. If not, the teacher can simply go down the roll and let each student have a turn at keeping the records. If you do not wish to use students as recorders, a teacher's aide might be recruited for this responsibility. In any event, we have found time devoted to record keeping not to be a major problem in contingency contract systems.

The type of record sheet that you use can markedly affect the efficiency of your recording system. You need a format that will permit you to tell at a glance how many points each student has gained or lost in each behavioral category each day. A record form that has the behavioral categories listed across the top of the sheet and the students' names down the side will allow you to do just that. You would then need one record sheet per day. If you have a weekly exam on Friday and wish to total the points accumulated by each student for the week, Friday's form will need to be slightly different from the Monday through Thursday forms. Friday's sheet would include not only a column for the daily total but a column for the weekly total as well.

In our studies, two types of record sheets have been used: (1) 8½″ × 11″ duplicated sheets (ditto or stencil) and (2) wall charts. When duplicated sheets are used, the records are periodically (at least once per class period) made available to the students. When wall charts are employed, each student's record is immediately accessible to the entire class. It is potentially quite reinforcing for a student to be able to see his record any time and to see other students looking at his record. An economical way to prepare wall charts is to put the names of your students and the behavior categories on cardboard sheets and then cover these sheets with a clear plastic. The points earned and deducted can be written in the appropriate spaces on the plastic sheet with a grease pencil. The same record sheet can be used again by simply erasing the pencil marks from the plastic surface.

In addition to keeping comprehensive records for the class as a whole, you may wish to let each student keep his own record, which would allow the students to be constantly aware of their progress in the class. Two preliminary studies (one with high school age normal students and the other with junior high school age educable mentally retarded students) suggest that individual record keeping facilitates appropriate behavior (Arwood, Long, and Williams, 1972; Long, 1972b). Individual record keeping would also be an excellent way for younger children to learn some basic mathematical concepts.

How do you determine the amount of credit to award or subtract for a particular behavior? That question appears simple, but we find it rather difficult to answer satisfactorily. These decisions are to some degree arbitrary, for research has not yet identified the optimal amount of credit to award or subtract for a given behavior. It would seem logical that in an academic setting more credit should be awarded for academic products than for purely social behaviors (e.g., coming to class on time, having appropriate materials).

Some teachers attempt to compute credit for an academic product by estimating how much time will be required to complete that product. Therefore, if assignment A is expected to take five times longer to complete than assignment B, A would carry five times as much credit. Since a student should be informed in advance how much credit can be earned for a particular product, the teacher must award credit on the basis of expected time, not the actual time, involved in completing the task. Another approach is to award credit according to the estimated difficulty of the work. A student would earn more credit for solving a difficult problem than an easy one, irrespective of the time involved. To summarize, we suggest that more credit be given for academic products than for social behaviors, for tasks requiring considerable time than those entailing little time, and for difficult than easy work. We realize that we have not provided a very precise answer to the question.

How many tokens or points should be required for a given grade or free-time activity? Regarding the issue of grades, let us say that evaluation standards should be based on specified academic and social criteria rather than competitive norms. The grading scale should be such that students who attend class regularly and manifest appropriate social behavior can at least earn passing marks. An A, on the other hand, should perhaps reflect high quality academic work. Appropriate social behavior would make it easier for a student to earn an A but would not be the major criterion of his attaining an A. We must remind you that we are generally opposed to the practice of giving grades and include these recommendations only because we realize that grades are still a fact of life in many academic settings.

The criteria for free time should be such that all students can frequently have access to free time activities. If students were placed on a self-paced schedule, every student could earn free time by finishing a specified amount of work. With this system, the slower students would be assured of eventually earning free time, though they would not earn free time as quickly or as frequently as the more precocious students. If the requirements for free-time activities are so high that only a few students can attain them, the offer of free time will obviously become an ineffective means of managing most students' behavior.

A question that you perhaps want to raise at this point is whether free time and grade requirement should be individualized; should you require more points for one student to earn an A than for another to earn the same grade? One commonly espoused educational doctrine is that we should grade according to a student's ability. In other words, if we think that Jack is a very slow child we would require less of him for a good grade than for a child judged to be brighter. Humane as this approach sounds, it is extremely difficult to implement. A major difficulty is accurately assessing a student's capability. We consider it precarious to base your judgment of a child's ability on his IQ scores, since many times students do much better on their academic work than their IQ scores would indicate. The problem is that if you cannot accurately establish what a child's ability is, you cannot assign credit according to his ability. You may also precipitate bad emotional reactions by using differential grading standards, i.e., Jack may feel that his A is a cheap A because less was required of him than of other students or Steve may feel that the teacher is being unfair in requiring more of him than of other students. Though applying uniform grading standards to a class is by no means ideal, it seems to entail fewer hazards than attempting to grade students according to their individual abilities. In reality, an ostensibly uniform grading system would still give the teacher considerable freedom to individualize credit. For example, when students are asked to give their opinion on an issue, Jack's opinion, though awkwardly stated, could be awarded essentially the same credit as Steve's opinion, which is much more fluently and logically stated.

Should free-time contingencies be on an individual or group basis? Why not use both types of contingencies? If you have identified high priority activities which are clearly of a group nature, and if you believe that peer reinforcement is a significant source of behavioral control in your class, group contingent reinforcement is definitely indicated. With group contingencies, you would be able to utilize the high priority group activities as backup reinforcers and would be able to mobilize peer support for appropriate classroom behaviors. Group contingencies have usually proven superior to individual contingencies

(Hamblin, Hathaway, and Wodarski, 1971; Long, 1972a). We have also found group contingencies to be quite effective for a wide variety of students. Such contingencies have been successfully employed with educable mentally retarded (EMR) students (Sulzbacker and Houser, 1968), with advantaged students (Wilson, 1971), with disadvantaged students (Long, 1972a), with first grade students (Wilson, 1972), with middle grade students (Hamblin, Hathaway, and Wodarski, 1971; Packard, 1970; Schmidt and Ulrich, 1969), and with junior high age students (Andrews, 1971; Long, 1972a).

Though group contingent reinforcement appears to have great potential, the logistics of implementing such a system could be quite cumbersome. The first decision is what criterion to use in dispensing the group payoff. Hamblin and his colleagues have indicated that the group reward may be based on (1) the average performance in the group, (2) the high performance in the group, or (3) the low performance in the group. In our own research, we have used a group contingency strategy in which a reward is offered to a group of students (perhaps the whole class) contingent upon every student's meeting a predetermined criterion of appropriate behavior. So if only one child fails to meet the prescribed criterion of appropriate behavior, the whole group fails to earn the specified reward.

Second, you need procedures for monitoring the group's behavior. If group rewards are based on points earned, the record-keeping system described earlier for individual contingencies could also be used. An ideal arrangement might be to make some activities (those which could be engaged in without disrupting others' work) individually contingent and other activities (those which involve person-to-person interaction) group contingent. A student could proceed to the individually contingent activities as soon as he earned the requisite number of points but could not engage in the group contingent activities until everyone had earned the required number of points.

When the group reward is based exclusively on disruptive behavior, it is still possible to use the same record-keeping system. You might specify, for example, that zero penalties would earn the class ten minutes of free time; one penalty, nine minutes free time, etc. If you keep public records (such as a wall chart), each student could readily see how the class stands with respect to penalties. A similar approach is to write the initial amount of reward time on a chalkboard and subtract from that time whenever a target behavior occurs. Or you might have a set of flip cards, with each card indicating a certain number of minutes. You could simply flip the cards as students exhibited disruptive behaviors. If you like to do things elaborately, you might prefer one of the mechanical devices that have recently been developed for monitoring group behavior. Schmidt and Ulrich (1969) employed a sound level meter and a kitchen timer to record intensity and duration of noise in the classroom. The students earned recess time for maintaining a noise level below forty-two decibels for the specified time period. Packard (1970) used a Cramer timer to monitor the studying behavior of kindergarten, third, and sixth grade students. When any student stopped attending to the learning activities, the teacher deactivated the timer and switched on a red light. Andrews (1971) and Wilson (1971) used a procedure similar to Packard's except that a buzzer was sounded whenever the clock stopped recording study time.

The major hazard in employing group contingencies is that one or more children may find it reinforcing to screw up the group. This kind of child usually has a history of disruptive behavior and low academic achievement. He may be very reluctant to relinquish his image of chief class disruptor and quite insecure about his ability to achieve teacher and peer approval through positive behaviors. Although the peer reinforcement strategy to be discussed in Chapter III may be helpful in working with this type of child, even it does not guarantee success. When one child habitually jeopardizes the viability of group contingencies, you hardly have any alternative except to exclude that child from those contingencies and deal with him on a completely individual basis.

When and where should free time be made available? It is best to have specified times during the school day when students can enjoy free time. In junior and senior high school classes, the last part of the period is considered the optimal time to have free-time activities. Another arrangement is to require the student to complete a specified amount of work, have free time, complete another segment of work, have free time, and so on. This approach would work exceedingly well with individualized learning packets and programmed instruction. It would also provide more immediate reinforcement for appropriate behavior than the giving of free time only at the end of the period. However, it may pose some practical difficulties. For instance, suppose that after completing a specified amount of work, the student can engage in five minutes of free-time activities. Who tells him when his five minutes are up? Some teachers follow a self-monitoring check in, check out system. If Betsy signs in for free-time materials at 9:24, she is expected to sign out at 9:29. We have found this self-monitoring system to work better after the students have first worked under external monitoring and then gradually made the transition to self-monitoring. Otherwise, you may find that many of your students are quite inept in controlling

their free time. Another difficulty in having free-time activities inter-
spersed throughout the period is that participation in these activities by
some students may be somewhat disruptive of other students' academic
activities. You certainly would have more disruptive movement in the
room by granting free time throughout the period than by restricting it
to the last part of the period.

The procedure that we have most frequently followed is to award
free time to each student after he has finished all his work for the
period. For example, if you were following the organization described
in Table 1 (checkup, learning activity, free time), you should plan the
agenda so that most students would finish the daily learning activity
with approximately ten minutes left in the period. Ordinarily a few
students would finish earlier than that and some later. Since each
student would have free time only after he had finished his work for
the day, you would not have the problem of getting students back to
work following free time. Although some students would still be
working on their assignments while others were engaging in free
time, the likelihood of students' work being disrupted is less near the
end of an assignment than at the beginning.

The second part of this question is where students should take free
time. Some students would like to take their free-time privileges outside
the classroom. Playing in the gym, going out of doors, or just messing
around the school building are suggestions often made by students.
You can immediately see the administrative hazards of sending students to unsupervised locales. However, if you can work out an
arrangement such that the student goes to a supervised area, such as
the library, gymnasium, or playground, it would increase the reinforcement potential of free time. Another possibility for free time outside
the classroom is to have a student lounge supervised by students.
Ideally, only those students who had earned free time could use the
lounge. The lounge could be a place where the students would have
refreshments, listen to records, dance, play ping pong, play cards, talk,
rest, and so forth. Since the lounge would be used by students other
than those in your class, the responsibility of supervision would
probably lie with elected representatives of the student body. Some
schools have used special activity rooms stocked with an array of
trinkets, games, art, and wood working materials. In an investigation
by McIntire, Davis, and Pumroy (1970), the activity room was
divided by colors into three areas. The most attractive activities were
placed in the red section, activities of lesser attraction in the yellow
area, and activities of least attraction in the white area. Contingencies
for getting in the red area were more stringent than those for entering
the yellow area and so on. Maintenance of a special activity room

would probably necessitate supervision. But if a teacher's aide or a responsible student aide could be recruited for this responsibility, the special activity room would be a highly desirable arrangement.

The most feasible arrangement for the majority of teachers is to provide free-time space within the regular classroom. The free-time materials should be kept in one place, such as a table at the back of the room, which is easily accessible to students. In some classes students go to this table, pick up free-time material, and return to their seats. Other teachers provide a special free-time area screened off from the rest of the classroom. In this case, a student gets his free-time material and takes a seat in the free-time area. This approach is good if you have enough space since it usually minimizes the amount of disruption that results from free-time activity.

Should students be permitted to accumulate free time over a period of several days? Presumably a student could earn an average of fifteen minutes free time each day, and save his free time until Friday, when he would have an hour's free time. If this were a junior or senior high school class, the student might simply take the period off on Friday. A major advantage of having free time each day, as opposed to accumulating large blocks of free time, is the immediacy of reinforcement for appropriate behavior. Yet, you may find that some of your students are able to delay gratification for extended periods and are more productive when allowed to accumulate free time. Two minor difficulties you may encounter in permitting students to accumulate free time are keeping the records straight for a period of several days, i.e., keeping up with who has or has not used his free time, and working out the mechanical details of when and where a student takes an extended period of free time. If the student takes his free time in your classroom, you will have to work out an arrangement so that his free-time activity does not interfere with the lesson activity of other students. If he takes his free time outside the classroom, you will have to arrange with the principal for the student to miss class, which entails certain administrative problems such as not counting the student absent when he takes his free time and providing an appropriate place such as the library or gymnasium for the student to utilize his free time.

How will I know if my behavior management system is effective? Your students will probably be in the best position to judge the effectiveness of your system. At least once every grading period a thorough evaluation of your system is in order. Students should be asked to evaluate your efficiency in implementing each component of the system, e.g., giving daily check-ups, giving free time, keeping grades posted. Needless to say, students should render their evaluations anonymously. The students are in essence giving you a grade on your consistency and fairness in implementing the system. We have found a pronounced correlation between the students' evaluation of a teacher's efficiency and the amount of appropriate student behavior in that teacher's class; that is, teachers who are judged as being very efficient produce the highest level of appropriate classroom behavior. So pay close attention to those student evaluations. They probably represent the one best source of feedback available to you.

Another good indicator of the quality of a plan is the effect it has on students' grades. Almost without exception teachers who are judged as highly efficient give higher student marks following the implementation of a behavior management system. If student grades do not improve after you instigate your plan, you probably have unrealistic grading standards or are inefficiently administering the system.

The one aspect of the system that needs to be examined most regularly and closely is free time. It is not uncommon for teachers to comment that after a few weeks students get tired of free time. A more accurate analysis might be that the specific free-time activities which have been provided have lost most of their reinforcement value. To minimize this saturation effect, change the free-time activities periodically. For example, if you're using comic books and magazines you should change your materials about once a week. Many magazine distributors will be willing to give you, free of charge, an abundant supply of magazines and comic books, so replenishing your materials frequently is not unrealistic. You might also allow your students to bring materials from home to use during free time. The concept of free time is workable only if the activities during free time remain highly reinforcing events.

What do you need to decide to get started with a contingency management system? If you are now thinking in terms of developing your own behavior management plan, there are several questions that you will need to answer. Will your plan be a proclamation, contract, or something in between? If a contract, how will you obtain student input in developing the plan? What types of behaviors do you want to reward under your behavior management system? Will the learning activities available under your plan be the same for all students or individualized and self-paced? What types of behaviors do you wish to minimize by the use of your plan? What will be the immediate consequences (e.g., points gained or lost) of appropriate and inappropriate student behaviors? What will be your procedure for recording points or keeping track of tokens? How will your conditioned reinforcers (e.g., points, tokens) be related to grades? How will your conditioned reinforcers be related to free-time reinforcers? Will your free-time contingencies be individual, group, or a combination of the two? When and where will the free-time activities be available? There are many other specific questions that will arise in the course of developing and implementing a behavior management plan, but these are the major ones that will have to be answered to get your plan developed and launched.

Undoubtedly, you've had enough of contingency contracting for a while. Answer the following questions and then take some free time. Reward yourself with a beer, a nap, your favorite television show, a hot fudge sundae, or by calling an old and dear friend.

1. Concerning the issue of record keeping in contingency management systems, the authors indicate that
   (a) Approximately half the teacher's time is taken up in recording points,
   (b) Students can assist in record keeping by serving as recorders,
   (c) Teacher aides make the best recorders,
   (d) No records should be kept lest they be discovered by the principal.

2. Which of the following would be most important in determining the amount of credit to award for a particular behavior?
   (a) Whether the behavior is academic or social,
   (b) Whether the behavior occurs in a public or private school setting,
   (c) Whether the behavior occurs in a natural science or social science area,
   (d) Whether the behavior is exhibited by a boy or a girl.

3. In establishing criteria for grades, you should
   (a) Us a norm-referenced grading system,
   (b) Award failing grades to students who fail to produce adequate academic products,
   (c) Grade each student according to his own ability,
   (d) Devise criteria so that students who attend class regularly and emit appropriate social behaviors can at least make passing marks.

4. A desirable free-time arrangement is to
   (a) Have only the top 5 percent of students to have access to free time,
   (b) Have free time at the beginning of a class period,

(c) Provide contingencies which would permit all students to periodically earn free time,

(d) Prohibit students from taking free time at different times.

5. Regarding the accumulation of free time, a teacher should
   (a) Allow students to accumulate free time for not longer than six months,
   (b) Permit students to take free time every day, come what may,
   (c) Categorically reject the possibility of accumulation,
   (d) Provide an accumulation option if space and time difficulties can be worked out.

6. It is clear from this chapter that Williams and Anandam
   (a) View contingency contracting as the only way for a teacher to get organized,
   (b) Are opposed to the concept of free time,
   (c) Are brilliant scholars,
   (d) Emphasize the use of the Premack principle in classroom management.

Chapter III

THE CLASSROOM FRATERNITY

An Analysis of Teacher and Peer Influences on Student Behavior

The behaviors that a child exhibits in the classroom are affected by variables other than points, grades, free-time activities, tangible pay-offs, and curricular materials. These additional variables fall within the social domain. The way that his teacher and peers socially respond to a child fundamentally affects his behavior. Inappropriate social reactions can largely negate the effectiveness of other potential reinforcers such as points, grades, and free-time activities. By the same token, appropriate social responses from teachers and peers can markedly enhance the potency of other behavior modification procedures.

Many social reactions occur somewhat automatically in the administration of a behavior management plan. For example, you may smile when you award points, or students may laugh and talk when they engage in free-time activities. Many other social behaviors take place apart from the formal implementation of a behavior modification system. These behaviors are often the most difficult to control systematically. Nevertheless, a child's behavior is continuously affected by the reactions it elicits from his teacher and peers.

Teacher Attention as a Means of Classroom Management

There are few moments in classroom instruction when the teacher is not attending to some type of student behavior. This attention may take many forms—smiling, giving a pat on the shoulder, hovering over a student, verbally praising a student, asking a question, listening to a student's response, nodding your head to a student, looking at a student, frowning, shaking your head, reprimanding a student, and striking a student. Predicting precisely how a particular type of teacher attention will affect a child's behavior is not always a simple task. Needless to say, some teachers are absolutely baffled by the impact their behavior has on their students.

While you might be inclined to assume that teacher approval would be reinforcing to students and teacher disapproval aversive, the very opposite is sometimes the case. The major purpose of this section is to delineate those variables—including the authenticity, the consistency, the frequency, the redundancy, and the specificity of a teacher's attention—which contribute to the reinforcing or aversive value of a particular type of teacher attention.

What determines whether a teacher's approval is perceived as sincere? The most important variable affecting the reinforcement quality of approval is probably the perceived sincerity of that approval. If you come across as a phony, your approval won't overwhelm your students. Although there is no way to determine with absolute certainty the sincerity of another's approval, none of us hesitates to make judgments in this area. If for any reason we suspect that another's approval is insincere, we are repulsed by that approval. The only exception may be when praise is given in jest and accepted in the same vein.

In judging the sincerity of others' approval, we perhaps first look at what is being approved. We are more likely to accept approval as genuine when it's directed toward something that we consider significant than something perceived as trivial. If someone praises your art collection, which you consider to be quite important, wouldn't you be more likely to accept that praise as authentic than if it were directed toward your discretion in choosing toilet tissue? In the process of establishing the credibility of your approval with a student, we suggest that you approve those behaviors that the student would most probably consider important. First give him credit for what he judges to be significant.

How do you determine what a student considers to be his significant behavior? Most students reveal these priorities via the kinds of activities in which they engage. For example, one child usually plays basketball during recess, another frequently talks about his model car collection, and a third paints during free-time activities. From these activities and from conversation, identify features that you can legitimately approve. For instance, if Will frequently plays basketball during recess, note what he does best in this activity. If his forte is rebounding, initially focus your praise on his rebounding ability. Suppose you note that another child readily expresses his views in class discussions but turns in very poor written assignments. It would initially be wise to comment on his facility in verbal discussion. If you try to praise any aspect of his writing performance, he will be more likely to see your praise as insincere.

Another important consideration in evaluating the sincerity of approval is the flamboyance of that approval. People tend to be skeptical of approval that is extreme or ostentatious. Judge for yourself: which of the following teacher reactions would you find more believable? "What you've said is undoubtedly the most articulate, creative, and insightful comment that has ever been made on this subject," or "What you've said seems to be an accurate analysis of the problem." Perhaps our example is a bit extreme, but some teachers do think of approval only in terms of the most eloquent accolades. As a result they use terms such as "the best," "the finest," "most intelligent," and "brightest" rather loosely. In reality there are few record-breaking performances. Repeated use of terms which imply that a child's performance is the *best* may convey to students that you are careless and insincere in the giving of praise. Most of us suspect that the person who slaps us on the back and tells us that we are the best looking, most intelligent, most dedicated, most stimulating person he has ever met will make the same pronouncement to the next person he meets.

Approval should be commensurate with the actual performance of the student. Approval should convey specific feedback to the child concerning the appropriateness of his behavior. For example, when Judy finishes her daily arithmetic assignment you need not say, "That's the finest treatise on mathematics I've ever read," but simply, "Judy, you got all the division problems correct today," "You worked two more problems today than yesterday," "It took you less time to finish your assignment today than yesterday," or "Your math scores are improving just about every day." Notice that Judy was given specific feedback about the kinds of problems she got correct, the number of problems she solved, the time it took her to complete her assignment, and her over-all progress in math. There were no extreme pronouncements made concerning her facility in math nor was her work compared with that of other students.

The sincerity of one's approval is sometimes viewed with suspicion because of the sheer redundancy of that approval. One of the most frequently used approval phrases is "very good." This phrase is fine when used sparingly but may lose much of its power after being used eighty-eight times in succession. You should specifically work on increasing your repertoire of approval comments. You may have to practice before a mirror, but try expressions such as "good thinking," "good work," "outstanding," "fine," "exactly," "that's correct," "you're doing better," "I'm pleased with your work," "you're really catching on," "you've learned this material well," "extremely good answer," "you're exactly right," "your point chart looks impressive," "I like the progress you're making," "you did well on today's checkup," and "you did a fine job on this assignment." We suggest that you begin by actually memorizing many of these expressions. Repeat them often enough to yourself that they become readily accessible to you. If you haven't been accustomed to using these kinds of phrases, you may feel a little artificial when you first begin to use them in the classroom. Remember, however, that as long as you're responding to behavior and accomplishments that you deem praiseworthy, there is no need to doubt your own sincerity. With continued use, an expression that initially sounds awkward to you may eventually sound downright natural. Anyway, saying nice things to people will be good for your blood pressure and hay fever.

The impact of verbal approval is often diminished by nonverbal behavioral cues that seem to imply nonapproval. For example, the teacher may say, "Fine, Fine," while simultaneously looking at something which is totally removed from the child who is supposed to be the recipient of the praise. Generally when people are pleased with our behavior, they look at us, smile at us, wink at us, come close to us, nod their heads to us, or touch us. The more these nonverbal behaviors accompany verbal approval, the more reinforcing your verbal approval will be. In fact, most of these nonverbal behaviors can be reinforcing in their own right. We usually respond positively to a smile, a gentle pat on the shoulder, or to a nod of the head. Conversely, praise which is administered without any of these nonverbal behaviors may be interpreted as blah or even insincere.

Nonverbal approval is also important in another sense. Occasionally a teacher encounters a student who appears to be uncomfortable about receiving any kind of verbal praise. It may be that the child has not experienced much approval in his previous relationships with people. By the time the child reaches your classroom, his perception of himself and his abilities may be so negative that he has difficulty accepting any kind of praise. Nonverbal behaviors such as a smile, a touch on the shoulder, and listening attentively while he speaks can convey to him, in a way that he can initially accept, that he counts with you. When it becomes obvious to you that these nonverbal behaviors are reinforcing to the child, you may begin to pair some very mild forms of praise with them.

A somewhat similar case is the child who is threatened by teacher praise because his peer group considers teacher approval taboo. Privately the child might relish your approval, but publicly act as though he loathes it. Some subtle nonverbal signs of approval may initially be acceptable to this child. The more confidentially these nonverbal cues can be expressed (e.g., smiling or nodding your head to him when the other children are not looking) the more likely he is to respond positively to them. Even verbal praise might be acceptable if it were given on a completely confidential basis (e.g., whispering to him when standing by his desk, talking with him at your desk, or leaving a note for him).

How can a teacher increase the reinforcement value of his approval? This question is closely related to the previous question on sincerity. One of the cardinal criteria of effective social reinforcement is consistency. Students must learn that certain kinds of behaviors will consistently be approved and others consistently disapproved or ignored. If what you praised yesterday is criticized today, students will legitimately conclude that your approval is more a function of how you feel than of their behaviors. In other words, sometimes you are likely to respond positively to practically anything students do and at other times respond negatively to essentially the same behaviors. When approval is used inconsistently, students may eventually stop caring whether they receive that approval. In contrast, when approval is paired daily with significant student behaviors, the message is conveyed that approval stands for something worthwhile. Now we know that having a fight with your husband or wife, having your car bashed in on the way to school, and being chewed out by the principal do not get your day off to an especially good start. But venting your hostility onto students will only compound your problems. And being nice in the midst of your adversities can sometimes reverse the course of your day's events.

A very difficult question to answer is how often to use approval in order to maximize its reinforcement value. Since most of us have not experienced a great deal of approval, we may initially be suspicious of the person who approves us frequently. So don't inundate your students with approval the first day of school. Instead, gradually increase the frequency and types of approval you employ. With this approach, you will find that approval acquires more reinforcement value over time. Since it is difficult to separate the question of frequency from that of consistency, perhaps the most definitive conclusion to draw is that consistent approval will become more reinforcing with use.

Another strategy for increasing the reinforcement value of approval is to pair that approval with something which is already reinforcing to the student. For example, if free time is reinforcing to him, you can express approval whenever you award free time. You might say, "Paul, you've done such a fine job that you've earned free time again today," "Paul, I'm glad that you've earned free time," or "Paul, I'm happy that you seem to enjoy free time." By being consistently paired with free time, approval will gradually acquire something of the same reinforcement potential as the free time. In much the same fashion, you can pair approval with good grades, points, tokens, tangible payoffs, or whatever is already reinforcing to the child. The consistent pairing of your approval with previously established reinforcers will emphasize the fact that *you* are the one who is awarding these other reinforcers. It follows then that you will become an increasingly significant person and your praise an increasingly significant event in the classroom.

A fourth strategy for enhancing the reinforcement value of your approval is to use that approval as a discriminative stimulus (S^D) for appropriate behavior that will lead to special kinds of payoffs. A discriminative stimulus indicates that a particular kind of behavior will be reinforced. To illustrate, assume that completion of arithmetic assignments typically results in the earning of free time. The discriminative stimulus could be something you say at the beginning of the arithmetic period which indicates that students will receive a special free-time privilege that day. Suppose you say, "Because you have been working so well recently, you may listen to your radio when you finish your arithmetic assignment today," or "Each of you has been making very fine progress in arithmetic, so when you finish your assignments today you can engage in group games." In either case, your approval has been the cue which indicates that doing the arithmetic assignment this particular day will result in unique privileges.

Toward what should a teacher's approval be directed? Our first contention is that the child *himself* should be the object of considerable teacher approval and that this approval should be administered on a noncontingent (unconditional) basis. Comments such as "I like you," "you're nice," "you're fun to be with," "you're very special," "you're a good friend," should not be reserved exclusively for those times when the child has exhibited extremely laudable behaviors. Instead, these affirmations can be made at times when the child has done nothing that is particularly praiseworthy (for example, the beginning of the day, lunch time, recess, and end of the day). Noncontingent approval of the child indicates that you like him irrespective of whether he meets your behavioral standards.

It is a common practice among some teachers and parents to approve children on a conditional basis. What effect does contingent approval have on children? In one case, parents frequently told their little boy they were proud of *him* after he manifested certain appropriate behaviors. The child soon began to respond to parental disapproval by asking them if they were still proud of him. The child had logically concluded that if his parents were proud of him when he behaved appropriately, they might not be proud of him when he behaved inappropriately. For this child, disapproval was tantamount to parental rejection. Contingently approving a child would undoubtedly be a powerful means of controlling his behavior. But such control would probably lead to poignant feelings of rejection when the child deviated from the behavioral standards set by his parents or teacher.

Contingent approval can profitably be used if it is directed toward behaviors and not the child. When a student completes his work, you can say, "Boy! You finished that in twenty minutes" instead of saying "You are a smart boy." Although some teachers swear that their students never do anything right, most students manifest many appropriate behaviors. The most disruptive child that we have ever systematically observed exhibited a baseline of 8 percent appropriate behavior; most students that teachers identify as highly disruptive emit 25 to 50 percent appropriate behavior during baseline. If you are quick to recognize and approve desirable behaviors, you will find that they increase in frequency. In responding to a child's academic and social behavior, be alert to any signs of improvement. This strategy will usually yield much greater dividends than your emphasizing mistakes and lack of improvement.

Of the situations that present opportunities for reinforcing appropriate behaviors, perhaps nothing has greater potential than class discussion. In facilitating class discussion, you need not direct your approval toward the accuracy of a child's comment; that is, you are not obligated to say, "That's right," "you are correct," or "I agree" following a student's comment. A teacher reaction which often proves to be highly reinforcing is to use a student's comment as the basis for further class discussion. Examples are: "Johnny has raised an extremely important question. How would others of you respond to it?" "Linda, that's a provocative opinion. Let's discuss the implications of that viewpoint." "Gary, what you've said brings up a crucial dimension of this problem." In each case you have recognized the worth of the student's comment without stating whether you agree or disagree with it.

A teacher reaction that not only reinforces class discussion but adds clarity to that discussion is the paraphrasing of student comments. When you paraphrase, you communicate to a student that he has been heard and understood. If a teacher has misinterpreted a student's response, this approach will give him the maximum opportunity for correcting that misinterpretation. Following a poorly worded comment, you might ask, "Pat, are you saying . . . ?" If the student indicates that you have correctly interpreted his comment, you can proceed to respond to that comment or ask other students to respond to it. If the student indicates that you did not understand what he was trying to say, you can then ask for a restatement of his comment. This approach should minimize the amount of misinformation that is propagated in the classroom. Clarification should not follow only poorly worded responses. If it did, it might cause restatement or clarification to assume a negative connotation.

Another avenue for enhancing class discussion is to approve certain categories of discussion behavior, e.g., asking questions, formulating answers, and expressing opinions. Consider the following teacher reactions: "I'm glad you're asking questions," "It's nice that you let me know when something is unclear to you," "It's good that you give us a reason for your ideas," "I'm glad that you let me know when you disagree with what I say," "I like the fact that you express your opinion," "The way you're speaking up pleases me," "I'm glad you're distinguishing fact from assumption," "It's nice that you're sharing the information you've gathered," "I'm pleased to see you react to Meg's argument." In each of these instances the student could assume that approval had a broader focus than the specific response he had just made.

You should attempt to reinforce positive emotional reactions as well as appropriate academic and social behaviors. A child may manifest a behavior that you consider appropriate, and he may also manifest that behavior with obvious zest. Instead of directing your approval exclusively to the behavior, e.g., "I'm glad you did that," you might also comment on the underlying affective response, e.g., "I'm glad you enjoy doing that," "I'm happy that you're pleased with your work." Expressing your delight when the child shows positive affect is an especially powerful way of conveying to him that his feelings matter to you. This strategy should also increase the frequency with which he expresses positive feelings. Far too little teacher attention is given to children's feelings. Some surveys show that less than one-half of 1 percent of the teacher's time is devoted to children's feelings, either positive or negative (Myrick, 1969).

Since there is more to life than just the good times, how should a teacher respond when the child feels angry, frustrated, anxious, or sad. First, it is completely natural and appropriate that you attempt to comfort a child who has experienced major trauma in his life (such as death in his family, serious illness, accident, separation of parents). Much more frequent, however, are the little day-to-day upheavals which engender confusion, frustration, anger, and anxiety. While there may be some value in giving the child an opportunity to externalize negative feelings, your response should mainly be directed toward relieving those feelings. In other words, it is more beneficial to attempt to alter those factors that are sustaining a child's frustration than merely to recognize that he is frustrated. With this approach you would primarily be reinforcing behaviors leading to resolution of negative feelings rather than the expression of negative feelings per se.

Before you point out the egregious weaknesses in our "feelings" strategy, give *us* the luxury of admitting those weaknesses. Some children may have extreme difficulty in expressing feelings, either positive or negative. In such cases, you will initially want to reinforce the externalization of feelings without regard to their positive or negative connotation. We are recommending an approach similar to that of Anandam, Davis, and Poppen (1971). These experimenters instructed the teachers to praise children (third graders) and to give them "feelings buttons" whenever they verbalized their feelings. A feelings button was a self-adhesive label with the feeling written on it. The child wore the button as long as he wished and then placed it in his feelings diary. While high school students might be insulted at the prospect of wearing feelings buttons, they could still benefit from an atmosphere in which expression of feelings was both encouraged and reinforced.

A second difficulty with our strategy is that some children may be able to externalize negative affect but not know what to do to alter that affect. It is not unusual to find that an anxious child cannot tell you why he is anxious or what to do to reduce that anxiety. We would have to admit that it is desirable to provide the setting events and reinforcement contingencies which will allow the child to express his anger, anxiety, or confusion, even when he has no idea about how to resolve those emotions. Under these circumstances, it is still possible to convey to him that your primary concern is helping him find ways to feel better. Seeking to get him involved in productive activity, asking him to think about what he might do to allay his feelings, and inviting him to participate in group discussions on feelings should help to accentuate that concern.

In the Anandam, Davis, and Poppen study, the experimenters employed a type of group discussion in which the primary focus was on reducing unpleasant emotional reactions. The following example from their research illustrates the tenor of those discussions. Cathy was identified by the class as a constant hitter. Jimmy, who sat directly in front of Cathy, had been the primary object of Cathy's physical abuse.

Cathy: It bothers me if Jimmy turns around and looks at me. So I hit him.

Experimenter: What can we do to help Cathy?

Student: Change Jimmy's seat.

Jimmy: I like my seat. Nobody is going to make me change my seat.

Experimenter: If Jimmy does not want to change his seat, what can we do to help him not bother Cathy?

Student: Ask him not to turn around.

Jimmy: I like to turn around.

Experimenter: Jimmy feels he should be allowed to do what he likes when he is at his desk. I wonder whether anything else can be done that would help Cathy not to hit Jimmy.

(Pause)

Cathy: I know what I can do. I can ask my teacher and change my seat.

Experimenter: I'm glad you have come up with a suggestion that would help you not to hit Jimmy.

Perhaps our response to this question has left the impression that the classroom teacher should be something of a therapist as well as an academician. That impression is intentional.

Should the teacher ever use disapproval? The emphasis of this chapter has thus far been on the use of approval as a technique for changing behavior. By now you may share the feeling of a disgruntled undergraduate who in the midst of her first course in classroom behavior management exclaimed, "I've just had too much of this positive reinforcement." You may be asking, "Don't you ever employ disapproval in classroom management?" Our answer would have to be a cautious "perhaps." Let us immediately qualify that answer by asserting that any classroom situation characterized by a high rate of teacher disapproval is a bad situation. On the other hand, we are not willing to say that you should never use disapproval.

Much of the behavior modification literature clearly implies that the most effective way to minimize inappropriate behavior is to ignore such behavior. We agree that attention (reprimands, threats, exhortations, pleas) to inappropriate behavior will usually increase the frequency of its occurrence. For example, if the teacher responds to the students' getting out of their seats with comments such as, "Sit down," "Get back to work," "Let's quiet down in here," "Stop that," "Don't get up again," he will increase the frequency of out-of-seat behavior (Madsen et al., 1968). Why? He is providing contingent attention to those behaviors. The attention which he construes as aversive is apparently reinforcing to students. The teacher is reinforced in his use of disapproval by the temporary reduction in disruptive behavior which follows disapproval. However, in a matter of two or three minutes the students may be disruptive again. When a teacher employs a great deal of disapproval, his disapproval usually *increases* the frequency of undesirable behavior. An exception is the teacher who is able to generate fear via his disapproval. His reprimands produce a subdued and anxious atmosphere in a class. Such disapproval not only impedes many productive student behaviors in *that* class, it may also diminish a child's capacity to respond in a relaxed, positive manner in other classrooms. Another problem in using disapproval is the effect that it has on children who are not the direct objects of that disapproval. These children may also become upset and disoriented in their work when they see other children reprimanded (Kounin, Gump, and Ryan, 1961). For these reasons, we strongly believe that the pervasive use of disapproval is never justified.

We implied earlier that there might be a time and place to use certain types of disapproval. Disruptive behaviors which involve attacks on students and property can hardly be ignored and therefore must be stopped through some type of restraint and disapproval. We feel that it is legitimate to disapprove of those behaviors which directly interfere with other students' learning activities. Hitting other students, throwing objects, and shouting would certainly fall in the disapprovable category. Probably the most efficient way to express disapproval is to take away credit toward established reinforcers. Deduction of points in a contract or proclamation system would be an example of this type of disapproval. Remember that such penalties should be issued in a very business-like fashion, e.g., "Pete loses two points for hitting Bev." No attempt is made to humiliate Pete or launch a personal attack on his character or competence. If you employ approval very frequently and *disapproval infrequently,* it is likely that your disapproval will effectively deter inappropriate behavior. McAllister et al. (1969) have shown that a combination of disapproval for specific inappropriate behaviors and increased praise for appropriate behavior is very effective in improving the behaviors of high school students.

Your disapproval should be directed toward the student's behavior and not the student himself. It is best to be very specific in stating which behavior you disapprove of and the reasons for your disapproval. For example, say, "your talking while I'm trying to give instructions to the class keeps both you and other students from understanding the instructions." This type of forthright statement as to why something is inappropriate is far better than attempting to communicate your message through sarcasm, "Well, Don, you're really helping us to get off to a good start, aren't you?" or through a personal attack on the child, "Don't you have any respect for others?" "I'm ashamed of you." "You've really disappointed me." These kinds of remarks may humiliate the child and take a heavy toll on his self-respect. In summary, we recommend that you employ lots of approval in your teaching, use little disapproval, and direct your disapproval toward specific behaviors, not the child.

Realizing that by now you may be fighting sleep, perhaps it would help matters if we could pose some challenging questions. If you are able to answer all ten questions, you know more than we do; if you answer at least eight questions, you've been dozing less than 10 percent of the time; if you answer only five questions, you've been fantasizing too much; and if you answer fewer than two questions, well, what can we say?

1. If the teacher's approval of a specific behavior leads to a decrement in that behavior, we can *definitely* conclude that
    (a) The teacher's approval is aversive,
    (b) The teacher's approval is eliciting peer reactions which are aversive,
    (c) The teacher is insincere,
    (d) None of the above.
2. A teacher's use of frequent disapproval is most likely reinforced by
    (a) The relatively permanent deceleration effect that disapproval has on disruptive behavior,
    (b) The temporary deceleration effect that disapproval has on disruptive behavior,

    (c) Behavior modification specialists,

    (d) The release of neuropsychiatric energy.

3. Under which of the following circumstances would teacher disapproval be most likely to impede disruptive behaviors permanently?

    (a) High frequency of disapproval in combination with minimal approval,

    (b) High frequency of disapproval in combination with no approval,

    (c) High frequency of approval in combination with minimal disapproval,

    (d) Random combination of approval and disapproval.

4. The authors contend that teacher approval is most likely to be perceived as sincere when

    (a) It focuses upon something which has not previously been considered important by the student,

    (b) It entails consistency between verbal and nonverbal cues,

    (c) It is given ostentatiously,

    (d) It repeats previously used approval statements.

5. Which of the following strategies would probably produce an increase in the reinforcement value of your approval?

    (a) Pairing approval with something which is already reinforcing to the child,

    (b) Using approval as an S^D for behavior that will lead to nonreinforcement,

    (c) Continuing to use a low frequency of approval,

    (d) Primarily employing noncontingent approval.

6. Regarding the use of contingent and noncontingent approval, the authors suggest that

    (a) The child should be approved on a contingent basis,

    (b) Behavior should be approved on a noncontingent basis,

    (c) The child should be approved on a noncontingent basis and behavior on a contingent basis,

    (d) Both the child and behavior should be approved on a noncontingent basis.

7. When attempting to reinforce appropriate participation in class discussion, a teacher should

    (a) Approve students only for giving correct answers,

    (b) Approve students for asking questions as well as for the specific questions they ask,

    (c) Always indicate if he agrees or disagrees with a student's response,

    (d) Praise students but not touch them.

8. Which of the following would the authors probably consider an acceptable way to reinforce a student for asking questions?
   (a) "John, your question is whether a person can get too much social approval,"
   (b) "John has raised a very important question about social approval. Would someone like to respond to it?"
   (c) "John, I like the way you're asking questions,"
   (d) All of the above.

9. An appropriate way for a teacher to respond to expression of affect is to
   (a) Ignore it since attention would make it worse,
   (b) Recognize and approve expression of positive affect,
   (c) Sympathize with the child when he expresses negative affect,
   (d) Approve expression of positive affect but give no attention to expression of negative affect.

10. Regarding the use of disapproval, the authors recommend that
   (a) Disapproval should never be used,
   (b) Disapproval of the child should be applied noncontingently and disapproval of behavior contingently,
   (c) Both the child and his behavior should be disapproved of contingently,
   (d) Disapproval should be applied only to behavior and not to the child.

Now that you've had such an easy time with our questions, let us pose a situation which might be a bit more difficult. Think of a class that you've taught or recently been in. Picture the students in that class who frequently misbehaved. That's not too hard to do, is it? We bet you've just identified at least three or four students. From among these, pick out the one who misbehaved most. He was the one who talked incessantly, forgot to do his assignments, tapped his pencil on the desk, talked back to you, etc. You name it and he did it. When school was out, you would say to yourself, "Thank God, I don't have to meet him again today." If you have this student identified, you are ready for our exercise. In the next three minutes, list *at least five* appropriate behaviors exhibited by this student in class.

    1.
    2.
    3.
    4.
    5.

Well, what happened? If you completed the list you know that even the so-called "bad" student manifests many behaviors which could legitimately be reinforced. The problem is to stop focusing on his bad behaviors long enough to see the good things he is doing. If you could not identify a single appropriate behavior, we suggest that you take off the blinders.

Peer Influences as Means of Classroom Management

The influences of peers in shaping, maintaining, and extinguishing a person's behavior are not unique to the twentieth century American classroom. Peer influence is as old as Adam and Eve. Was it not peer influence that led to Adam's sudden affinity for apples? Many behaviors in everyone's repertoire have been shaped by peers in one fashion or another. Honestly examine how many of your own behaviors are being maintained by the reactions of peers. Even groups such as hippies who break away from the societal norms seem to be strongly affected by the peer influences within their own culture.

Although peer influences are not new to the present century, the concept of systematic manipulation of peer influences to elicit and maintain desirable behavior is fairly new. The Russians have used peer support as the principal means of modifying student behavior (Bronfenbrenner, 1970). In the United States the concept of individualism may have impeded experimental investigation of peer influences. We know of one instance where the community's resistance to systematic manipulation of peer influences ran so high that the headlines in the local daily read something to the effect of: "Beware of psychologists who make your children sit in circles—these are communistic activities." In resisting the use of peer controls, we are ignoring a vital source of behavioral management.

There are four notable ways by which peer influences can be brought to bear upon a student's behavior: (1) interactions with peers can be used as reinforcement; (2) direct peer attention can be manipulated to decrease inappropriate behavior and increase appropriate behavior; (3) peers can be used as models for other students; and (4) peers can be used to tutor other students.

Interactions with Peers as Reinforcement

From infancy, man seeks contact with other human beings. Although many variables can contribute to the reinforcement value of that contact, human interaction appears to be reinforcing in its own right. Over an extended time, almost any kind of interaction would probably be preferable to no interaction. If individuals happen to be of the same age with similar interests, interaction becomes even more reinforcing.

It is reasonable to expect, therefore, that peer interactions can be exploited as a top level reinforcement for modifying classroom behavior.

How can the teacher use peer interactions to reinforce appropriate behavior? A few opportunities for peer interaction already exist in most schools. These include playing during recess, sitting at the same table for lunch, and numerous out-behind-the-barn type opportunities that our censor would not permit us to discuss. In the classroom, occasions for peer interaction can be deliberately arranged by the teacher. These planned opportunities, just as other types of rewards, can be made contingent upon appropriate behavior. For example, you might say, "As soon as you finish the math assignment, Bob, you can work at the puzzle with Tom." Before making such a statement, you would need to be sure that: (1) Tom is someone with whom Bob wants to work the puzzle and (2) Tom is likely to finish the math assignment by the time Bob finishes. Peer interaction can also be used as a reinforcer for the whole class. You could say: "You have ten arithmetic problems to solve today. As soon as you complete them and have them corrected by me, you can spend the rest of the class period playing." Such an approach would encourage most students, if not all, to speed up, and you would not have the responsibility of deciding who is liked best by whom.

Proximity to liked peers is a privilege that can be used in some cases as a reinforcer for ongoing academic activity. Let's say that Tom and Bob like to be deskmates but are not necessarily engaging in task-relevant behavior. Under these circumstances you can tell them, "I know you two guys like sitting together. I want you to have that privilege and I have no reason to deny it except when you goof off." You can then make their sitting together contingent upon their completing specified amounts of work.

Can peer interaction help to make learning activities more reinforcing? Yes, it can. Activities which entail peer reactions in written or oral form are highly reinforcing to many students. For example, you can choose a controversial topic such as "Should abortion be legalized on a national basis?" and find out which of your students say "yes" and which "no." Pair a "yes" student with a "no" student and let them engage in a written dialogue of presenting their cases to each other, challenging each other's statements, and so on. By pairing the students, you avoid the possibility of a few students dominating the discussion. By having them write, you avoid the possibility of having too much noise. Their written dialogues will also provide you with tangible evidence as to the quality of the learning experience. After you have read their dialogues, you can praise students for providing factual information to support their points of view, providing a rationale for their argument, etc.

It might be difficult for elementary students to handle a highly controversial issue like abortion, but that doesn't rule out the possibility of written dialogues. You can give each pair ten words from their vocabulary list and request them to come up with a story which contains all ten words, each student writing a sentence alternately. It is fun for the students to see how their story develops because neither is sure what the other one is going to write.

When small group discussions are arranged, the general expectation is that each group will present a report to the class or turn in a written report to the teacher. With oral reports, the teacher's inquiry "Any questions on the group report?" usually falls flat. It could be that students are not inclined to listen to such reports or that students are too intimidated to question the work of their peers in front of the whole class. Both of these weaknesses can be eliminated if two groups exchange their reports and react by writing comments and questions about the content of the report. In our use of this approach with college and high school students, we have noticed that students not only get a kick out of reacting to another group's report but in seeing their peers' comments concerning their own work. You can bet that students are consummate artists at interjecting humor in their comments!

One way to make large group discussion more reinforcing is by eliciting peer reactions to student comments. Under such circumstances, teacher approval becomes less important in facilitating the discussion. In one study with fourth and fifth graders, we found that students could carry on a discussion by making comments such as: "Chuck, I have a question for you. How do you think you can use the electric power if there is no manpower?" or "I disagree with Jane, Dan, and Lee because manpower will be replaced by other types of power," or "Why do you think man will become lazy if he invents too many machines?" or "I disagree with myself because I see what Chuck is saying." In the early stages of the study, the teachers had to ask for peer responses. Toward the end of the project the number of times students responded to each others' comments outnumbered the teachers' requests for peer reactions.

When students were asked to express their feelings about the discussion atmosphere in this classroom, they gave the following kinds of responses: "I liked it because it was fun agreeing and disagreeing." "I like the way we are doing it, because everyone gets to take part. If someone has a question, maybe a classmate could get through to him

better than the teacher." "In one way I like the discussion. It is that
I like to hear other boys' and girls' opinion about what we are talking
about. In one way I do not like it. It is that sometimes you get bored.
But I want to keep discussion." "I like the way we can discuss and
work together and I like the way we can ask and answer questions. I
hope that we will always do it this way."

It is time for you to engage in some reinforcing peer interactions.
You don't have to tell us what they are. Just answer the following
questions, and you have our blessings to interact as you will. (Our
nonjudgemental attitude is sometimes shocking even to us.)

1. Interactions with peers should be
    (a) Permitted only after task-relevant behaviors are completed,
    (b) Minimized in antiquated buildings since the noise level may
         bring down the roof,
    (c) Made a built-in feature of learning activities,
    (d) Allowed only with members of the same sex.
2. Peer interactions can make a learning activity more reinforcing if
   students are given
    (a) An opportunity to react to each other's responses in writing,
    (b) Controversial topics to discuss,
    (c) A chance to make projections for the future,
    (d) All of the above.
3. In attempting to make large group discussion reinforcing for the
   students, the teacher should
    (a) Refrain from making any comments whatsoever,
    (b) Nod his head to every response that is made,
    (c) Tell risqué stories,
    (d) Elicit peer reactions to what is being said.

Modifying Behavior through Peer Attention

The effectiveness of contingent teacher attention in changing a student's behavior is sometimes negated by the reactions of peers to that
behavior. The teacher may painfully train himself to ignore a student's
clownish behavior only to find that everytime the student engages in
that behavior, he gets a big laugh from the other students. Peer attention is often reinforcing enough to maintain an undesirable behavior
no matter how consistently the teacher ignores or punishes it. If peer
attention can outweigh the potency of teacher-provided consequences
and can maintain a student's disruptive behavior, it stands to reason
that (1) withdrawal of peer attention can help reduce disruptive behavior and (2) contingent peer approval for appropriate behavior can

increase that behavior. We shall now entertain your questions in these two areas.

How does one initiate a systematic peer reinforcement program in a class? Perhaps a good beginning point is to discuss with the students how they can contribute to the desirable behavior of their peers. Try to conduct the discussion in such a way that students suggest the appropriate reactions rather than have you telling them how to react. You can certainly shape the strategies students suggest by asking the right questions and selectively reinforcing appropriate responses to these questions. You should ask questions such as "Since we have already agreed that there are certain behaviors which interfere with the work of others, why do you suppose some students continue to exhibit these behaviors?" "When a student misbehaves, what kind of reaction from the rest of us would make a recurrence of his misbehavior less likely?" "When a student behaves appropriately, what could we do to encourage him to continue behaving appropriately?"

If you respond neutrally to inappropriate comments offered by students and emphasize suggestions which are consistent with reinforcement principles, you will probably be able to piece together an adequate description of peer reinforcement from their suggestions. Here are the major propositions which you should be quick to emphasize: (1) Disruptive behavior is often maintained by peer attention even though much of this attention may be negative, e.g., "shut up," "get to work," "go to hell." (2) Completely ignoring disruptive behavior would be an effective way of reducing that behavior. (3) Responding by approving appropriate behavior would be an effective way of increasing such behavior. Perhaps these suggestions should be written on the board as students offer them. At the end of the discussion you might summarize the basic principles of peer reinforcement and list the payoffs the class will receive if it can increase appropriate behavior and decrease disruptive behavior.

The next phase in implementing a systematic peer reinforcement program is to select certain students who will serve as major peer reinforcers in the class. We shall refer to these youngsters as the *control students*. Suppose that you wish to select one control student to work with each of the target students. Your objective is to identify a specific student who would be quite influential with the target. To achieve this objective, it is probably best to choose a control student who already frequently interacts with the target. In this case, you would have a behavioral basis for assuming that the control student's attention would be reinforcing to the target.

A second consideration in the selection of control students is the extent to which *your* approval would be reinforcing to them. The best indication of the reinforcement value of your approval is the past behavior of these students. If a student has previously volunteered to do things for you, has been quick to comply with your requests, and has responded positively (e.g., smiling) when you praise him, it is likely that your approval is highly reinforcing to him. This consideration is important because your approval is probably the major reason why the control student will work toward becoming an effective peer reinforcer.

A third consideration in the selection of control students is the extent of their influence with students other than the targets. Selection of control students who are popular with their peers will increase the likelihood of other students emulating the control students' reactions to the targets. In this case, other students would enhance the effectiveness of the control students rather than negating that effectiveness.

In summary, you should select as controls those students whose attention is already reinforcing to the targets, students for whom your approval is already reinforcing, and students who appear to be reinforcing to other members of the class.

Once you have selected your control students, how do you enlist their assistance in working with the targets? A completely candid approach is probably the best. Arrange to see these students privately and explain to them as fully as possible why they have been selected and what you want them to do. Emphasize the contributions they will be making to you, to the target students, and to the class by becoming peer reinforcers.

Training the selected students to be efficient reinforcers will require more than simply providing a verbal explanation of their new role. Some of the expected modes of behavior may initially seem quite awkward to them. Most students, like most adults, are not used to praising people for behaving appropriately. We have found it useful to follow a verbal explanation with role-playing exercises in which the control students practice giving contingent approval to one another. Some of the controls can initially assume the role of target students and others the role of peer reinforcers. These roles can be interchanged as the control students develop skill in showing contingent approval. If you have video-taping equipment available, you might also tape the role-play sessions and let the students see first-hand how they were responding to each other. The video tape would give you an excellent opportunity to point out specific instances of appropriate peer behaviors (e.g., approving desirable target student behaviors). Continue the role-play sessions until the students meet your criterion for responding contingently to target student behavior.

The most crucial phase in the training of control students comes when they attempt to exhibit their new behavior in the classroom. At this point you must be willing to shape their behavior and give them a great deal of verbal support for responding appropriately to the target students. Their initial attempts to be reinforcing may elicit some rather unusual reactions. One control student was recounting to us his first attempt to praise a target. According to his story, the target student (a female) was drawing a picture when he leaned over her shoulder and whispered, "That's a really good drawing." At this point in the account, we eagerly inquired as to how the target student had responded to his praise—to which he replied, "She took a swing at me!" So you must be prepared to reinforce your control students when their peer reinforcement tactics are not ostensibly paying off.

If possible, have someone (e.g., teacher's aide, guidance counselor) to observe the interaction between the controls and the target students. The observer would primarily need to record how many times a control student responded to appropriate target student behavior and how many times to inappropriate behaviors. The observer, when possible, should also record the kind of attention given to the target, e.g., praise, smile, touch, reprimand. You can use these observational data as a basis of daily feedback to the controls concerning their proficiency as peer reinforcers. Such data will allow you to be highly systematic in reinforcing the controls for their peer reinforcing behavior.

Another source of reinforcement to the controls will be the positive changes that eventually occur in the target students' behavior. If the targets begin to contribute more to the attainment of group rewards, if their academic work improves, and if they become less disruptive in class, that would be definitive evidence that peer reinforcement is paying off. For that reason the control students should be systematically informed of changes that occur in the target students' behavior.

How can the teacher get the class as a whole to ignore inappropriate behavior? We've already suggested a general class discussion in which you attempt to emphasize the prudence of not attending to undesirable behavior. A few of your students will probably take this counsel to heart. When you introduce your systematic peer reinforcement program, a few more students will follow the control students' lead in not responding to poor behavior. Nevertheless, there still may be a considerable amount of peer attention to inappropriate behavior. Where does a teacher go from here? Ackerman (1972) has used what he calls "differential reinforcement" to help students ignore the disruptive behavior of their peers. Tokens were given only to those students who ignored others' inappropriate behavior and who continued in their work. When the other students realized they were losing out on the tokens "the performer suddenly lost his audience" (p. 103). Since students (like teachers) have been attending to inappropriate behaviors all of their lives, you should not expect instantaneous success with the Ackerman approach. Furthermore, the time required to dispense the tokens may negate some of the gains from peers' ignoring undesirable behavior.

Another approach for reducing peer attention to inappropriate behavior is a procedure called *time out*. Under this arrangement the misbehaving student is removed for a short time period from the situation in which he manifested the inappropriate behavior. It is virtually impossible to eliminate the reinforcing reactions that certain behaviors elicit in a classroom setting. For example, Patty hits Rock, causing him to cry. Rock's crying may be a major source of reinforcement for Patty's aggressive behavior. Removing that source of reinforcement from the situation may be a Herculean task. It would be possible, however, to remove Patty from the classroom situation immediately following her aggressive behavior. If she is so removed, she will not have the prolonged satisfaction of hearing Rock cry. So if a behavior naturally produces a great deal of peer reaction, time out may be an effective way to minimize the reinforcing effects of that reaction.

Since time out should immediately follow the behavior it is designed to weaken, the time out space must be close to the regular classroom setting. Some teachers use a nearby cloak room and others partition off a part of the regular classroom for a time out space. No, we will not endorse using a cold, damp, and dreary cellar for the time out area. The purpose of time out is not to frighten children. The time out area is simply to be a dull space in which the student is removed from whatever was reinforcing his disruptive behavior. Ideally, it should be an area in which the child is visually and auditorily cut off from what is happening in the regular classroom. Otherwise, he can still be reinforced for his disruptive behavior by what he sees and hears through the cracks. You must also make certain that the child carries nothing with him to time out. One child emerged from time out with an obvious look of delight on his face. When the teacher looked inside the large refrigerator box used for the time out space, she found the walls a veritable panorama of colors. A student should take nothing, not even his crayons, to time out. Otherwise, time out may become an ecstactically reinforcing activity.

For time out to be effective, a student need not stay isolated forever and always. Usually a period of five to ten minutes is sufficient for the teacher to reestablish a calm atmosphere in the classroom (i.e., quiet Rock's crying, pick up the broken glass, get the other children back to work). The dissident student should stay in time out until this calmness has been achieved. Sometimes a child will react to the time out area rather violently. If this happens, the child must be left in time out until his aggressive behavior has abated. If you remove him from time out while he is screaming, crying, and kicking, you will reinforce the incidence of those behaviors. In using time out to reduce a preschooler's aggressive behavior, Allen (1972) found that in the early stages 80 percent of the time out occasions evoked tantrums. Continuation of the time out strategy produced a drastic reduction in both aggressive behaviors in the classroom and tantrum behaviors during time out.

It is probably apparent to you that the time out procedure is better suited for children at the kindergarten or primary level than for older students. With older students, you run the risk of physically not being able to place the student in time out for the appropriate time period. He may simply refuse to go to time out or he may decide to leave the time out area before the set time has elapsed. Under these circumstances, you may be physically unable to prevent him from carrying out his intentions. However, with young children you would usually have the wherewithal to remove the child from the regular classroom area and keep him in time out for the appropriate time period. Time out simply represents a way of minimizing the reinforcing effects of peer reactions on disruptive behavior when the peers are too young to implement a systematic peer reinforcement strategy.

Some teachers have confused time out with a procedure often employed in calming hyperactive or agitated children. Some children seem to benefit emotionally from being moved to a quiet area. It may be that the child is being overly stimulated by all that is occurring around him in the regular classroom. As a result, he is unable to concentrate on his work and may become visibly agitated by the interfering activities. Certainly, this child could benefit from being transferred to an area where there are fewer interfering stimuli. This procedure is *not* equivalent to what behavior modification specialists call time out. In using time out, you remove the disruptive child from the situation that is reinforcing his disruptive behavior. In the case of the hyperactive or agitated child, you change the *setting events* (concurrent activities) which seem to be provoking his hyperactivity and irritation. If you're going to use a quiet area, we suggest that it be different from the time out area. For a quiet area, the child need not be totally cut off from the rest of the class. He also may take his lesson materials with him to the quiet area.

Okay, let's see how well you've been following our discussion on the modification of student behavior through peer attention. Unless you've been engaging in excessive transcendental meditation you should have no problems with the following items.

1. In setting up a systematic peer reinforcement program, the teacher should
    (a) Explain to the students how they are reinforcing bad behavior,
    (b) Explain the peer reinforcement contingencies to the target students but conceal the contingencies from the controls,
    (c) Let students suggest procedures for facilitating appropriate behavior from their peers,
    (d) Enlist the aid of the custodial staff.

2. Which of the following might be used as a criterion for selecting a child to serve as a control student?
    (a) The child has previously interacted quite frequently with one or more of the target students,
    (b) The child has previously been cooperative with the teacher,
    (c) The child has previously evidenced popularity with students other than the targets,
    (d) All of the above.

3. In the implementation of a peer reinforcement program,
    (a) Interaction between control and target students should be systematically monitored,
    (b) The teacher should avoid making any comments which might affect the behavior of the control students,
    (c) The target students should be told that they are the object of a special behavior modification program,
    (d) The superintendent should be called in to analyze the situation.

4. You can help peers to ignore a student's disruptive behavior by
    (a) Reprimanding them each time they attend to disruptive activity,
    (b) Utilizing Ackerman's differential reinforcement system,
    (c) Ignoring the peers' attention to disruptive behavior,
    (d) Sending students who give you a hard time to the office.

5. The time out procedure can be used most efficiently at which of the following academic levels?
    (a) Primary,
    (b) Secondary,
    (c) College,
    (d) Graduate.

6. Under which of the following circumstances would time out be indicated?
   (a) Teacher attention is sustaining disruptive behavior,
   (b) Disruptive behavior is eliciting peer reactions which can not be eliminated from the situation,
   (c) The dissident child wants to be alone,
   (d) The child is engaging in nondisruptive, time off task activity.
7. In response to the question of how long a child should stay in time out, it was suggested that
   (a) Five to ten minutes would always be sufficient,
   (b) The child should remain in time out until a calm atmosphere can be reestablished in the situation from which he was removed,
   (c) The child be removed from time out if he starts screaming and kicking,
   (d) The child stay in time out until he's sorry for what he's done.

Peers as Models

A child's behavior is not exclusively a function of the consequences which directly follow the responses he exhibits. His behavior is often affected by the behaviors he observes in others. When a child manifests a behavior as a result of observing someone else displaying that behavior, we refer to his response as *imitative* or *role-modeling* behavior. The person the child observes exhibiting the behavior is termed the *role model*. Though the teacher is probably the most potent role model in most classrooms, peers run a close second. With such a powerful source of behavior management on the loose, you would certainly want to mobilize it for the edification of other students.

What can the teacher do to help students develop desirable behaviors through peer modeling? You will not be surprised to learn that the concept of reinforcement is useful in accounting for peer role modeling. One type of reinforcement that is fundamental to modeling is vicarious reinforcement. Suppose that David never raises his hand before blurting out a comment. While you might attempt to change that behavior by ignoring all such comments, an additional strategy would be to make sure that David observes Bill being reinforced for raising his hand before commenting. For example, "Bill, you have your hand up. What's your comment? [Bill comments.] That's an extremely important question, Bill." You have approved of Bill's handraising and have given him an opportunity to obtain additional approval via his comment. Your reactions to Bill should affect the frequency of David's raising his hand before commenting. Cormier (1970) has demonstrated that attending to the appropriate behavior of target students has a positive impact on the behavior of other students.

It is not always necessary for a behavior to be reinforced before it will be imitated. If a student's previous behaviors have generally been reinforced, his present behaviors, though not directly reinforced, will probably be imitated. Apparently, other students assume that most anything the model does is the right thing to do. Advertisers frequently employ this strategy in getting famous people to endorse their products. Though it's improbable that movie stars would be experts on detergents, coffee, and toothpaste, we may still associate the fame and fortune achieved in other ways with the use of these products. Teachers can produce a peer modeling effect merely by arranging for a student who has consistently been reinforced for desirable behavior to manifest a specified appropriate behavior in the presence of his peers.

There is a third way that reinforcement can affect peer modeling. If a peer has previously been the source of considerable reinforcement to a child, the peer's behavior has probably acquired substantial reinforcement value for that child. Consequently, the child may find the mere act of behaving like the model reinforcing. One strategy that should increase the role-modeling potential of peers is to use them as control students in a systematic peer reinforcement program. Indirect support for this postulation comes from Feshbach's study (1967), which showed that a teacher who approves correct responses is imitated more frequently by students than one who emphasizes negative feedback.

Proximity seems to be a factor that can increase the effectiveness of peer modeling procedures. Students tend to imitate peers who are closer to them. You can periodically rearrange the seating patterns of your students so that students who are inclined to behave inappropriately sit closer to those who behave appropriately. Similarly, you can assign an habitually disruptive student to a group project on which several productive students are working. Proximity in combination with the reinforcement procedures described earlier should pay off handsomely in producing a positive peer modeling effect.

How effective is negative peer modeling? Some educators have felt that an effective way to decrease deviant behaviors is to make an example of children who manifest such behaviors. Research has shown that when a child observes a model being punished for a specific behavior, he will be less likely to show that behavior (Bandura and Walters, 1963). Nevertheless, this strategy does entail certain risks. For example, a teacher may administer very harsh public criticism or physical punishment to the child who has attacked another child. But in so doing, the teacher serves as a role model for the very behavior he is attempting to discourage. The teacher demonstrates that he also handles frustration by responding aggressively—and the teacher's behavior goes unpunished. Another disadvantage of using negative role models is that in other settings the child may be reinforced for the very behavior he sees punished in the classroom. So witnessing the model's behavior allows the child to add another negative response to his repertory of "bad" behaviors.

Sometimes the behavior of a role model is sequentially followed by both reinforcing and aversive consequences. This helps to explain why reinforcing the behavior of a role model in the classroom is not always effective in changing other students' behavior. It may be that the very behavior which is reinforced in the classroom is punished outside the classroom. For example, the academic accomplishments which are approved by the teacher and peers in the classroom may be severely criticized by the peer group outside the classroom. The possibility of such conflicting contingencies is one reason why you must be aware of the major contingencies which exist in the child's home and community milieu. Unless some of these external contingencies are altered they may largely negate the most appropriate of contingencies within the classroom.

While a reinforcement–punishment sequence following a role model's behavior may decrease the incidence of a desired response, a punishment–reinforcement sequence may increase the frequency of an undesired response. For example, a student may continue to manifest an inappropriate behavior until he finally gets the payoff he's seeking. As a result, the effects of your initially aversive reactions are negated by the reinforcement he ultimately receives. If Cathy raises so much hell in your class that you finally acquiesce to her demands or send her on an errand, you can shortly expect a deluge of hell raising from other students.

Well, it's that time again. Your answers to the following questions will indicate whether you've assimilated the substance from this discussion on peers as role models.

1. Under which of the following circumstances would a child be likely to imitate the behavior of a role model?
   (a) Model is rewarded for the behavior in question,
   (b) Although model is not rewarded for the behavior in question, he has frequently been rewarded for other behaviors,
   (c) Model has been the source of considerable contingent reinforcement for the child,
   (d) All of the above.

2. A major difficulty in using punishment in the role-modeling paradigm is that
   (a) Punishment has no effect on the likelihood of a child's imitating a role model,
   (b) The child may later be reinforced for the behavior he sees punished in the classroom,
   (c) Punishment serves to make the role model more compassionate,
   (d) Punishment puts fear and trepidation into the hearts of one and all.

Peers as Tutors

There are few educational endeavors which have generated more reports of success than the use of student tutors. Educators who have tried student tutoring almost without exception feel that it results in a plethora of benefits. In fact, we have been unable to identify any report in the literature which casts student tutoring in a disparaging light. However, our endorsement of student tutoring is tempered somewhat by the nature of the reports dealing with this issue. Practically no report treats tutoring within a precise operant framework. Most discuss it in such global terms that you cannot determine precisely what occurred in the tutoring experience.

A second major limitation of the student tutoring reports is their lack of sound experimental design in appraising the effectiveness of tutoring. Few of these studies have non-tutored control groups and few present hard data to support the efficacy of tutoring. Most depend on the testimonies of teachers, tutors, and tutees. In dealing with your questions in this area, we will attempt to extract from the published reports what seem to be the principal factors contributing to the success of student tutoring. And we won't be above throwing in a few speculations of our own occasionally.

What are the benefits of utilizing students as tutors? At this time, there is modest empirical evidence that students benefit academically from tutoring other students (Davis, 1972; Fleming, 1969) and from being tutored by other students (Conlon, Hall, and Hanley, 1972; Davis, 1972; Harris, Sherman, and Henderson, 1972; Willis, Crowder, and Morris, 1972). Consider first the academic benefits which may accrue to the tutor. A sixth grader might be absolutely insulted at the prospect of reading first or second grade materials for his own benefit, but quite willing to work with these materials when tutoring a first or second grade student. As far as the tutee is concerned, he experiences a degree of individualized instruction which would not be attainable in most traditional classrooms.

The obvious benefits of student tutoring may lie in the personal and social domains. Almost without exception, writers on this topic mention tutoring's facilitative impact on the self-esteem of both tutor and tutee. Asking a child to assume the role of tutor is analogous to saying, "We think you're important"; "We believe you have something to contribute to someone else"; and "We can trust you with responsibility." The tutoring relationship communicates a similar message of personal importance to the tutee. The tutor, first of all, provides lots of personal attention to the tutee, a commodity all too scarce in public education. Second, that attention has the connotation of friendship more than of authority. In fact, some schools refer to tutors as "friends" or "teaching buddies" in order to convey the image of a helper rather than an authority figure.

Published reports on student tutoring strongly suggest that it also enhances a child's attitude toward school, toward his teachers, and toward teaching as a career (Davis, 1972; Fleming, 1969; Frager and Stern, 1970). It allows the child to experience first-hand what it would be like to be a contributor to society. It makes knowledge and academic skills important in an immediate and tangible sense. Knowledge becomes something more than facts to memorize and regurgitate on final examination. Instead, the tutor's knowledge and academic skills allow him to make an observable change in another person's (tutee) behavior. Some reports (Thelen, 1969) suggest that tutoring results in such an increase in morale that the tutor's dress habits, cooperativeness with the teacher, consideration of other students, and his own affinity for learning all change for the better. Now you know that something which sounds that good couldn't be all bad.

Who should tutor whom? The typical arrangement is for junior and senior high school students to tutor primary level students. This age difference should minimize the threat experienced by the tutor since he is dealing with someone who is much smaller physically and someone considerably less sophisticated in the ways of the world. This age difference may also maximize the reinforcement value of the tutor for the tutee. Receiving extensive attention from an older child is apparently a very supportive experience for a young child.

If tutor–tutee relationships are arranged so that a child who is receiving help in one area is giving help in another, then children of similar ages can productively tutor each other. A convincing illustration of this point is provided by Harris, Sherman, and Henderson

(1972). In their study, the whole class divided itself into groups of two to four members and students within each group helped one another for about ten minutes before a spelling quiz. Since grouping, leadership within groups, and tutoring procedures were a matter of spontaneity, they changed rather substantially from day to day. The spelling performance of the entire class improved.

You may be inclined to think that you should select your smartest students to be the tutors. Surprisingly but fortunately, the achievement level of the tutors seems to have little impact on the degree of learning attained by the tutee. Davis (1972) found that remedial students of a higher class could successfully tutor remedial students of a lower class. Even more surprising is Fleming's (1969) finding that low average and borderline (IQ assessments) students of one age level could effectively tutor high average students of a much younger age. We recommend that you select your tutors primarily on the basis of their desire to serve as tutors. If you don't have enough volunteers, you can set up a contingency in your contract system to award points to any student who tutors other students.

Exactly what does student tutoring entail? In programs where the emphasis is on friendship rather than teaching, the tutor is someone with whom the younger child can talk, play games, read, and get academic help. Under these circumstances, tutoring is a relatively unstructured experience in which tutor and tutee define the nature of their relationship on a day-to-day basis. At the opposite end of the continuum are arrangements in which tutors instruct children in very specific academic skills via precisely delineated academic activities. For instance, the sixth grade tutors in the Frager and Stern (1970) study used the McNeil ABC Learning Activities (1966) in working with first and second grade students. Perhaps the most common arrangement is for the tutor to formulate his own lesson plans under some degree of teacher supervision. We suspect that the tutor would be a bit more enthusiastic about using activities he had worked out than those prescribed by the teacher. In many cases, tutors have essentially assumed the role of teacher aides. Their responsibilities may include making presentations to an entire class, leading small-group discussions, helping a group put on a dramatic program, providing individual assistance to students, developing instructional materials, correcting homework, and operating audio-visual equipment. The individualized learning packages to be described in Chapter VI make extensive use of tutors to assist less advanced students with the mechanics of the program and specific instructional activities in the program.

You're naturally wondering when students would engage in all these fantastic activities. Although many schools have used recess time, study periods, and after-school periods for tutoring, we recommend the scheduling of tutoring sessions as a regular part of the academic day. Since student tutoring seems to hold as much promise as most other academic activities, what is not legitimate about incorporating it in the regular schedule? In a conventional school setting, tutoring can most easily be scheduled by having members of an entire class work individually with members of another class at a set time during the school day. Schools engaged in full-fledged tutoring programs appear to be spending two to five hours a week in tutoring activity. Whether more or less time would be advantageous is an unresolved empirical question.

What type of training should student tutors receive? In general, we would say that the procedures for training tutors are not too dissimilar from the techniques for training teachers. A first step in the training process might be to have the student observe in the classroom in which he will later be tutoring. Use of an observation scale similar to that shown in Table 3 of Chapter IV should sensitize the tutor-to-be to different modes of interacting with children and the effects of these behaviors on the child's responses. A second activity used in many training programs is the role playing of appropriate tutoring behaviors, such as presenting the learning activities in a logical sequence, approving desirable tutee behavior, and minimizing criticism of the tutee (Davis, 1972; Willis, Crowder, and Morris, 1972). Role playing of this type should be conducted with groups of prospective tutors, so they can criticize each others' behavior.

The actual tutoring sessions should be carefully evaluated by having an observer record the nature of the interaction between tutor and tutee, by asking the tutor to keep a log of his activities, and by having the tutee fill out an evaluation of the tutoring sessions. Feedback derived from the various sources should be shared with the tutor. Some authors suggest that providing time for tutors to get together and compare notes is one of the most crucial elements of a tutor-training program.

That tutor training can make a difference is clearly evidenced in an investigation by Niedermeyer (1970). His Tutor Observation Scale differentiated between trained and untrained tutors on the following points: (1) trained tutors engage the pupils in more friendly conversation than do untrained tutors; (2) trained tutors verbally confirm correct pupil responses more frequently than untrained tutors; (3) trained tutors praise pupils more frequently than untrained tutors;

(4) trained tutors show the pupil the correct response when he is incorrect more frequently than do untrained tutors; and (5) trained tutors get correct responses from the pupil before proceeding to the next item more frequently than untrained tutors.

What types of behavior management programs would most readily incorporate peer tutoring? The group contingent reinforcement procedure described in Chapter II would lend itself very nicely to peer tutoring. Under this arrangement, everyone stands to gain from helping his peers. This is a far cry from the traditional competitive atmosphere in which students succeed at the expense of their fellow students. Hamblin, Hathaway, and Wodarski (1971) have demonstrated rather unequivocally that certain types of group contingent reinforcement automatically result in peer tutoring behavior. One warning: under group contingencies students sometimes copy rather than learn from one another. You can take care of this possibility by making the reinforcement contingent not only upon finishing assignments but passing teacher-monitored tests over those assignments.

What Ackerman (1972) calls "reinforcement sharing" should also promote tutoring. Reinforcement sharing is a situation in which reinforcement for the group is contingent upon one or a few students' performances. The underlying assumptions are that most students will approve a peer's behavior that leads to their own reinforcement and/or will assist that student in learning the specified behavior (peer tutoring). Evans and Oswalt (1971) have successfully used the reinforcement sharing technique to improve students' academic performance in spelling and arithmetic. In the first instance, the class was dismissed for recess immediately if subject one or two could correctly spell a specific word. The performance of these two students improved substantially on weekly spelling tests. A similar contingency using early dismissal of class for story-reading time improved the performance of two students in arithmetic. In both of these cases, the authors anecdotally reported many attempts by peers to influence the behaviors of the target subjects (e.g., urging the targets to do their work, offering assistance with their work).

By now, you've heard so much discussion of teacher approval, peer reinforcement, peer modeling, and peer tutoring that you would probably regurgitate at the mere mentioning of these terms. Answer the following questions, and we promise not to speak of these concepts again in anything above a whisper.

1. Published reports dealing with student tutoring
   (a) Are of the highest empirical quality,
   (b) Primarily contain testimonies from teachers and students about the effects of tutoring,
   (c) Indicate that tutoring is of great value to the tutee but of minimal value to the tutor,
   (d) Are pretty pessimistic about the prospects of tutoring.
2. The section on student tutoring indicates that
   (a) Tutors are usually several years older than tutees,
   (b) Only very bright students make effective tutors,
   (c) Teachers should plan all the activities used by tutors,
   (d) Tutoring should take place only during recess and study periods.
3. Regarding the training of student tutors, Anandam and Williams suggest
   (a) Role playing of appropriate tutoring behaviors,
   (b) Periodically monitoring the tutor's interaction with the tutee,
   (c) Providing time for tutors to get together and compare notes,
   (d) All of the above.
4. Student tutoring would most likely *not* be facilitated by
   (a) A norm-referenced grading system,
   (b) Pairing students so each will be responsible for the other's behavior,
   (c) Using reinforcement sharing during special occasions,
   (d) Implementing a group contingent reinforcement program.

Chapter IV

BEYOND THE SKINNER BOX
Procedures for Empirically Analyzing Classroom Behavior

Few psychologists would deny the stupendous impact of B. F. Skinner on the study of human behavior. His contributions in the areas of programmed instruction and application of reinforcement concepts to societal problems are among the most significant in the field of applied psychology. These contributions are exemplified by books such as *Walden Two* (1948), *Technology of Teaching* (1968), and *Beyond Freedom and Dignity* (1971). Although these works focus on the behavior of human beings in applied settings, they were preceded by approximately two decades of laboratory research with animals. The major contribution of Skinner's laboratory experiments was the delineation of the operant conditioning paradigm and the parameters which affect the strength of operant behavior. His laboratory research was typified by an apparatus containing a simple response mechanism such as a lever, bar, or key which the animal could manipulate to obtain reinforcement. That type of apparatus has acquired the infamous title of "Skinner Box," a label which even Skinner disavows.

In the last twenty years, perhaps in part due to Skinner's influence, increasing numbers of behavioral psychologists have moved their experiments from the laboratory to applied settings. Their efforts have not yet produced unequivocal success. Many educators have been highly resistant to a behavioristic analysis of the teaching–learning process. These educators are quick to point out that a child is quite different from a rat in a Skinner Box. The critics are certainly correct on one point: educators cannot control the child's environment nearly so precisely as psychologists can the rat's environment. These limitations are painfully felt each time we attempt to systematically analyze some portion of students' behavior. Despite the difficulties involved, numerous psychologists are now engaged in a serious study of classroom behavior. The procedures being used by these psychologists will be the focus of this chapter.

At the risk of losing some of our readers, we must say that this chapter is intended for the serious student of behavior management. By "serious student" we do not simply mean graduate students in Educational Psychology or those who have done extensive reading in the area of behavior modification. Instead, we are talking about that individual who wants to pursue a systematic analysis of classroom behavior on a first-hand basis. The principal who wants to investigate the relative merits of various operant techniques for his school, the counselor who wishes to demonstrate the efficacy of behavior modification strategies to his colleagues, and the teacher who aspires to become a skilled behavioral engineer all fall into the "serious student" category.

Basic to a systematic functional analysis of behavior is the process of describing behaviors precisely, quantifying their occurrences, delineating the situations (setting events) in which they occur, and identifying the events (consequences) which follow their occurrences. These activities constitute what we call the assessment of behavior. A behavior modifier would rarely stop with just making an assessment of behavior. Prompted by his behavioral assessment, the behavior modifier would attempt to alter setting events and consequences which he believes elicit and maintain inappropriate responses. His quest would bring him face-to-face with questions such as: Did the alterations make any difference in behavior? How much? In whom? When? And for how long? In attempting to answer these and similar questions, the behavior modifier sets foot into the arena of research strategies. An appropriate research strategy will allow you not only to determine that a change in behavior has occurred but to infer what caused that change in behavior.

Assessment of Behavior

There are two types of assessment we make of students' behavior: product and process. A product assessment simply specifies a product of a person's behavior without describing the behaviors the person emitted in arriving at the product. Product assessment might include dimensions such as the percentage of items answered correctly on a weekly examination, the number of frames of programmed materials completed in a prescribed time period, the number of assignments done correctly, and level of performance on a standardized achievement test. In each case, we have some type of product from the student on which to base our evaluation of his progress.

Although product assessments are of prime importance in evaluating academic productivity, they often fail to provide the information needed to improve a student's performance. A product assessment will tell you that Johnny did not complete his in-class assignment but it will not specify the behaviors he manifested during the assignment period which interfered with his lesson activity. An answer to that question requires a process assessment, i.e., a description of Johnny's ongoing behavior during the assignment period. Only by finding out what Johnny was doing during that period and changing those behaviors can the teacher expect a better product from him. For instance, Johnny might have been doodling or daydreaming while he was supposed to be working on his assignment. Through process assessment, you can readily identify behaviors which facilitate or impede the attainment of a satisfactory academic product.

In making process assessments of classroom behavior the pivotal word is "observation." Most of what we know about behavior modification has resulted from thousands and thousands of hours of systematic observation. Pavlov, the eminent Russian physiologist who provided the first experimental demonstration of classical conditioning, attributed great significance to the power of observation. It is said that he had the words OBSERVE, OBSERVE, OBSERVE inscribed in large letters at the entrance to his laboratory (Babkin, 1949). We wonder how many are aware of the years Skinner and his disciples have invested in systematic observation. The book on schedules of reinforcement by Skinner and Ferster is a report of 70,000 hours of actual observation (Reese, 1966). That's only a mere eight years of data collection! Undoubtedly, observation will prove to be just as useful in the classroom as it has in the laboratory.

A deficiency frequently noticed in classroom management research is the fact that process assessment is rarely accompanied by product assessment. This is not to say the process assessment *per se* does not merit our time and efforts. It is important that Mary not move around the room while the teacher is instructing. For one thing, the teacher and the other students could concentrate far better on the teaching–learning activity if Mary would get back to her seat. However, what if Mary stopped roaming around but showed no progress whatsoever in solving math problems? What we are saying is that concurrent assessment of process and product behaviors is more desirable than either to the exclusion of the other.

How does one develop a procedure for making process and product assessments? Permit us to address ourselves to product assessment first since it is the simpler of the two. In your instructional objectives, you would have identified the terminal behaviors you expect of your students and when you expect them to occur. Therefore, in product assessment, you need only to make a record of the occurrence or non-occurrence of these terminal behaviors at/by the designated times. To illustrate: the student did or did not score above the cut-off point on the College Entrance Exam; the student did or did not answer correctly the required number of items on the weekly examination; the student did or did not turn in the required number of homework assignments; the student did or did not correctly solve the problems during an in-class study period; the student did or did not finish the assigned number of frames of programmed materials. Most teachers customarily maintain records on product assessment, at least on a weekly or semester basis. We feel that daily product assessment is far more helpful in monitoring students' progress than weekly or semester assessment. You will recall that the contingency contract system described in Chapter II included provisions for making daily assessment of student products.

In the case of process assessment, you will have to develop a system for observing students' ongoing behavior. You might be interested in only one type of student response. For example, Danny's jumping behavior is driving you up the wall. Under these circumstances, you need not agonize over formulating a complex observational system. Just get your pencil and start counting jumps. In most instances, however, you will need to get a much more comprehensive picture of a child's behavior. In this case, a behavior rating system with clearly delineated behavior categories should be devised. As a first level of differentiation, you can classify student behaviors into two major categories, appropriate and inappropriate. What you consider as appropriate and inappropriate behavior is to some degree a matter of personal judgment. A teacher in the primary grades may have quite different behavioral expectations from a teacher in junior or senior high school. Or, the same teacher may attempt to produce very different behaviors from one situation to the next.

A two-way classification of behavior would seldom provide sufficient information for you to devise an intervention strategy. Let's assume that your observations show that a student spends 50 percent of his class time in inappropriate activity. Where would you begin in modifying his behavior? You need to know the kinds of inappropriate behavior the student is exhibiting and the frequency of each. The more specific your behavior categories, the more precisely you can identify the behaviors that need changing. It follows that the next step in developing a behavior rating system is to define subcategories of appropriate and inappropriate behavior. Table 2 indicates the classification system we have used in several behavior management studies.[1]

TABLE 2

Student Behavior Rating System

Behavior category	Behavior description	Behavior code
Task relevant	Includes answering or asking questions (must be lesson-oriented), writing when directed to do so, looking at book when directed to do so, hand raising to get teacher's attention, looking at teacher while he is lecturing, looking at another student who is participating in lesson activity, and any other behavior that is consistent with the ongoing lesson activity.	Tr
Appropriate social interaction	Includes talking, laughing, playing games, telling jokes, or just sitting at one's desk when students *have not been instructed to engage in lesson activity* and when these behaviors are not expressly forbidden by the teacher. This behavior would usually occur during free time.	S
Time-off task	Includes just sitting at one's desk without appropriate materials or attempting to get appropriate materials, looking at non-lesson material, gazing out the window, or looking around the room *when lesson activity has been assigned.* The student, however, is not distracting another student by his inattention.	To
Disruptive behavior	Includes any behavior that disrupts the academic performance of another student.	
	a. Motor behaviors—getting out of seat, walking around, gesturing without talking, showing object without talking, throwing objects, looking at another student, turning toward another student, turning around when another student	M

---

[1] A number of our subcategories were adapted from a behavioral rating system developed by Thomas, Becker, and Armstrong (1968).

TABLE 2 (*continued*)

Behavior category	Behavior description	Behavior code
	hits him, or any disruptive movement without noise.	
	b. Noise making—tapping feet, clapping hands, tearing papers into pieces or crumbling paper, tapping pencils on desk, flipping pages without looking at book, dragging chair or desk, or any other non-verbal noise producing behavior.	N
	c. Verbalization—crying, screaming, whistling, singing, laughing, coughing, or talking with other children, getting teacher's permission to be excused from class or sharpen pencil.	V
	d. Aggression—hitting, pushing, shoving, pinching, slapping, striking, poking with objects, grabbing objects from another child, destroying objects.	A

In rating disruptive behavior, distinction should be made between three situations in the classroom.

Situation I includes lecturing, conducting total group discussion, showing a film or film strip, playing an audiotape or any such activity involving the whole class. During Situation I, if behaviors listed under *a* through *d* occur, they should be rated disruptive.

Situation II includes seatwork, taking test, or small group discussion. During Situation II, all behaviors listed under *a* through *d* except the following should be rated disruptive:

Getting out of seat,
Looking at another student,
Walking around,
Asking permission to do something,
Talking to another student.

These behaviors will be rated disruptive only if the teacher verbally calls attention to them.

Situation III includes preparing to use audiovisual aids, getting ready for small group discussion, passing or collecting papers, taking roll, or any other situation when the teacher has not specified what the students should do. During Situation III, behaviors listed under *a* through *d* should be rated disruptive *only if* the teacher verbally calls attention to those behaviors.

In building up categories for an observational system, it is important to arrive at mutually exclusive categories. If the observer has to debate where to put behavior X because it seems to fall under more than one category, the reliability of observation will be appreciably diminished. Any time you provide criteria that distinguish one category from another, you are likely to have more reliable data. In our own rating system, these criteria are provided in the descriptions of the categories. We must admit that such criteria do not entirely eliminate difficulty in using the system. One big problem is rating the borderline behaviors. Identifying the level of noise necessary to rate a movement behavior as N rather than an M, determining whether a verbalization between students is lesson-related or village gossip, and distinguishing between a playful slap and an aggressive slap on the back represent some of the borderline situations you will encounter. Fortunately, we have found that less than 10 percent of the behavioral situations which present themselves are borderline cases. Perhaps the most difficult behavior that we ever attempted to log was when Henry Jones pulled out his "unmentionable" and indiscreetly shook it at the girl in front of him. It just seemed that an M rating didn't do justice to that behavior.

Somewhat similar to the question of borderline cases is the dilemma of what behavior to record when several behaviors occur simultaneously. Suppose a student is looking at his book and singing at the same time. The rule that we have followed in such instances is to rate only the inappropriate component. The rationale for this policy is that as long as there is an inappropriate component to a child's behavior, some behavior modification is necessary. In the case of disruptive behaviors that occur simultaneously, we have established a rating priority from most to least disruptive (A, V, N, M). Consequently, any time aggressive behavior occurs in combination with other disruptive activity, an A rating would be given. Conversely, movement would be rated M only if it entails no A, V, or N.

What kinds of observational methods are available for process assessment? The three major approaches are numerical occurrence (frequency count), time duration (logging time), and numerical occurrence in terms of time (time interval). Each method has a place in classroom observation, but each also has certain limitations. In the next few pages, we shall describe these three methods and indicate the strengths and weaknesses of each.

The frequency count approach consists of tabulating the number of times a particular behavior occurs. Suppose you suspect that Johnny is not completing his work because he talks during much of the assignment period. You could test this hypothesis by observing Johnny's behavior during a specified portion of that period. Your strategy would be to quantify Johnny's talking behavior by counting the number of times he speaks to other students. When you are tabulating only one behavior, it is not necessary to limit your observation to one student. As a matter of fact, if you are recording a behavior such as "answering teacher's question" (which is usually exhibited by one student at a time), you can make a frequency count observation on all your students. Needless to say, behaviors such as "talking to peers" would restrict your observation to fewer students. In some instances, you will be interested not in one behavior exhibited by several students but in several behaviors exhibited by the same student. For example, you may want to record the different types of disruptive behavior displayed by Julie. Whichever way you choose to use the frequency count method, simple mechanical devices are available to help in the recording process. A multicounter, compact enough to fit comfortably in the palm of a hand, can be used to simultaneously log one behavior for several students (up to five) or multiple behaviors (up to five) for one student.[2] A wrist-type golf score counter can also be used to maintain a frequency count of behavior(s). And let us not forget the good old paper-and-pencil technique for recording the frequency of responses.

The frequency count method is not without limitations. One difficulty is delineating the beginning and end of an instance of behavior. Suppose that Julie talks to one student and then turns abruptly to speak to another student. Do you count this as one or two instance(s) of talking? Suppose in talking to one student, she momentarily (three seconds) pauses in the midst of the conversation. Does that pause signify the end of a behavioral episode? Obviously, these things have to be defined prior to observation in order for you to be consistent in logging Julie's behavior.

Another limitation of the frequency count system is that different instances of a behavior may not be equivalent. Julie may speak briefly on five separate occasions to other students and then speak continuously to one student for a longer period than was subsumed by the first five instances combined. A simple frequency count would treat the sixth instance in the same manner as the first five. Quantification of behavior by frequency count provides no means of weighing instances of a behavior. This difficulty suggests that behaviors occurring frequently but momentarily could be most reliably studied by this method.

In many instances, the amount of time a student engages in a particular behavior is of greater importance than how many times he engages in it. A time duration assessment would be appropriate in this

---

[2] A multicounter can be obtained from Lafayette Radio and Electronics, 111 Jerico Turnpike, Syosset, L.I., New York 11791.

case. Generally, the nature of a behavior will suggest which method
to use. For example, hitting will lend itself to a frequency count more
readily than crying, which in most instances needs to be recorded on
a time basis. If the focus of your attention is on the duration of *one*
behavior, you can simply use a stopwatch to record the cumulative
time the child engages in that behavior. In the event you don't have a
stopwatch, don't close the book. We do have alternate ideas. You may
use an ordinary watch and jot down the number of minutes for each
occurrence and then add them up at the end of the observation. A
similar method would be to record the starting and stopping time
whenever the behavior occurs. After the observation is over, you can
calculate the total number of minutes the behavior lasted during the
observation. (We hope you're a good mathematician!) Although this
is a rather cumbersome procedure for calculating the total time, it has
one advantage. In case you should be interested in more than one
behavior of a student, you can record the behaviors in sequence. After
the observation is completed, you would have to calculate the total
number of minutes spent by the student in each of the behaviors.
Using this procedure, you would also be able to chart the number of
episodes for the various behaviors.

Unless a behavior to be observed specifically demands the use of
either a frequency or duration type of assessment, it makes little difference which method you use. As measurements of behavior, they seem
to be highly correlated. Adams (1970) obtained thirty-two video-
recorded lessons and had them rated by both frequency and duration
rating scales for predetermined behavior categories. When the occurrences of behaviors in these categories were rank ordered for each
lesson by both methods, 78 percent of the correlations between rank-
ings were higher than 0.74.

An observation system that yields information in terms of both
frequency and duration is time interval assessment. This is the case
because interval assessment equates instances of a behavior with respect to time. Using this approach, you would arrange to record
behavior at specified time intervals, e.g., every five to ten seconds.
Three variations are possible in using the time interval method: (1) at
the beginning of each time interval you note the first identifiable
behavior, (2) at the end of each time interval you record the principal
behavior which occurred during that interval, or (3) at the end of each
time interval you note all the behaviors that occurred during the
interval. The first variation necessitates observing only at the beginning
of each time interval, while the other two methods require observing
for the entire interval. The second method is generally very difficult to
employ because of the complexity of determining what behavior con-

stitutes the principal activity during an interval. We usually consider the behavior that occurs for the longest time in an interval to be the principal behavior. However, when several behaviors occur in a single interval, you may have a lot of difficulty judging which was the longest in duration. If you insist on using this method, employ an interval of no longer than five seconds. And even during a five-second interval enough behaviors can occur to make it laborious to decide which behavior to record.

Perhaps you feel that the best solution to this problem is to record all the behaviors that occur during an interval. This approach would generally be feasible only if you have a short interval and very few categories of behavior, e.g., two or three. Using this approach, you would simply note at the end of each interval which of the specified behaviors had occurred. When long intervals are used, a multiple-event recorder which allows you to record each behavior as it occurs would be extremely helpful. A multiple-event recorder is made up of a series of typewriter-like buttons and corresponding pens. The arrangement is such that each button can be pressed independently and held down until the behavior is terminated. By designating a button for each behavior, the experimenter can obtain a running account of both the frequency and duration of behaviors.

By now, you might have guessed what type of time interval scale we prefer. Our preference is recording the first behavior that occurs during the time interval. We call this type of time interval assessment *on-the-count* assessment. In this case, a tape recorder is unnecessary, particularly if you use an interval as long as ten seconds. This approach entails (1) looking at your watch until ten seconds have passed, (2) looking at the student you are observing (target subject) to determine what kind of behavior he is emitting at that moment, (3) looking down at your record sheet and recording the behavior, (4) looking back to your watch to determine how much time has elapsed in the ten-second interval (usually five or six seconds at this point), (5) looking back at the target subject at the end of the ten second interval, and so on.

A criticism that is often leveled against on-the-count assessment is that you miss too much of the student's behavior this way. In a ten-second interval the total amount of actual observation time is only one to two seconds. Also, it may be highly frustrating to you not to record those very important behaviors that occur near the end of an interval. We can assure you that we have been quite concerned about these weaknesses in on-the-count assessment, yet have adopted it as our primary technique for logging behavior in behavior management research. We have made this decision for two reasons. First, it is easier to establish agreement between observers through on-the-count assessment than through almost any other technique of assessing behavior. If there is a definite and restricted time space (e.g., one or two seconds) in which different people are observing the same person, it is easier to get agreement as to what the person was doing than if the observers have to identify principal behaviors in longer time intervals (e.g., five or ten seconds). A second reason for adopting on-the-count assessment is that over an extended time it usually yields essentially the same distribution of different behaviors as does recording the major behavior or all the behaviors during the intervals, even though those two methods are based on considerably more actual observation time. In other words, the three variations would yield an equivalent percentage of different behaviors over an extended time period. Since it is easier to develop skill in recording behavior via on-the-count assessment, why struggle with a more laborious approach?

Which students should be observed? Usually you would decide to launch a behavior modification program in your class because you had had it with certain students. Occasionally, you might want to assess the efficacy of an operant strategy in improving the behavior of the entire class. In either case, it would probably be feasible to observe up to four students for ten minutes each during a fifty-minute class period. Even though in our own research we have typically observed four students per class, we do not consider it reprehensible to observe fewer students for longer time periods or more students for shorter time periods. The restriction on the number of students you can observe naturally poses the problem of which students to select for observation. If you are concerned about the disruptive students, then you would choose the most disruptive ones to observe. If your interest lies in the whole class, then you should randomly select students for observation.

What types of assessment should be made of teacher behavior? Observations in a classroom are seldom conducted on students alone. Teacher behaviors are assessed simultaneously in order to establish a functional relationship between student and teacher behaviors. The concept of functional relationship entails identifying the sources which are maintaining particular student behaviors. Observations can be arranged in three different ways to provide data concerning the functional basis of behavior. In the first method, which we shall call the *concurrent* method, one observer would rate the student and another the teacher during the same time period(s). (See Table 3 for a description of a rating system that could be used in monitoring teacher behavior.[3]) Data gathered in this manner would show the functional relationship on a global rather than a contingent basis. Observational data for four days are presented below in terms of the percentage of time intervals in which each category of behavior occurred. The student and teacher were observed independently by two separate observers during the same class periods.

	Student's task-relevant behavior	Teacher's praise of appropriate behavior
First day	7.8	0.6
Second day	85.6	6.7
Third day	37.2	0.6
Fourth day	60.0	3.3

These data indicate that the teacher used substantially more praise on days two and four than one and three. Not surprisingly, task-relevant behaviors for the target student were highest on days two and four. In a very global sense, it appears that there might be a functional relationship between the teacher's praise and the student's task-relevant behavior.

TABLE 3

Teacher Behavior Rating System

Behavior category	Behavior description	Behavior code
Approval	Includes praise (e.g., "That's good," "correct," "right," "fine," "okay") and nonverbal gestures (e.g., smile, head nod, pat on the back). Praise— P Nonverbal— N	
Instruction	Includes anything that has to do with instruction such as lecturing, writing on the board, pointing out information on a chart, asking a content question, answering a student's question, listening to a student's comment, checking a student's work in the immediate presence of that student, giving a quiz, taking up papers, returning papers, recording test points.	I

[3] Again, some of the subcategories are taken from Thomas, Becker, and Armstrong (1968).

TABLE 3 *(continued)*

Behavior category	Behavior description	Behavior code
Neutral attention to appropriate behavior	Includes looking at a student who is working, walking in an area where students are working, looking toward the class while students are working.	NA
Disapproval	Includes verbal or auditory reprimand, threat, or penalty (e.g., yelling, scolding, raising voice, belittling or being sarcastic with a child), facial reprimand (e.g., frowning, grimacing, hard stares, side to side head shaking, and gesturing), and corporal punishment (e.g., grabbing, hitting, spanking, shaking, slapping, or pushing a student).	D
Neutral attention to inappropriate behavior	Includes looking at or in some way attending to a child who is misbehaving without conveying disapproval of the child's behavior. The teacher's behavior would usually entail the teacher's routinely looking at a child who is misbehaving without stopping his (the teacher's) current activity.	A
Routine tasks	Includes taking the roll, making announcements, listening to intercom, collecting money.	R
Socializing	Includes any kind of interaction (e.g., talking, laughing, smiling) between teacher and students which is not related to academic issues.	S
Time out	Includes any behavior that removes the teacher from instructing or from any other interpersonal interaction with the class (e.g., counting money, reading a book, grading papers, leaving the room, talking to someone outside the class).	T

Contrast the global nature of the functional relationship described in the previous paragraph with a specific contingent analysis of the same relationship. The specific contingencies between teacher and student behaviors can best be established through what we call a *consecutive* method of observation. Using this method, the observer rates the teacher during one time interval and the student during the next time interval (Cormier, 1970). This observational method allows you to determine how the teacher is behaving immediately prior to and following a particular category of student behavior. For example, you may find that the teacher praised the target student ten times during a class session. Immediately after his praise, the target student exhibited task-relevant behavior nine out of the ten times. In this case, we can be quite confident that an increase in teacher praise would produce an increment in task-relevant behavior. Using the consecutive method of observing we have found in one classroom that a teacher admonished her class 13, 12, 11, and 15 times respectively during four forty-minute periods. Her admonitions were: keep quiet, turn around, sit still, behave yourself, etc. We also found that during the ten second intervals immediately following her admonitions, the target student was misbehaving 12, 11, 11, and 15 times respectively. In effect, her exhortations were obtaining results exactly opposite of what she intended.

A third method of observation, the *simultaneous* method, also provides data concerning the functional relationship on a contingent basis. In this method, the student and the teacher are observed by the same person for the same time intervals. Having to observe two persons at a time would markedly limit the number of behaviors you could record. Researchers who use this method are usually interested in only one or two target behaviors in each person. Hall, Lund, and Jackson (1968) employed this method in their investigation of "studying" behavior. The student's behavior was rated as "study" or "nonstudy" and the teacher was observed for his verbalization and proximity (within three feet) to the target student. A one-minute sample of their observation form is given below:[4]

Seconds

	10	20	30	40	50	60
Student behavior	N	S	S	S	N	N
Teacher verbalizations						T
Teacher proximity			1			1

Row 1 N Nonstudy behavior
          S Study behavior
Row 2 T Teacher verbalization directed toward pupil
Row 3 1 Teacher proximity within three feet

---

[4] From R. V. Hall, D. Lund, and D. Jackson, "Effects of Teacher Attention on Study Behavior," *Journal of Applied Behavior Analysis*, 1:1 (1968), p. 2. Copyright 1968 by the Society for the Experimental Analysis of Behavior, Inc.

From the data obtained through this method, the experimenters were able to say that 55 percent of the teacher attention directed toward the target student followed nonstudy behavior. It is quite likely that teacher verbalization and proximity were actually reinforcing nonstudy behavior. Although this method obviously restricts you to a few behaviors, it does allow you to obtain precise information about the functional relationship between these selected behaviors.

How is a person trained to record classroom behaviors? In conducting training sessions for observers, we have found it more helpful to use video-recordings of classroom interactions than to visit in the actual classrooms. As Peterson (1967) explains, the opportunity to look, to discuss what one has seen, and then look again greatly improves objectivity. In order to ensure that all behaviors included in your behavior assessment system are exhibited on the video tape, you may find it profitable to simulate a classroom situation using ten to twelve students who are specifically instructed to exhibit as many behaviors as possible from your system. In an actual classroom, many of the target behaviors might not even occur during a training session. Furthermore, the sound quality of a simulated recording could be quite superior to that of a regular classroom.

At the beginning of the training session, you should discuss the behavior categories with the observers, mainly to identify the criteria which distinguish one category from another. Some categories immediately stand out as distinctive, while others appear to overlap until the distinguishing criteria are clearly specified. For example, a time-out behavior such as sitting at one's desk and grading papers is distinguished from a routine behavior such as sitting at one's desk and calling for students' grades by the fact that the former entails no observable interaction between the teacher and students. In order to clarify such differentiating criteria, the trainer can present some written examples of behavior and request the observer–trainees to independently categorize them. Their ratings can then be checked against the trainer's. Discussion about disagreements should further clarify the distinguishing criteria for each category.

In our experiences with training college students, we have found that some students question the appropriateness of including particular behaviors in certain categories. They may argue that a student is thinking when he is looking up at the ceiling and hence his behavior should be rated as "task relevant" instead of "time-off task." In such instances, we have found it helpful to say "You could be right. The student *may* be thinking, but since he is not visually oriented toward his academic work, we arbitrarily classify his behavior as 'time-off task.'" When we use statements to this effect, the observer recognizes that we do not view our system as an absolute one. This realization appears to facilitate achievement of inter-rater agreement. In one study (Webb and Brown, 1970), it was found that teachers who felt negative toward the theory on which an observational system was based scored lower in reliability and agreed more with one another and less with the trainer than those who felt positive. It appears that people allow conflicts with an observational system to affect their perception of behaviors. If that be the case, the time you initially invest in reducing observer resistance may save considerable time later on when you're attempting to achieve an acceptable level of inter-rater reliability.

At the end of the preliminary discussion, the video tape can be played, with the trainer and observers simultaneously rating behaviors. You can start by rating one-minute segments of the tape and then progressively increase the length of the segments. Following each time segment, the ratings of observers are compared with those of the trainer. Inter-rater agreement is assessed by dividing the total number of behavior instances into number of agreements between trainer and trainee. In time-interval assessment, the trainer's and trainee's ratings are compared interval by interval. An agreement is counted only when they have the same code for an interval. When all the behaviors occurring in an interval are being recorded, the disagreements within intervals are added together to arrive at the total number of disagreements between the trainer and trainee. In this case, the total number of behaviors rated will be greater than the number of time intervals used. The minimal level of agreement between raters is usually set at around 85 or 90 percent.

How can you be sure that an observer is reliably recording behavior in an actual classroom setting? Reliability of observation can never be taken for granted. A high degree of inter-rater agreement during training sessions does not assure accuracy of observation in the classroom. For this reason, inter-rater agreement should also be established in the classroom setting and at several different times. These reliability checks would necessitate having at least two observers simultaneously rate the same child or teacher's behavior. The second observer can be the trainer or another person of essentially the same research sophistication as the first observer.

A major source of bias in classroom observation is a desire to please the experimenter or teacher. If observers are aware of the expected effects of treatment conditions, they may distort their observations in the expected direction. In extreme cases, observers have been known to fabricate data in order to please the researcher. These errors were usually detected later when other researchers attempted to replicate the findings. Rosenthal's (1966) extensive research on this problem of "observer bias" provides sufficient evidence for its existence. If it exists, what can the researcher do to minimize its effects? Using several observers and periodically cross-checking observations should help to reduce the observer bias. In addition, care should be taken not to communicate to the observers what the treatment conditions are, exactly when they are being introduced, and what the expected outcomes are. Some researchers (Patterson and Harris, 1968) advocate misinforming the observers, but misinformation is likely to bias the observation as much as accurate information, though in a different direction.

Do persons being observed behave as they generally behave? Many people are hesitant about accepting observational data as the "truth." You may be wondering if the way a person behaves when he is being observed accurately reflects how he behaves when he is not being observed. If we could arrange the situation so that a person is not aware he's being observed, we should get an accurate reading on his behavior. This arrangement is sometimes accomplished through one-way mirrors or secretive video taping. However, in many behavior management studies the observer is in the same physical setting as the observed. Under these circumstances, it is certainly possible that a person would become aware that he is the object of observation. That people who are being observed may initially behave differently is supported by Patterson and Harris' study (1968) of parent–child interaction. In the academic milieu, we find that most teachers report that things are back to normal after observers have been in the room for two to three days.

Reestablishing normalcy depends on a number of factors, not the least of which is *who* is doing the observing. The more the observer is viewed as an authority figure in the school, the less the likelihood of normal behavior. For example, behavior would probably get back to normal faster if the counselor did the observing than if the principal assumed this role. Another important variable is how unobtrusively the observer carries out his task. It would be difficult for any of us to behave normally if we felt that evil eyes were constantly staring at us. For that reason, the observer should sit near the back of the room and out of the direct line of vision of the person being observed. How the observer's presence is explained to students can also affect his impact in the classroom. If students are told that the observer is there to scrutinize Tony's weird behavior, it is not likely that Tony will behave normally. He may go all out to give the observer his money's worth or he may drastically reduce his bizarre responses. We suggest the no-fanfare approach in which students are informed that so-and-so will be sitting in the class for a few days to see how a fifth grade class functions. One point is imperative: observational data should never be used as a basis of disciplinary action. If that is ever done, students will become super-sensitive to having any external observer in the classroom.

There is one way to avoid answering the question. What we are usually concerned about in behavior modification research is not an absolute quantification of behavior but rather establishing functional relationships between teacher and student behaviors. The latter can be accomplished even though teacher and students may not be behaving in a completely normal fashion. For instance, one teacher requested our assistance with a student who talked incessantly. Our initial observations indicated that the student talked only about 50 percent of the time. Despite the apparent reduction in talking behavior, we discovered through observation that the talking usually occurred when the teacher was engaged in prolonged conversation with another student. When the observational data were shown to the teacher, it didn't take long for her to recognize the changes that needed to be made in her behavior. In short, the search for functional relationships lessens our preoccupation with the "true" behavior and, correspondingly, our concern with effects of being observed on the observed.

Who will do the observing? This is the kind of question that brings us back to earth. While university researchers can usually find graduate students who are willing to record student and teacher behaviors in behavior management research projects, it may be much more difficult for you as a classroom teacher to find willing and able observers. And in the absence of observers, many of the lofty recommendations of the previous pages go for nought.

Perhaps the best prospect for a competent classroom observer is the school counselor. We are quite certain that most counselors would be willing to help you, if you would request their help. If a school counselor is not available, there are several other possibilities. If you are lucky enough to have a teacher's aide, he could assist with observation. Another possibility is a cooperative student from another class. Most schools use students as office workers, hall monitors, library assistants, etc. Assisting a teacher in analyzing classroom behavior would certainly be as educational as any of the more traditional duties assumed by students. We have found principals quite willing to make student observers available to teachers who are attempting to improve their teaching procedures. What about training responsible students in your own class to serve as behavior observers? This responsibility could be shared by several students so that no one student would have to engage in observation to the detriment of his own academic performance. A final possibility is to exchange observation time with another teacher, i.e., you assist him (during your planning period) in analyzing behavior in his classroom and he assists in your classroom.

We hear someone saying, "You don't realize the conditions in my school. We don't have a counselor or teacher aides. The principal will not let us use the students. And *I* don't have a planning period. This may sound unbelievable, but it is the truth." We believe you. When worse comes to worst, the teacher may have to do his own observing. Needless to say, the reliability of data is likely to be reduced by the observer bias discussed earlier. On the other hand, some research (Patterson and Harris, 1968) suggests that it takes longer to obtain stability of behavior when outside observers are used than when someone from within the group does the observing. So there may be some advantages in being your own observer. That the teacher can be a reliable observer has been shown by Hall and his colleagues (1971) who found that agreement between teacher and teacher aide ratings ranged from 84 to 100 percent over thirteen different occasions; that the reliability of observation was 100 percent when the teacher logged talking-out behavior using a wrist counter and a fellow teacher later rated a tape recording of the same class; and that agreement between simultaneous teacher and student ratings ranged from 60 to 91 percent.

If the teacher should decide to be his own observer, a few tips are in order:

1. It is not always necessary to observe for an entire class period. You may choose a time period as brief as ten minutes per day and still be able to collect valuable data. Stillwell, Harris, and Hall (1972) report a study in which teacher observations were conducted daily for ten minutes during an individual work period. This teacher recorded a particular behavior during a very brief but specific period of time and therefore was able to demonstrate a functional relationship in a five-phase study.

2. Unless process behaviors are your immediate concern, you will find it far less frustrating to keep up with product behaviors as dependent variables.

3. A frequency count method would lend itself more readily to teacher use than would time duration or time interval assessment. While in the act of teaching, you can see the occurrences of behavior more easily than you can see a clock or wristwatch. In addition, mechanical devices like the wrist and golf counter

allow the teacher to make a frequency count without taking his eyes off the students.

We've been logging your behavior as you read this section and, quite frankly, the results are disturbing. So far we've recorded 29 minutes of sleep, 10 minutes of staring into space, 9 minutes of talking on the phone, 8 minutes devoted to making a sandwich, and 12 instances of outright profanity. Oh yes, we also recorded 27 seconds of task-relevant behavior. Since task-relevant behavior is usually highest when students are taking a test, think of the following items as the final examination in the course. If you can't answer the items, just consider yourself a behavior mod reject.

1. Which of the following procedures would most likely be used in making a process assessment of student behavior?
   (a) Tabulating scores on weekly tests,
   (b) Appraising students' homework,
   (c) Computing final grades,
   (d) Observation.

2. In developing a scale for appraising process behaviors, you should
   (a) Strictly follow the classification system presented in this book,
   (b) Delineate mutually exclusive subcategories of appropriate and inappropriate behavior,
   (c) Identify no more than five types of student behavior,
   (d) Be content with a two-category (appropriate and inappropriate) classification system.

3. While working on his assignment, Johnny is engaging in a couple of extraneous activities, singing in a barely audible tone and kicking the girl in front of him. According to the Anandam and Williams classification system, his behavior would be rated as
   (a) Tr,
   (b) M,
   (c) V,
   (d) A.

4. A major weakness of the frequency count observational method is that
   (a) You can't observe more than one student at a time,
   (b) You can't observe more than one behavior at a time,
   (c) Different instances of the same behavior may not be equivalent,
   (d) It's the most complex of all rating scales.

5. In doing an on-the-count time interval assessment, you would record
   (a) The first identifiable behavior that occurs during the interval,
   (b) The major behavior that occurs during the interval,

(c) The last behavior that occurs during the interval,

(d) All the behaviors that occur during the interval.

6. The major reason for observing teacher behavior is to

(a) Keep the teacher on edge,

(b) Establish a functional relationship between teacher and student behavior,

(c) Make the students feel less self-conscious about being observed,

(d) Establish reliability between the teacher and student observers.

7. Regarding the training of observers, it was suggested that

(a) Observers should initially be trained in an actual classroom setting,

(b) A video tape of a simulated classroom situation should initially be used,

(c) The rating system should be presented as infallible,

(d) Objections to the rating system should be ridiculed.

8. In response to the question of whether persons being observed behave as they generally do, the authors contend that

(a) Students behave in their normal fashion after the observer has been in the room for two or three days,

(b) A functional relationship can be established between student and teacher behavior even though students may not be behaving in a completely typical fashion,

(c) The more the observer is viewed as an authority figure in the school, the less the likelihood of normal behavior,

(d) All of the above.

Behavior Modification Research Strategies

The assessment procedures described in the previous section allow you to describe what is taking place in the classroom and postulate certain hypotheses as to why these behaviors are occurring. Assessment procedures *per se* do not provide unequivocal evidence that a particular intervention is responsible for the change in student behavior. We could have very precise assessment procedures and yet be unable to specify what caused the recorded changes in behavior. Inferences about cause and effect take us beyond assessment into the realm of research design.

Behavior modifiers have developed research strategies which are somewhat different from the mainstream approaches employed in educational research. These behavioral researchers have utilized small samples (many studies focus on the behavior of a single child), have made little use of control groups, and have seldom employed parametric or nonparametric designs. In fact, graphs depicting frequencies or percentages of behavior have been the major means of presenting their data. An advantage of this approach is that people without extensive background in statistics can readily comprehend the findings.

The question is: why such simple procedures in behavior mod research? Are behavior modifiers just inherently simple folks? Or did they flunk statistics in graduate school? We believe there are more complimentary explanations for behavior modifiers' affinity for the simple life. The basis for their research procedures is primarily derived from Murray Sidman's *Tactics of Scientific Research* (1960). Although Sidman's book focuses on laboratory research, behavior modifiers have applied many of his concepts in educational settings. Sidman's thesis is that behavior is exhibited by a single organism and therefore must be explained in the context of a single organism. Large group trends can never compensate for the failure to understand behavior in the individual case.

The antithesis of Sidman's idiographic approach is the nomothetic approach, exemplified by analysis of variance. In analysis of variance designs, you are essentially comparing variability between treatment groups to the "natural" variability within treatment groups. If you have a significant effect, the between-group variability is considerably greater than the within-group variability. Unfortunately, analysis of variance designs do not tell us how many people in the treatment group behaved in line with the treatment effect. Most probably, some subjects in the treatment group performed more poorly than some subjects in the control group. However, these cases get buried under variances and standard deviations. Another weakness of many analysis of variance designs is that the various treatment conditions are applied to different groups of subjects. Consequently, variables other than the treatment conditions may differentially affect the groups. Even random assignment to groups does not ensure that extraneous factors will affect the groups in a similar manner.

To counteract all the evils of analysis of variance, behavior modifiers have chosen to explain behavior in the context of the single organism. The key term in behavior management research is "intrasubject variability." The major issue is whether the subject behaves differently when the treatment is applied compared to when the treatment is *not* applied. Another key term is "intrasubject replication." The more times we can turn a behavior on and off by successively introducing and withdrawing a treatment, the more reliable the treatment effect. It would never be sufficient to simply demonstrate *one time* that behavior is different under baseline and treatment conditions.

In behavior management research, the focus is clearly on internal validity, i.e., unequivocally establishing that the treatment condition (independent variable), not something else, accounted for the change in the student's behavior (dependent variable). Behavior modifiers believe that external validity (generalizability of findings) is enhanced more by a high degree of internal validity than by large samples or random sampling. This is not to say that we can indiscriminately generalize from the behavior of one individual. A relationship established in subject one may not immediately be replicated in subject two. Failure to produce that relationship in subject two does not mean that the original finding was spurious. Other factors may be overriding the effects of the independent variable in the case of subject two. The original relationship may eventually be established in the second subject by reducing the potency of extraneous variables or increasing the potency of the treatment variable. Let's say that token reinforcement has been used to increase the amount of time children devote to reading. A child who has developed a high degree of proficiency in reading may not be affected by X amount of token reinforcement for time spent in reading. Since you cannot very well reduce this subject's reading proficiency, you will have to increase the potency of the token reinforcement procedure. Raising the potency to level Y may demonstrate a relationship between token reinforcement and reading time even with the highly proficient student.

Enough on the basic assumptions underlying behavior modification research strategies. Now to the specific procedures.

What types of designs can be used to establish the effectiveness of a treatment condition? The basic design used in the functional analysis of behavior is called an ABAB design.

A—Baseline Phase—Record of behavior(s) before treatment is introduced.

B—Treatment Phase One—Record of same behavior(s) after treatment is introduced.

A—Reversal Phase—Record of same behavior(s) when treatment is removed.

B—Treatment Phase Two—Record of same behavior(s) after treatment is reintroduced.

The rationale for collecting baseline data is to establish a point of comparison for assessing the effectiveness of the treatment. Baseline data should be collected before the experimenter makes any attempt to alter the behavior in question. What happens to the behavior when the treatment is introduced is, of course, the focus of any behavior management study. We cannot automatically conclude that improvement in behavior concomitant with the introduction of treatment is a function of that treatment. The behavior change may actually be a function of extraneous factors which are operative during the treatment period. The reversal phase (withdrawal of treatment) will indicate rather conclusively whether the behavior change was a function of the treatment. If indeed it was, the behavior will probably revert to baseline level.[5] The reversal demonstrates that improvement in behavior was not a function of extraneous variables which inadvertently entered the picture during treatment. Since no teacher wishes to leave a behavior at the baseline level, most experimenters reinstate the treatment condition following completion of the reversal phase. The ability to improve the behavior by again implementing the treatment adds to the reliability of the treatment effect. This final phase also proves to be a powerful selling point for behavior modification. Reinstatement of the behavior indicates the high degree of external control that a teacher can exercise through operant methodology.

Some teachers vehemently object to the use of reversal strategies. After Dolly's knife-fighting has been brought under control, teachers are not too anxious to see that improvement eroded through reversal of the treatment. Another type of difficulty encountered with reversal is inability to recover baseline behaviors, i.e., withdrawal of the treatment does not alter the dependent variable. This state of affairs, to express it euphemistically, leaves the experimenter with his pants down. Failure to achieve a reversal may indicate that something besides the treatment variable produced the improvement in behavior, that the treatment variable produced the improvement but that the improvement is now being sustained through other types of consequences, or that the treatment produced a change in behavior which is inherently irreversible.

To illustrate, suppose you are using contingent teacher approval to increase the time Peg spends in reading. During treatment, Peg spends an hour a day in reading as opposed to only ten minutes during baseline. In the reversal phase you stop approving Peg for reading, but she continues to read about an hour a day. Why? One possibility is that the use of approval entailed other changes in your behavior which

---

[5] Sometimes the behavior does not completely revert to a baseline level, but does change in the direction of the baseline. We would still consider this change a reversal. Most likely, the behavioral changes during treatment have produced changes in the environment which are partially sustaining the improvement in behavior even when the treatment condition has been withdrawn.

actually produced the increment in reading time. (We have noticed on several occasions that teachers become more organized in presenting their lessons when they attempt to implement any treatment systematically.) A second possibility is that Peg's reading is now producing reinforcement other than your approval. Perhaps her father plays with her more since she developed such an avid interest in reading. Or the enjoyment she acquires from reading itself may be sufficient to sustain extensive reading. Behaviors which come to be intrinsically reinforcing are very difficult to reverse. In some instances, the dependent variable may represent a skill, e.g., ability to spell certain words, solve certain math problems, or read at a certain proficiency level, which is not likely to be reduced by removal of the treatment.

Experimenters can circumvent the hazards of reversals by using a design which entails *multiple baselines.* There are several ways in which multiple baselines can be established.

1. Baselines can be established for more than one person for the same dependent variable (reading time). Treatment (teacher approval) can then be introduced for one student at a time. If the increments in reading time are correlated with the introduction of the treatment, it is fairly safe to assume that the independent variable made the difference. This approach involves the introduction of the treatment at different times for the different students. If the treatment were introduced at the same time for all students, you could not determine whether behavior changes were a function of the treatment or other variables operative during the same time period. Staggering the implementation of the treatment for the different students minimizes the possibility of a common extraneous variable accounting for the changes in reading time.

2. Baselines can be established for two or three different behaviors of the same individual. The independent variable can then be introduced for each of the dependent behaviors but at different times. If changes in dependent behaviors correspond to the introduction of the independent variable, it is legitimate to assume that the independent variable accounted for those changes. To use this method, you must assume that the baseline levels of the various behaviors are similar, that the behaviors are independent of each other, and that the behaviors are equally accessible to change.

3. Using one person and one behavior, the experimenter can establish baseline in two or more situations. Again, the independent variable is introduced in each situation but at different times. If changes in the behavior in the different situations coincide with

the introduction of the independent variable, it is fairly reasonable to claim the efficacy of the independent variable.

The three types of multiple baseline are well illustrated in a series of studies conducted by Hall et al. (1970). In one study, quiz grades of three students were recorded for baseline, after which the same consequence of staying after school for *D* and *F* grades was applied successively for each student. Poor grades were eliminated only when contingencies were applied. In the second study, simultaneous measurement was made for three different behaviors (clarinet practice, project work, and reading). The same consequence of going to bed early for less than thirty minutes spent in each activity was applied successively for the three behaviors. Marked increases in the respective behaviors were noted at the points where the contingencies were applied. In the last study, a fifth grade teacher concurrently measured the same behavior (tardiness) in three different situations during the day. Behavior reduced at the points where contingencies were applied.

The multiple baseline design has also been successfully used by Long (1972a) in implementing complex treatment variables in a junior high setting. He used the same group of students but in different settings— math and geography classes. He carried the students through the same sequence of experimental conditions in both situations, but introduced each condition eight or nine days later in the geography than in the math class. The sequence of experimental conditions was as follows: baseline, structured lessons (providing a mimeographed handout of the day's lesson to each child as he entered class), group contingent free time, individually contingent free time, structured lessons, and accumulation of points without free time. In both classrooms, appropriate behavior was highest in the group contingent free time condition but also very high during individually contingent free time. In the true style of multiple baselines, Long's study demonstrated that appropriate behavior could be very high (90 percent) during a treatment phase in one class and concomitantly (for the same students) very low (20 percent) in a non-treatment phase in another class (see Figure 3).

What types of designs can be used to compare the effectiveness of two or more treatments? Since a teacher cannot simultaneously apply all the behavior management procedures known, some decision has to be made as to which procedure(s) would be the best to apply. Should you use a behavior contract or behavior proclamation, group contingent free time or individually contingent free time, criterion-referenced grading or norm-referenced grading? These decisions cannot adequately be made without some direct comparisons of treatment procedures. To make these comparisons and yet stay within the framework

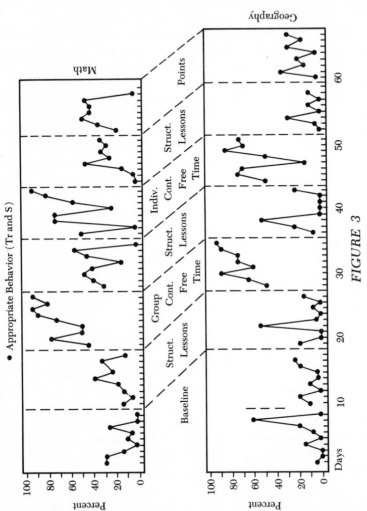

FIGURE 3

Multiple Baseline Design of an Inner-City Junior High School Student's Responses to Various Contingency Management Systems

From J. D. Long, The comparative utility of structured lessons, group and individually contingent events, and conditioned reinforcers in modifying classroom behaviors (Ed.D. diss., The University of Tennessee, 1972a). Reprinted with permission.

of intrasubject analysis, we could sequentially introduce the treatments to the same subject(s). With the sequential arrangement, we might have an ABACABAC, ABABACAC, or BCBC type design. It is important to introduce each treatment at least twice and to look for consistency between the two applications of the same treatment. If each treatment were introduced only once, as with an ABAC arrangement, you could not determine if the effect produced by treatment C is really any different from the effect that would have been achieved from a second implementation of treatment B. If each treatment is introduced at least twice, you can then draw some conclusions about the relative potency of the two procedures. For instance, if the B phases are consistently higher than the C phases, you may conclude that B is superior to C. However, if you don't achieve consistency between different phases of the same treatment, you've got problems. More about those later.

If the treatments are likely to produce a carry-over effect, it is necessary to impose baseline periods between treatment phases. Otherwise, what happens during C may in part reflect the influence of B. You would be much more likely to get a carry-over effect when comparing behavior contracts and proclamations (since they involve many similar operations) than when comparing contracts and teacher approval. It might be defensible in the latter case to employ a BCBC type design with no baselines between the treatment phases. Remember, you're comparing treatments to each other, not one treatment to a baseline.

You may be wondering how we control for sequence effects with the types of designs we've discussed. A student's response to C may be affected by his having operated under B. The effects of a behavior proclamation could be quite different, depending on whether the student had previously operated under a contracting system. With an intrasubject design, there is no way to control for the impact that the first treatment phase has on the effectiveness of subsequent treatments. However, by the time you get to the second application of each treatment, every treatment will have been preceded by every other treatment. So if the effect from the second application of B is consistent with the effect from the first application of B, the sequence of treatments is apparently not affecting the potency of treatment B. Because B always preceded C, we cannot apply the same test to treatment C.

One possibility for controlling sequence effects is to counterbalance the order in which treatments are presented, i.e., to employ something like an ABACACAB design. Wilson (1971) used this approach in his investigation of the relative effectiveness of a buzzer (signaling inappropriate behavior) and a clock (signaling accumulation of free time for appropriate behavior) on the task-relevant behavior of elementary students. The sequence of treatments used in his study was: baseline, buzzer, clock, buzzer plus clock, baseline, clock, buzzer, and buzzer plus clock. The finding that is relevant to our discussion is that the clock condition produced more appropriate behavior than the buzzer, regardless of whether the buzzer preceded or followed the clock phase.

Perhaps the best way to establish the relative effectiveness of various treatments, and yet control for sequence effects, is to employ inter-subject as well as intrasubject comparisons. One subject or group of subjects might receive an ABACABAC sequence of treatments, whereas a second subject or group of subjects might receive the sequence of ACABACAB. If the effects of B and C are consistent across the two subjects or groups, sequence is apparently making little difference. However, if the effectiveness of a treatment differs with its position in the sequence, it's probable that you've identified a genuine sequence effect.

How long should assessment be continued within treatment phases? Irrespective of the kind of design you use, you will have to make some type of process or product assessment within each treatment phase. Ideally, assessment should be continued within phases until stability of behavior is achieved. If stability is not attainable, you should continue observation until some type of order can be extracted from the fluctuations in the data. By order, we mean the identification of conditions under which high and low frequencies of the behavior are being obtained.

Some of the events which cause fluctuations within phases cannot be avoided. Nearness of vacations, civil disorder in the city, and unusual weather conditions can dramatically affect student behavior, though you may have little control over any of these. This lack of control should not negate your attempting to specify how such occurrences affect student behavior. You may obtain an extremely high level of appropriate behavior on all except one day of treatment. On that day, you note that students spend lots of time looking out the window and engaging in disruptive behavior. The fact that a hurricane is raging outside may have no small impact on their responses that particular day.

There are other types of events—guest speakers, tests, seating arrangements—which are not a part of your treatment condition but which can markedly affect student behaviors. Since you have some control over these events, you should attempt to describe the unique impact that each has on student behavior and introduce the same number and type in all treatment phases. If you give weekly tests during baseline, give weekly tests during treatment.

Achieving stability and order within treatment phases simplifies the process of establishing the relative potency of treatments. Suppose behavior is fluctuating wildly during baseline and you have no earthly idea as to the reasons for those fluctuations. You then introduce the treatment, at which time appropriate behavior jumps to an extremely high level. What can you conclude? Since two or three baseline days also produced a high level of appropriate behavior, you cannot immediately determine if you're getting a treatment effect or just another baseline fluctuation. If you know that such high levels of appropriate behavior occurred during baseline only on test days, you can readily assume that the treatment behavior (on a nontest day) represents something more than a baseline fluctuation. You obviously have to observe over an extended time period to identify representative types of fluctuations within a treatment period. We consider one week of observation to be the absolute minimum for any treatment phase. Even then, fluctuations may be occurring that you can't account for. In the case of a product assessment such as weekly test scores, you will obviously need to continue a treatment phase much longer, say for a six- or nine-weeks grading period.

So far, we've been talking about stability in the dependent variable. What about stability in the independent variable? Some researchers prescribe in advance how long a treatment phase will continue. Wilson (1971), for example, planned to use the buzzer five days, the clock five days, and a combination of the two for five days. This approach is feasible where the treatment conditions are totally manipulatable by the experimenter. On the other hand, independent variables such as teacher approval and peer reinforcement are not completely under the control of the experimenter. One day the teacher uses approval frequently and the next day not at all. Under these circumstances, a reasonable level of approval is predetermined; if this level is maintained for five, six, etc. consecutive days, the treatment is considered to be implemented. What is considered a reasonable level of treatment implementation may be considerably above the baseline level of that treatment. It is very important in this case to use the technique of successive approximations in getting the treatment implemented.

Are behavior modification research designs ever used in combination with parametric and nonparametric analyses? Yes, but probably not often enough (Birnbrauer, 1971). Some behavior modifiers are moving toward larger samples and the conventional statistical designs. However, these researchers have not abdicated the charting of data. In practically all behavior modification studies, you can find one or two nice graphs indicating how the behavior changed under the various treatment conditions. Why have some behavior modifiers decided that the conventional charting of data is not sufficient? Perhaps they have developed a sensitivity to the word "significant." Someone always wants to know if the differences between treatment phases are statistically significant. So maybe behavior modifiers want to be able to say that they obtained not only consistent differences between treatments but significant differences.

One study that has used parametric procedures in addition to the graphing of data is Glynn's (1970) investigation of self-determined reinforcement. Glynn used analysis of covariance to compare classes operating under different treatments. Baseline means for each subject were used as the covariate. An analysis of variance–mixed design was used to assess the differential effect of treatments across days, with days serving as the repeated measure. A significant group by days interaction would have indicated some type of divergence or convergence between the classes across days.

Long's dissertation (1972a) represents one of the strongest combinations of functional and statistical analyses that we have encountered in the behavior modification literature. He used an intrasubject design in which all treatments were applied to the same subjects in the same setting and different settings. In other words, he combined an ABA and multiple baseline procedure. Because he monitored the behavior of eight subjects, he was also able to apply a nonparametric analysis to his data. The Friedman test was first applied to determine the presence or absence of an over-all treatment effect. Having obtained significance with the Friedman, Long then used the Wilcoxon Matched Pairs Test to determine the specific nature of treatment differences. His ABA, multiple baselines, and nonparametric analyses yielded essentially the same conclusions about the effectiveness of the treatments.

We believe that behavior modification research will profit from the use of parametric and nonparametric analyses. In many instances, the teacher is concerned about the performance of an entire class. He needs to know if the class as whole will perform better under procedure X or Y. Under these circumstances, some type of parametric or nonparametric analysis is almost imperative. We are not recommending that behavior modifiers stop charting their data or stop nonstatistically analyzing fluctuations in their data. However, we would like to see some type of statistical analysis (e.g., trend analysis) applied even to the behavioral graphs.

Congratulations! You have stayed with us through a rather difficult chapter. Your behavior indicates to us that you are indeed "serious" about classroom behavior management. But after such an exacting investigation, we all need some rest. The following questions represent our last words on behavior modification research procedures.

1. A behavior modification research study would most likely entail which of the following?
   (a) A single subject with the various treatment conditions successively administered to that one subject,
   (b) A large stratified random sample,
   (c) A control group,
   (d) A multivariate analysis.
2. Behavior modifiers employ reversals to
   (a) Irritate teachers,
   (b) Demonstrate that the dependent behavior is intrinsically reinforcing,
   (c) Demonstrate that the dependent behavior is under the control of the treatment,
   (d) Demonstrate that the improvement in the behavior was actually a function of extraneous variables.
3. Which of the following might account for the failure to achieve a reversal?
   (a) Something besides the treatment variable produced the improvement in behavior,
   (b) The treatment variable produced the improvement but the improvement is now being sustained through other types of consequences,
   (c) The treatment produced a change in behavior which is inherently irreversible,
   (d) All of the above.
4. Which of the following would be a multiple baseline design?
   (a) Baselines are established for two or three behaviors being exhibited by the same individual. The independent variable is then introduced for each of these behaviors but at different times,
   (b) Baselines are established for the same person and behavior in two or more situations. The independent variable is then simultaneously introduced in the various situations,
   (c) Baselines are established for the same person and behavior on three separate occasions. The treatment is introduced following each baseline,
   (d) Baselines are established for two groups. The treatment is then introduced to one group but not to the other.
5. In comparing the effectiveness of two treatments via intrasubject analysis,
   (a) It is sufficient to introduce each treatment one time,
   (b) You should introduce each treatment at least twice,
   (c) You should eliminate all sequence effects,
   (d) You should always use a multi-element manipulation.

6. Baselines between treatment phases would be *least* necessary in which of the following instances?
   (a) You're attempting to establish the effectiveness of a single treatment,
   (b) You're comparing the effectiveness of two very dissimilar treatments,
   (c) You're comparing the effectiveness of two very similar treatments,
   (d) You're comparing treatments which are likely to interact.
7. Assessment should be continued within each treatment phase until
   (a) The treatment has been consistently implemented for a period of several days,
   (b) The dependent behaviors have stabilized,
   (c) The experimenter can account for fluctuations in the data,
   (d) All of the above.
8. You're implementing a behavior mod program designed to increase biracial interaction in your classroom. Things have been going beautifully until one day a racial disturbance occurs on the playground. For the next three days, the biracial interaction in your class is near zero. Following this three-day period, biracial interaction gradually increases to its formerly high level. In reporting the study, you should
   (a) Average in these three days with the rest of the treatment days,
   (b) Graph all the data but indicate on the graph when the playground disturbance occurred,
   (c) Forget about those three days since you know that the behavior was a direct result of the playground disturbance,
   (d) Recommend the closing of playgrounds.
9. Regarding the application of parametric and nonparametric analyses in behavior modification studies, Williams and Anandam take the view that
   (a) All parametric analyses are sinful,
   (b) Such analyses will broaden the generalizability of our findings,
   (c) Such analyses should be used in lieu of conventional behavior mod research strategies,
   (d) Such analyses are exactly what Sidman was recommending.

Chapter V

SOMEONE TO LEAN ON

The Roles of Principals, Counselors, and Parents in Classroom Management

We now venture into perhaps the most difficult area of classroom behavior management—dealing with those agents outside the classroom who may profoundly affect a student's performance in the classroom. Although the teacher is the person most directly responsible for a student's in-class behavior, the teacher's efforts can be significantly facilitated or impaired by what happens outside the classroom.

In dealing with the role of helping agents, we will have to lean quite heavily on anecdotal information. Many critical questions about the contributions of supporting agents have not been systematically studied. So pardon us for being somewhat speculative and subjective in discussing the issues in this area.

The Role of the Principal

The principal is probably the most important person in determining what happens in a school. He has greater potential for modifying teacher behavior and, indirectly, student behavior than any other person in the academic milieu. It is our personal judgment that few principals come close to maximizing their effectiveness as behavior modifiers. We are aware that many of the situations with which the principal must deal are not exactly the kind that make you sleep well at night. A college of education dean who exchanged his position for two weeks with the principal of an inner-city school succinctly conveyed the tension that surrounds the principalship—"I had a feeling that I was walking on a live volcano" (Cunningham, 1969, p. 124). In dealing with the perplexities brought to him by teachers, students, and parents, the principal frequently is able to accomplish little more than a temporary truce. As a result, there is probably no one who is happier to see the school day end than the principal. The strain of dealing with interminable frustrations eventually takes a heavy toll on the principal. The most likely consequence is that he becomes a perturbed and frustrated person himself. This frustration often causes the principal to exhibit behaviors which contribute to additional problems in the school. It sounds like a vicious cycle and it *is*.

We believe there is a happier and a more beneficial role for the principal to assume than the traditional one. We aren't suggesting that the principal close his doors and go fishing, but rather that he intervene at a point where behavior problems can be prevented. Under the existing system, the principal deals with most problems only after they have already occurred. The factors which habitually precipitate the problems may, therefore, go completely unattended. He spends most of his time putting out brush fires and devotes minimal time to changing the conditions responsible for igniting the flames. Since many problems arise from mismanagement in the classroom, the frequency of problems brought to the principal's office should be affected by the training of teachers in behavior management.

You would probably agree that training teachers to manage their classes efficiently is a commendable endeavor. Nevertheless, you may have some misgivings about involving the principal in this process. Shouldn't the assistant principal, the guidance counselor, the school psychologist, the curriculum specialist, the custodian, or someone else assume responsibility for working with the teacher? Perhaps most of these people should be involved in classroom management, but not to the exclusion of the principal. The principal probably has more reinforcement potential than anyone else in the school. We have found most teachers to be quite sensitive to his expectations. Because the principal makes recommendations concerning hiring, firing, and tenure, teachers are inclined to listen rather closely to what he says. Approval and disapproval from the principal have a greater impact than similar comments from almost anyone else in the school setting. Therefore, the more actively a principal can be involved in a behavior management program, the more likely it is to succeed. For this reason, the proposal of the directors of the National Association of Secondary School Principals (NASSP) Administrative Internship Project (1969) that the principal invest three-quarters of his time in improving teaching and learning is very much to our liking.

In what ways can the principal directly assist teachers in classroom management? Training teachers to be effective managers of behavior requires more than simply explaining behavior modification procedures to them. It begins with the principal's directly approving desirable teaching behaviors. The major focus of the principal's approval should be improvement rather than perfection in classroom management. To illustrate our point, let us assume that the principal had requested Ms. X not to send students to his office for disciplinary action. Although Ms. X is slow to heed his requests, one day she sends only two kids instead of her usual six to ten. That's not perfection but it is improvement. So the principal definitely needs to communicate to Ms. X his appreciation of that improvement. If the principal is quick to recognize signs of improvement in teacher behavior, he will magnify teacher effectiveness many-fold.

What are the specific ways by which a principal can communicate his approval to teachers? In the case of Ms. X, it might be worthwhile to actually seek her out at the end of the day and say something like "You must have had an awfully good day because I find that only two of your students were sent to my office." We realize that finding Ms. X is not the principal's only task as a school day approaches an end. However, a very good substitute for a face-to-face expression of approval is a written note placed in the teacher's mail box in the main office. It would be worthwhile for the principal to take fifteen to thirty minutes at the end of each school day writing notes to his teachers. What he would mainly want to write is an expression of his appreciation for behaviors such as implementing a new teaching strategy, going beyond the call of duty in helping students, sharing their ideas at a faculty meeting, and sending frequent notes to parents about their children's progress. Notes would also be a good way to pass on positive comments that the principal had heard about the teacher from other teachers, students, and parents.

If note passing is distasteful to a principal, he can still express his appreciation to teachers without interrupting their classes. Teachers usually come to school earlier than students and leave later. Perhaps the principal could use the intercom during these times to mention specific accomplishments of various teachers. Identifying teachers by name could help to create positive role models on his teaching faculty. Delineating specific accomplishments should serve to strengthen those accomplishments instead of other types of teacher responses. It should also embellish the perceived sincerity of the principal's approval. Most any of us can pat someone on the back and say, "You're a real great guy." Few of us take enough interest in another person to point out the specific things that impress us about that person. The principal will be viewed as far more sensitive and sincere if he's specific.

In training teachers to use behavior modification procedures, the principal should devote some time to actual classroom observation. First-hand observation may give the principal far more ideas about what teacher behaviors need to be modified and reinforced than could ever be acquired through out-of-class contacts. In systematically observing teacher behaviors, the principal might find the behavior rating scale described in Table 3 in Chapter IV quite useful. When a principal observes in a classroom, he should communicate to the teacher his specific perceptions of what he is doing appropriately and his ideas for improving his teaching methods. To elucidate his suggestions, the principal should demonstrate the use of them in the teacher's classroom. A demonstration usually provides a clearer picture of a methodology than does a verbal description. It also conveys something very important about a principal's commitment to a strategy and a teacher. A principal doesn't put himself on the line for a technique he believes to be ineffective. Neither does he take time to demonstrate a procedure to a teacher unless he's committed to helping that teacher. The impact of this type of assistance from the principal has been clearly substantiated in a recent study by Stephens (1972).

Another possibility for the principal's involvement in classroom management is for him to act as a source of reinforcement for appropriate student behavior. One principal spent fifteen minutes a day playing basketball with a third grader as a reward for the reduction in disruptive behavior (Brown, Copeland, and Hall, 1972). This positive approach proved highly facilitative in improving the child's performance in the classroom. Traditionally, the boy would have been sent to the principal for disciplinary action. In another study (Copeland, Brown, and Hall, 1972), the principal's approval was made contingent upon students' academic achievement. The principal went to the target class twice a week to announce which students had shown improvement in their math assignments the previous day and to approve these students publicly. It took the principal three minutes or less to complete each visit, but the payoff was improvement in math performance for the entire class.

Perhaps you're feeling threatened by the very thought of having the principal in your classroom. However, if the principal is exhibiting the kind of reinforcement we've recommended, he should be a rather pleasant person to have around. Threat to teachers can be minimized by the principal's deemphasizing the fact that he is the principal. We envisage a colleague-type relationship between principal and teacher rather than a superordinate–subordinate relationship. What we are proposing is that the principal depend on the merits of his recommendations rather than his rank as principal to enlist teacher cooperation.

What kinds of resources can the principal make available to assist teachers in classroom management? If a principal could only mobilize the resources available within his own faculty for helping new or struggling teachers, he could obtain some fantastic results. One possibility is to ask teachers to assist each other in analyzing their instructional behaviors. The main purpose of the interteacher program would be for teachers to systematically observe each other's classroom operations and exchange ideas as to how each can improve. The principal's approval will be a crucial determinant of the success of this effort. He can convey his interest by casually inquiring about their observations and discussions, bringing relevant literature to the teachers' attention, observing the classes where the teachers feel a change is taking place, and mentioning the highlights of the interteacher projects at faculty meetings.

Another extremely valuable resource person in the school is the guidance counselor. In the next section, we will describe the contributions a counselor can make to classroom management. For the counselor to actually do many of the noble things that we recommend, he will have to be freed from the myriad trivia in which he is frequently immersed. No one can remove that trivia more swiftly and decisively than the principal. If the principal chooses to let the counselor do most of the on-the-job training of teachers, it is imperative that the principal regularly approve the counselor for his efforts, approve teachers for working with the counselor, and visit classrooms often enough to demonstrate that he is committed to the behavior modification training program. It is hard for a principal to convince the counselor and teachers that a program has his blessings if he never gets out of his office to see that program in action.

Educators are now becoming quite sensitive to the tremendous contributions that paraprofessionals can make to classroom management. In their report on the Winooski Model Cities Program, Hanley and Perelman (1971) provide empirical evidence as to the usefulness of paraprofessionals in improving both academic and social behaviors. We feel that the success of the Winooski program was primarily a function of the fact that eleven teachers, one guidance counselor, one librarian, two school secretaries, and fifteen paraprofessionals together attended a two-week workshop in applied behavior analysis. Customarily teachers receive information on how to utilize paraprofessionals and the paraprofessionals are told how to work *for* the teachers, but they never receive training together. Securing the paraprofessionals and organizing workshops for teachers and paraprofessionals are the responsibilities of a principal. If a principal can recruit people from his community to serve as paraprofessionals and then beg, borrow, or steal funds from his budget for training and hiring them, he can really have a ball!

How should the principal organize the activities of the school day in order to promote effective classroom management? A teacher's effectiveness in the classroom can be severely impaired by adverse setting events in the school, not the least of which is external interruptions. In many schools, intercom announcements are scattered throughout the school day, students are called out of class to go hither and yon, and assembly programs are called on the spur of the moment. We once heard a principal read the names of two hundred students over the intercom and request that teachers send these students to the auditorium for psychological testing. Another principal made it a practice of turning on the intercom every time he administered corporal punishment in his office. So at least five or six times during the school day, the intercom would come on with a "Wham!" "Wham!" "Wham!" Such an experience made it easy for students to concentrate on their studies and, no doubt, contributed immeasurably to the reinforcing atmosphere of the school!

Our recommendations are that the principal eliminate unscheduled assemblies, set aside a short period at the beginning and end of the school day for all intercom announcements (except absolute emergencies), refrain from and prohibit others from calling students out of class for all kinds of piddling jobs around the school (e.g., "Mr. Smith wants Joe down in the gym to help count the cracks in the floor"), and schedule all major events such as assembly programs, club activities, and aptitude testing at least one day in advance.

How can teachers help the principal to manage the school effectively? In our treatment of ethical issues, we emphasized the reciprocal nature of behavior modification. This is certainly the case when it comes to principal–teacher interaction. Just as the principal can markedly alter your behavior, you can markedly alter his. Like students, teachers, guidance counselors, custodians, and cooks, the principal is a person. Yes, we really believe that. It is not unreasonable to affirm that the same principles of behavior modification which a teacher should apply in working with students should also be applied in relating to the principal.

To accomplish very much in working with the principal, you must establish yourself as a source of reinforcement for him. This can best be achieved through noncontingent support for the principal as a person and through consistent expressions of appreciation for the facilitative aspects of his professional behavior. We aren't saying that you should never express grievances. But grievances should be fewer in number than positive inputs and should be expressed in a manner that would not impugn a principal's competence or integrity. A prudent approach is to emphasize *your* reactions to a situation, e.g., "I'm confused," "I'm upset," or "I feel let down," rather than enumerate all the mistakes the principal has made.

Now that we have dissected, analyzed, and synthesized the principal's role in behavior management, it's time to see how fully you have comprehended this discussion.

1. The appropriate posture for the principal to assume regarding disciplinary problems is to
   (a) Give the guidance counselor sole responsibility for discipline,
   (b) Assume responsibility for handling all problems which teachers can't handle,
   (c) Exercise a preventive function by assisting teachers with classroom behavior management,
   (d) Be tough as nails.
2. In dealing with teachers, the principal should
   (a) Avoid giving noncontingent approval,
   (b) Give teachers objective feedback concerning their in-class behavior,
   (c) Emphasize the fact that he is the principal,
   (d) Emphasize the mistakes that teachers are making in the classroom.
3. Teachers are
   (a) Likely to treat their students as they (the teachers) are treated by the principal,
   (b) Less responsive to the principal's approval than that of the guidance counselor,
   (c) More inclined to work hard for a principal who uses lots of disapproval than one who primarily employs approval,
   (d) Most impressed by principals who don't take crap from anyone.
4. Principals should
   (a) Occasionally call spur-of-the-moment assembly programs to keep teachers and students on their toes,
   (b) Confine their intercom announcements to specified times during the school day,

(c) Call students to their office whenever they wish,

(d) Administer discipline over the intercom.

5. Teachers can work most effectively with the principal if they
   (a) Butter him up,
   (b) Express their appreciation for the facilitative aspects of his behavior,
   (c) Pressure him to do better,
   (d) Never express their dissatisfactions to him.

6. The principal can help his teachers apply behavior modification strategies in their classes by
   (a) Hiding himself in his office,
   (b) Using his administrative authority to make teachers apply behavior modification strategies,
   (c) Organizing the school activities in such a way that teachers are busy and find no time to gossip,
   (d) Promoting interteacher exchanges in areas related to behavior modification programs.

The Role of the Counselor

Counselors have traditionally operated as if the problems of teacher–student interaction lay primarily with the student. Therefore, it was the counselor's job to modify the student's behavior so he could operate more comfortably and productively in the classroom. The counselor spent considerable time working with students on an individual or group basis. Yet if many student problems are actually a function of inappropriate contingencies within the classroom, then perhaps the counselor should focus most of his attention on changing *teacher* behaviors. This responsibility would require the counselor to act as a behavior management consultant to the teacher. We shall now attempt to specify the logistics for assuming that role. To give you an overview of the good things in store for the counselor, we have a six-step consultation model developed by scholars of "international reputation" (Anandam and Williams, 1971). The six steps include:

1. Meeting with the teacher to find out what behaviors he considers appropriate and inappropriate in his classroom;

2. Observing the teacher's and students' behavior in order to identify the contingencies leading to the inappropriate behavior;

3. Conferring with the teacher to discuss possible ways to reduce inappropriate behavior;

4. Obtaining suggestions from students for eliminating inappropriate behavior;

5. Executing the plan of action derived from activities 1 through 4;
6. Evaluating the effectiveness of the plan of action and making further recommendations.

How does a counselor establish sufficient rapport with teachers in order to change the contingencies within the classroom? At a faculty meeting early in the school year, the counselor could succinctly describe some of the ways he could assist teachers with classroom management problems. The gist of the counselor's message would be that most teachers periodically face classroom problems for which it would be helpful to get an outsider's point of view. The counselor's role would be described as one of helping teachers formulate alternatives for dealing with these problems. The counselor should indicate that he will be able to provide more realistic suggestions if he can actually observe the "problem" child in the classroom setting. He should explain that observation will allow him to pick up clues for dealing with a problem which a second-hand report might not show.

After initially describing his consultative role, the counselor should not expect to be inundated with requests for assistance. The very thought of having someone observe in their classroom strikes mortal fear in the hearts of many teachers. In his contacts with teachers outside the classroom, the counselor can do much to allay that anxiety. If the counselor can establish a reputation for being a competent, congenial, and supportive person, teachers are likely to request his assistance. To achieve this image, the counselor must first take advantage of opportunities in the cafeteria, teacher's lounge, etc., to convey his regard for teachers as human beings. This goal might be accomplished by his expressing interest in the significant, nonacademic aspects of their lives. Discussion of their families, hobbies, and vocational aspirations would help to communicate the value that he attaches to them as persons.

As the conversation with teachers shifts to the school, the counselor should take care to pass on any good comment he has heard about teachers from students, parents, other teachers, or the principal. For instance, he might say, "I heard the principal commenting on what a tremendous job you are doing with forty-two students in your class." At least two benefits could result from this kind of comment. The teacher may feel elated that his work is being recognized and he may also feel very positive toward the counselor for being sensitive to the fact that he has to work with forty-two students.

If in these beginning discussions a teacher chooses to relate some of his classroom experiences, it is advisable for the counselor to respond either nondirectively or approvingly. A nondirective reaction will allow the teacher to get some things off his chest, clarify his own perceptions of problems, and perhaps feel that he has found an ally in working with those problems. If the counselor has reading materials related to the teacher's concerns, he might pass those on to the teacher. In selecting the materials, the counselor must make sure that they don't convey the message that the teacher is wrong. Let's say the teacher is concerned about Johnny's nonparticipation in class discussion. The counselor might give him the article on "The Role of Social and Material Reinforcers in Increasing Talking of a Disadvantaged Pre-school Child" (Reynolds and Risley, 1968) with a note saying "Wonder whether this would work with Johnny." Such a gesture on the counselor's part provides an invitation for the teacher to seek him further. As a teacher continues to discuss his concerns, it may then be appropriate for the counselor to ask permission to visit the teacher's classroom.

Despite the counselor's efforts to set the consultative relationship in positive terms, teachers may interpret his coming into their classroom as an indication of their inadequacies. This perception might become particularly rampant if the counselor initially visits only those teachers known to be having serious difficulties in their classes. Identifying teachers who could serve as role models for other teachers early in the school year can be an extremely important part of the counselor's consultative program. If the counselor is new to the school, he should first identify the individuals who are generally regarded as competent teachers in that school. He will need to be very honest in communicating to these teachers that he is attempting to prevent any stigma from being attached to his consultative assistance. Therefore, working with the very best teachers should indicate that his assistance is not to be equated with teacher inadequacy. We predict that this strategy will help teachers who are having considerable difficulty with their classes to not feel embarrassed at asking for the counselor's help.

Should the counselor make decisions about what student behaviors are appropriate or inappropriate? Obviously, one of the first tasks in improving a classroom situation is to identify the behaviors that need to be strengthened or weakened. Should the counselor assume that responsibility? How would the counselor feel if the principal were to tell him that it is inappropriate for a counselee to make certain types of statements in his (the counselor's) office? He might just tell the principal where to go. The teacher would probably feel much the same way if the counselor were to enumerate the behaviors which the teacher ought to consider appropriate or inappropriate.

Suppose the teacher identifies behaviors as inappropriate which the counselor does not perceive as undesirable, or includes goals that are not observable (e.g., honest attempt). Under these circumstances it might be legitimate for the counselor to ask questions such as: "I wonder why you consider this inappropriate?" or "How do you think we will know when a student has made an honest attempt?" We have found that questions like these help the teacher to clarify his own thinking and to come to some logical decisions about what should be done in his class. It is crucial for the teacher to experience a feeling of personal control over his own class, which can best be achieved by asking appropriate questions rather than telling teachers what to do.

Often the behaviors identified by the teacher as inappropriate include both process and product behaviors. If the teacher identifies an academic deficiency as the primary problem, the counselor must first help him define the academic products he wants from students. Several excellent resources are available on the preparation of measurable product objectives (Mager, 1962; McAshan, 1970; Kibler, Barker, and Miles, 1970). In addition, the counselor might refer the teacher to one of the many sources of commercially prepared objectives (Baker, 1970; *Behavioral Objectives*, 1971; Popham, 1970). Following the designation of desired academic products, the counselor and teacher should attempt to identify the process behaviors that would facilitate or impede the attainment of those products. Most behavior management strategies which evolve from counselor–teacher consultation will focus on both process and product objectives.

In helping teachers identify appropriate and inappropriate behaviors, the counselor should not forget the students. Just as the teacher is more likely to cooperate with the counselor if he (the teacher) participates in the delineation of desirable and undesirable behaviors, students are more likely to cooperate with the teacher if they participate in the designation of appropriate and inappropriate behaviors. Procedures such as those described on pages 45–46 of Chapter II would help in obtaining students' input.

How can the counselor help teachers decide on strategies to change the contingencies in the classroom? We hope we have given you some ideas about how the counselor can help the teacher identify the behaviors he wishes to change. Having accomplished this objective, how does the counselor go about helping the teacher alter the environmental contingencies which are contributing to the problem? A common-sense approach is to begin by collecting baseline data on the target behaviors and then sharing these data with the teacher. Before the counselor offers any solutions, the teacher should be asked what he thinks could be done to alter the target behaviors. We have found that the temptation is often great to just tell the teacher what to do. Invariably the teacher would agree to try our approach and invariably he would call back to say that it didn't work. Painfully but profitably we have learned that it pays to explore possible consequences of a number of strategies without identifying any one approach as *the* strategy.

Earlier in the book, we discussed token reinforcement, behavior contracting, teacher approval, peer reinforcement, peer tutoring, group contingent reinforcement, and modeling. These constitute the major strategies that a counselor would discuss with a teacher. It might be obvious from the baseline data that the contingencies of teacher attention should be altered. Even so, the counselor may find some teachers saying "Well, that seems the logical thing to do but I'm not sure it will work in my class." What do you do? Throw up your arms in exasperation and leave? That's one possibility. In order to see what other possibilities exist, imagine that the consultative conference is a one-to-one counseling situation. That calls for some nondirective acceptance of the teacher's feelings. Given this kind of atmosphere, the counselor will probably find that what the teacher means is "I am not sure that I can train myself to attend only to appropriate behavior" or "I am afraid other kids will think that I am showing favoritism toward one student." Helping teachers overcome their feelings of doubt, fear, and anxiety is a vital factor in getting them to try behavior modification strategies.

How can the counselor help in implementing a behavior modification strategy? Whatever strategy the teacher and the counselor decide upon, certain changes in the teacher's behavior are almost always necessary. The most effective technique for modifying teacher behavior appears to be live modeling in the teacher's classroom. Anandam employed this approach in helping a third grade teacher increase her attention to appropriate behavior during math period. Anandam taught the class for the first half of a thirty-minute period while the teacher observed; the roles were exchanged in the second half. A fifteen-minute session was long enough to demonstrate several ways of approving children when they behaved appropriately. Using this modeling procedure, Anandam increased the amount of teacher approval from a weekly average of 1.4 percent to 10.2 percent in approximately six weeks. About the same time, an attempt was made to increase the approval rate of another third grade teacher. This time, the training procedure consisted of observational feedback and weekly conferences. During a six-week period, teacher approval increased from an average of 3.9 percent to 6.3 percent, which was less than the improvement achieved through the modeling arrangement. Other research (Stephens, 1972) supports our findings that live modeling in the teacher's classroom is more effective than simply providing direct feedback to the teacher. Obviously, the two techniques can be used together.

Some behavior modification strategies require a teacher to behave in ways which are alien to his conventional mode of operation. For example, a teacher who has habitually chastised students for misbehaving may find it very difficult to approve students for behaving appropriately and to ignore them when they behave inappropriately. In this case, helping the teacher to role-play in a situation outside the classroom may be useful in making the transition from conventional to behavior modification methods. Such practices allow the teacher to become accustomed to hearing himself exhibit approving behaviors. They also present situations in which making mistakes would not have catastrophic consequences and in which behaviors could be analyzed immediately after they occur.

Following these role-playing sessions, the teacher should be ready to try out the strategy in his classroom. In order to ensure a fair degree of success for the teacher, fair enough to encourage him to continue, the technique of successive approximations should be employed. The counselor should begin by asking the teacher to make changes which would be easy for him to make. Otherwise, the counselor may lose the teacher. Suppose a counselor encounters a teacher who appears to have extreme difficulty in being complimentary toward students. This teacher has never been known to make a kind remark to students, and he has expressed concern about being perceived as acting artificial if he attempts to be complimentary. Rather than initially asking this teacher to praise students for their appropriate behavior, the counselor should begin by asking him to do things such as listen closely when students comment in class, use students' comments as a basis for further class discussions, and nod his head to indicate approval of a student's comment. After these behaviors have begun to occur frequently, the counselor might then ask the teacher to indicate verbally when he feels that a student has responded particularly well. This verbal indication might entail little more than short phrases such as "That's good," "I like that," "Your work is improving." Eventually, the teacher may be able to verbalize highly specific approval of a student's behavior and the reason for the approval, e.g., "What you've said about . . . is an extremely important point because . . ."

As the teacher attempts to implement a behavior mod procedure, the counselor should provide objective feedback to that teacher concerning his behavior and student reactions to that behavior. Without feedback, the teacher can be totally oblivious to mistakes he is making or may even become discouraged about things he is doing effectively. This feedback usually takes the form of meeting with the teacher at least once a week, going over observational data with him, specifying the well executed episodes of teacher–student interaction, and, in the case of inappropriate episodes, suggesting more desirable ways of responding. Changes in student behavior should receive particular emphasis in these counselor–teacher discussions. Such changes will be a powerful selling point for teachers who are highly suspicious of operant tactics. In one study skeptics who initially called the behavior modification strategy hogwash are reported as having a change of heart when they were shown observational data indicating improvement in their students' behavior (Packard, 1970).

We have now reached that exciting juncture where once again you can demonstrate your knowledge by responding to a set of challenging questions. We know that you approach this task with the greatest of anticipation, but do try to keep your excitement within reasonable limits.

1. Counselors should primarily
    (a) Administer aptitude and interest tests,
    (b) Counsel with individual students,
    (c) Consult with teachers concerning classroom behavior management problems,
    (d) Consult with the principal regarding school board policies.
2. In establishing rapport with teachers, the counselor should
    (a) Explain his role as consultant to the teacher,
    (b) Communicate his regard for teachers as human beings,
    (c) Deal with the classroom problems which the teacher deems important,
    (d) All of the above.
3. In reacting to a teacher's description of a classroom situation, the counselor should
    (a) Point out all mistakes the teacher is making,
    (b) Employ only approval,
    (c) Primarily respond nondirectively,
    (d) Tell the teacher exactly what to do.
4. Once the counselor has gained access to a teacher's classroom he should
    (a) Initially collect baseline data to assess the severity of the problem,
    (b) Quickly identify an appropriate behavior modification technique to be applied in the classroom,
    (c) Examine the baseline data to identify the contingencies which are maintaining the problem behavior,
    (d) Both (a) and (c).

5. In helping teachers decide on appropriate intervention strategies, the counselor should
   (a) Indicate that he has read the classic books in the field of behavior modification, e.g., Skinner's *Beyond Freedom and Dignity*, Williams and Anandam's *Cooperative Classroom Management,*
   (b) Get the school board to make tenure contingent on teachers' working with a counselor,
   (c) Simply refer teachers to research materials on behavior modification,
   (d) Discuss observational data in such a way that teachers can make their own decisions about what operant strategy to employ.

The Role of Parents

You may think that we are now ready to negate the theme which we have promoted throughout the book—namely, that the school is primarily responsible for a child's academic success or failure. Not so. Discussion of the parents' role is not to be equated with absolving the school of responsibility. We are simply recognizing that parents can enhance or impede the efforts of the school. We will now focus our attention on how teachers, principals, and counselors can work with parents to optimize parental contributions to classroom management.

How can the teacher establish sufficient rapport with parents to enlist their cooperation in facilitating their children's academic growth? Establishing rapport with parents in middle-class suburbia may pose no big problem. Rapport may be accomplished as simply as inviting parents to attend a P.-T.A. meeting, to visit their child's classroom periodically, or to serve as teacher aides. If their child is not doing well at school, most middle-class parents would probably take the initiative of contacting the school to discuss the problem. Our perception is that most middle-class parents are anxious (sometimes overly anxious) to see that their children do well in school. They want to know what they can do to help and will try most anything that has a reasonable chance of succeeding.

What can be accomplished very easily in middle-class suburbia may be painfully difficult to attain in an impoverished inner-city setting. P.-T.A. meetings may attract no more than 1 percent of the parents; straight *F*'s for a child may not even elicit as much as a phone call from his parents (Daniels, 1971). It is our conviction that many inner-city parents (or guardians) are concerned about their children's academic progress, but have such hostility, distrust, and insecurity with respect to the school that they are not able to interact comfortably with teachers and administrators. Many of these parents have themselves had excruciating failure experiences in school. Furthermore, most have had little communication from the school except when their children were doing poorly.

In the face of the distressing facts described in the previous paragraph, what is a teacher to do? In establishing a trusting and cooperative relationship with inner-city parents, you must somehow convey to these parents that you genuinely care about their children. A step in this direction is to communicate something positive about those children. A succession of negative comments not only fails to help a child, it makes both you and the school aversive to the parents. We recommend that instead of contacting parents primarily when their children are doing badly, contact them when they are manifesting improvement.

Another way that you can demonstrate genuine concern about their children is to give parents feedback concerning the child's progress more frequently than at the end of the traditional six- or nine-week grading period. It is important to indicate that this feedback doesn't go on a child's permanent record but is simply to keep parents well informed about the child's performance at school. An outstanding program for providing frequent feedback to parents has been developed by the Anne Arundel Learning Center (AALC) in Maryland (Cohen et al., 1971). Teachers in this center introduced the idea of "Good Friday" and "Excellent Friday" letters to parents, informing them that their child had been doing good or excellent work during the week. The student had to earn a "Good Friday" or an "Excellent Friday" letter by completing a certain number of academic tasks. The reinforcement value of the letters was further enhanced by pairing them with high-priority activities at school. The "Good Friday" letters were worth ten Skinnerians and "Excellent Friday" letters worth twenty Skinnerians. The Skinnerians were redeemable for various reinforcing activities. Oh yes, a Skinnerian was a token printed in the form of a dollar bill with a picture of Skinner on one side and the words "In Behavior We Trust" on the other.

At some point you may wish to invite parents to the school to see their children's classes in action. This invitation should be preceded by the types of communication mentioned above, or you will probably get little response from the parents. When a parent arrives on the scene, you should make every effort to let him see his child functioning positively. If the parent comes during an evening session, be sure to have some of the child's productive work ready to show the parent.

In what ways can the teacher respond to a parent when the confrontation seems unpleasant? It would be nice if all teacher–parent interactions could be serenely reinforcing. Realistically, that will not always be the case. Parent–teacher encounters tend to become unpleasant when a parent accuses the teacher of negligence, favoritism, prejudice, and so on. When a parent takes such a stand, it is quite natural for you to feel hostile toward that parent. How can a parent be so insensitive to the incredible effort you expend in your teaching? One reason why a parent may accuse you is to direct attention away from his own inadequacies. In other words, the parent's accusation is an attempt to keep you off his back. By defending yourself, you do exactly what the parent expected and probably reinforce his accusing behavior.

When you are confronted with accusations from a parent, we recommend that you acknowledge his feelings by saying something to the effect of "I didn't realize you felt that I've been . . . Could we talk about why you feel that way?" We can hear you muttering, "I can't do it!" We recommend that you have some practice sessions in which you cognitively structure these situations and then verbalize the responses you would make to a parent. You might practice in front of the mirror, when you do your make-up, trim your beard, or just survey your attractive countenance.

Probably the most unpleasant type of encounter with parents is when they issue threats because of something which has happened at school. These threats cause different types of teacher reactions, including fear, hostility, self-pity, or a "to hell with it all" kind of resolve. It is legitimate for you to have these feelings. Before you act, however, we propose that you think about the following: the parent who seeks you, whether in a positive or a negative way, is probably more concerned about his child than the parent who never seeks you. Your response to the parent should recognize and reinforce that concern. Since the parent perceives what is going on in the classroom differently from the way you perceive it, it would probably be constructive to acknowledge his perceptions and explore how he came to those perceptions.

How can the teacher explain a behavior modification program to a parent? The ways in which you can explain behavior modification programs to a parent are dependent upon the kind of parent you encounter: the "informed," the "uninformed," or the "misinformed."

The informed parent is one of those rare individuals who knows the in's and out's of behavior modification. In all probability this parent will question your rationale for designating certain student behaviors as inappropriate or for employing certain types of operant procedures. For instance, you may have decided that "getting out of seat without permission" is inappropriate student behavior. However, a student may be delayed in his work by five minutes or more trying to obtain your permission to sharpen his pencil. If an informed parent should bring this point to your attention, you'd better explore alternate suggestions with him.

The uninformed parent is somewhat naive about behavior modification techniques and programs. He might become curious about the points his daughter is receiving, about free time, etc. This parent may call you or come to school to find out what it's all about. You can overwhelm this parent with sophisticated talk about behavior modification, but such a strategy is sure to sever whatever tenuous relationship you might have managed to establish with the parent. How, then, should a teacher respond to an uninformed parent? Express your appreciation for his calling you or visiting your class and indicate that you will be happy to discuss his child's progress with him. In maintaining a conversation with this parent, you should attempt to find out what he has heard from his child and to elicit his questions regarding what's happening in the classroom. Also, it is desirable that you not resort to the use of technical language like *successive approximations, aversive stimuli,* and *contingent,* but instead use words like *step-by-step, unpleasant consequences,* and *immediately.*

We move now to the highly reinforcing misinformed parent. By misinformed, we mean that the parent has heard about behavior modification, but has a very distorted conception of what it entails. He is hung up on words like *control, manipulation,* and *bribery.* How do you think such a parent would react when he learns that you have introduced a behavior contract in your class? He may call the principal and complain that, as a parent, he objects to his son being bribed and controlled by the teachers. It is the principal's problem at this point; but it will quickly become yours if the principal insists that you change your program in order to get the parent off his (the principal's) back.

Occasionally, you will find a parent who, instead of calling the principal, writes to the local newspaper. His article may carry a title such as "Do you want *your* children to be treated like rats?" Something similar to this once happened to us following a workshop on behavior management. The writers of the article recommended that parents and teachers categorically reject the behavior modification techniques which had been taught in the workshop. Our immediate feeling toward these parents was to make their criticisms look as ridiculous as we possibly could. Self-control eventually prevailed; we responded by applauding their concern for the quality of their children's education, by emphasizing the importance of the issues they had raised, by discussing the issues in a direct fashion, and by inviting the parents to additional study in the area of classroom management. To our knowledge, there was no further comment in the local papers.

When parents complain to the principal or news media about your teaching, it is very important for you to establish face-to-face communication with those parents. Go ahead and call them. Indicate that you would like to get to know them and learn more about their ideas for improving the school. How do you predict they will respond to your invitation? Common sense dictates that they will either come in to see you or quit complaining about your teaching. If they continue their extracurricular protests, it would probably be best simply to ignore those complaints. We must hasten to add that if our new-found critics have political power, your ignoring them may not get them off your back. Under these circumstances, you could face the following consequences for continuing with the behavior modification programs: non-renewal of contract, if under probation; transfer to another school, if under tenure; nonrecommendation for salary increase; and additional tasks such as lunch room duties and hall duty. Whether you are willing to incur these consequences for employing operant procedures rests with your judgment. Remember that these consequences are not peculiar to behavior modification programs. You may confront them any time you significantly deviate from the status quo.

What can parents do to enhance their child's success at school? First, they can help to keep the child in school. It is unlikely that the school can help the child very much if his attendance is highly irregular. The parents may contend that if school were interesting, their child would stay in school. No one can refute this. Yet parents can help in identifying activities that would make school stimulating and reinforcing to their children. Where possible, these activities should become a part of your classroom program. Unfortunately, many of the privileges which would be the most reinforcing to students are not available for use in the school setting. Some of these privileges, such as watching TV, being with peers, attending movies, going to the pool hall, attending an athletics contest, and purchasing new clothing are at least partially under the control of parents. It is your task to get parents to use these privileges to reinforce the child's attendance at school.

By telephone or home visit, you or the school counselor can arrange a "deal" between parents and children. This parent–child deal would bring some of the aforementioned privileges to bear upon appropriate behaviors such as attending school (MacDonald, Gallimore, and Mac-Donald, 1970) and completing assignments (Cantrell et al., 1969). One of the first tasks in negotiating this agreement is to identify the specific privileges which will serve as reinforcers for the child. A common-sense way to acquire this information is to ask the parent or child what he spends most of his time doing, what he would like to do if he had a chance, and what things he would work to obtain. It is likely that some of the things would already be accessible to the child on a noncontingent basis. In arranging a deal, it would be advisable to depend primarily on new privileges. Otherwise, the child may feel that he is getting a raw deal, i.e., he is now having to work for things which were formerly freely available.

As a part of the deal, procedures should be delineated for recording the child's attendance or achievement and dispensing the reinforcing privileges. The teacher is in the best position to keep the records. Initially, reinforcement should be given as frequently and as immediately as possible. If week-end movie privileges are being used as reinforcers, the teacher could give the child tokens each day that he attends school and completes his assignment. The tokens would be redeemable at the end of the week for money or a movie ticket. The contingencies should be such that a child has something to gain each day he attends school and does his work. If a perfect record is required to earn reinforcers, once the child misses a day he has nothing to gain by attending the rest of the week.

In what ways can the principal help to establish a positive relationship between the school and parents? Our experience shows that when parents do not understand or agree with what the teacher does in the classroom, they usually call the principal to express their dissatisfaction. How common it is for principals to take the telephone and hear a high-strung voice at the other end saying "What's going on in my son's class? It is ridiculous for him to be working for points," or "I send my son to learn for himself and not to learn for others. Why on earth does he have to wait till others finish?" or "Mr. Smith, you know I am a very tolerant woman. I hardly ever complain. But I can't keep quiet when my child has to study while Johnny is raising Cain in the class and the teacher doesn't do anything about it."

We feel that it is important for the principal to know what is going on in the classrooms and the rationale behind those activities so that he can, without any delay, respond to the parent's complaint. The fact that he is cognizant of what is happening would tend to calm the parent. On the other hand, if the principal were to say "Well, Ms.

Jones, I don't know what you are talking about—you better talk to the teacher," the parent will, in all likelihood, get more uptight. She will assume the principal has little control over his school or that she is getting the proverbial run-around. The suggestions we presented earlier in this chapter on the role of the principal should be helpful in keeping the principal abreast of classroom activities.

Day after day, parents contact the principal to express their concerns and complaints. It would be highly beneficial for the principal to keep some type of record of parental concerns. Let us assume that over a period of a week or two, the principal's record looks something like this:

Date	Parent's name	Teacher's name	Concern	Rationale
10/6	Ms. A	Ms. M	Working for points	It is like bribing.
10/7	Mr. B	Ms. M	Working for points	Children should work without any such rewards.
10/7	Ms. C	Ms. N	My son loses points because someone else misbehaved.	It's just not fair.
10/10	Ms. D	Mr. O	Working for points	They never did that to us when we went to school.

From this record, you can see that three out of four parents are concerned about "working for points," no matter who the teacher is. Would this not suggest that at the earliest opportunity, perhaps at the next P.-T.A. meeting, the principal should arrange for someone (the teachers, himself, or a consultant) to respond specifically to that concern? No doubt keeping a log on parental complaints would be time consuming. But if this approach results in the satisfactory resolution of most of these complaints, the principal will spare himself a multitude of headaches. As a result he can take five less aspirins and two less tranquilizers during the course of the day.

Is there any way the counselor can help in developing a positive relationship between the teacher and parents? In our estimation, the counselor has a unique opportunity to receive all kinds of information from various people, including the students, the parents, the teachers, and the principal. The counselor can sort and sift among this information, pick out the pieces that would facilitate positive relationships, and transmit that information to the appropriate party. Information from the parent or teacher expressing appreciation for the other is the main thing that should be communicated. We aren't suggesting that the counselor necessarily take time to record this kind of information, or write notes to teachers and parents. But we do recommend that he develop an orientation that would make it very natural to pass on such information to others when he meets them in the hallway, at lunch time, in the parking lot, before faculty meetings . . .

It's time to terminate our discussion on the role of parents. Parents can profoundly affect the nature of the educational process, but little research has been conducted to identify exactly what their contributions ought to be. In the absence of extensive empirical data on the issues, we have formulated recommendations which appear to be consistent with what we know about behavior modification in other settings. With that confession, we now pose these exacting questions for your consideration.

1. The authors obviously feel that
   - (a) Most parents have nothing to contribute to the educational process,
   - (b) Middle-class parents are interested in their children's academic progress but lower-class parents are not,
   - (c) Parents are more responsible for children's academic progress than is the school,
   - (d) Parentally controlled rewards should be used in fostering school attendance and completion of academic assignments.

2. Teachers in inner-city schools should
   - (a) Stay as far away from the students' parents as possible,
   - (b) Communicate with parents primarily through P.-T.A. meetings,
   - (c) Not become personally involved with their students,
   - (d) Communicate with parents primarily when they (the teachers) have something positive to say about their children.

3. In arranging a deal between parent and child, the teacher should
   - (a) Identify privileges controlled by parents which can be used as rewards for behaviors such as attending school, completing assignments, and doing homework,
   - (b) Make sure that all privileges are administered noncontingently,
   - (c) Specify that all privileges are to be administered by the teacher,
   - (d) Avoid letting the parent feel that he is making an important contribution to the child's academic progress.

4. When parents threaten a teacher for the poor performance of their children, the teacher should
   (a) Give them a lecture on all that he has done to help their children,
   (b) Assume that these parents are less concerned about their children than those who never complain,
   (c) Confront the parents with all the inadequacies he has detected in how they have brought up their children,
   (d) None of the above.
5. Williams and Anandam claim that since parents generally call the principal when they have a complaint about the teacher, the principal should
   (a) Hook up a prerecorded tape to acknowledge their complaints,
   (b) Be very diplomatic in directing them to talk to the teacher,
   (c) Let the parents know that he (principal) is aware of what is going on in the classes,
   (d) Tell the parent that he should bring his complaint up at the next P.-T.A. meeting.

Chapter VI

THE RIGHT TO KNOW
The Use of Operant Procedures to Promote Academic Behaviors

In defending their coverage of highly distressing events, news reporters often speak of "the public's right to know." Being patriotic Americans, we endorse that concept. Our citizens should be well informed about what's happening in these perilous times. In most instances an informed citizenry can act far more responsibly than an uninformed one.

There is no institution in society in which the concept of "the right to know" should apply more unequivocally than in the school. Tragically, the conditions within many schools appear to permanently damage children's desire and ability to know, in spite of the fact that the field of education has experienced its share of "messiahs." With the emergence of every new teaching strategy has come visions of something which would dramatically accelerate the rate at which students learn. But in too many instances, the new strategies have not helped children learn to read better, to write better, to speak better, or to more accurately understand the world in which they live.

We have even been asked some rather embarrassing questions about the efficacy of operant procedures in facilitating academic achievement. It is true that most behavior modification research studies have been directed toward changing undesirable social behaviors (e.g., temper tantrums, fighting, throwing objects, disruptive talking). We're tempted to affirm that improvement in social behaviors is accompanied by improvement in academic achievement. Distressingly, we have found little empirical evidence to substantiate this contention. So it may be that teachers are using operant techniques more to produce "nice" students than academically productive students. We would be the last to oppose students' being nice, but we wonder if the attainment of socially acceptable behavior per se justifies extensive use of operant methodology in the classroom. We suspect that you share our interest in seeing behavior modification techniques demonstrate their merit in the area of academic behavior. In appraising this merit, we shall examine three different dimensions of academic performance: studying behavior, scholastic achievement, and creative responses.

Studying Behavior

By studying behavior, we mean what was identified in Chapter IV as task-relevant behavior. Studying behavior refers to any process activity in which the student is observed as attending to designated academic stimuli. Usually, the behavior is classified as "studying" or "task-relevant" only if the child appears to be oriented to assigned academic activities, such as looking at a book when reading has been assigned, looking at the teacher or taking notes during a class lecture. Quite a number of behavior modification studies have focused solely upon studying behavior; a great many more have included it as one dimension of appropriate classroom conduct.

Can studying behavior be manipulated in the same fashion as other process behaviors? Yes. Most of the operant techniques which have been used to improve social conduct have been applied with equal success to "on-task" behavior. Teacher attention, points, tangibles, group contingencies, and peer monitoring are the major strategies which have been used to increase study behavior (Broden et al., 1970; Bushell, Wrobel, and Michaelis, 1968; Coleman, 1970; Ferritor et al., 1972; Hall, Lund, and Jackson, 1968; Surrat, Ulrich, and Hawkins, 1969). The typical arrangement is for the reinforcing consequences to be contingent upon a specified amount of study behavior. In the case of shaping procedures, the amount of study time required for the pay-off is progressively increased. Although peers have been used to monitor study behavior, the teacher usually assumes this responsibility.

Is an increase in study behavior accompanied by improvement in academic performance? Not necessarily. Sulzer and her colleagues (1971) demonstrated that token reinforcement for on-task behavior during a reading class produced both a high level of desirable behavior and an increase in reading rate. Unfortunately, accuracy in reading was lower during this token condition than when correct reading responses were specifically and directly reinforced. Even more distressing, results obtained by Ferritor et al. (1972) show that increments in on-task behavior produced by token reinforcement were not accompanied by improvement in arithmetic performance. Apparently, some children are quite astute in giving the appearance of working without actually being productive. Looking at the issue from the opposite perspective, it appears that children can also be productive without seeming to be studying (Ferritor et al., 1972). However, Kirby and Shields (1972) did find that a combination of praise and immediate feedback not only produced an increase in arithmetic response rate but a concomitant increase in study behavior. We must admit that the answer to the question is ambiguous. Differences in reinforcement procedures, in types of responses being modified, and in the kinds of subjects being used may account for some of these inconsistencies in research findings.

Before proceeding to our weighty discussion of academic achievement, we must appraise your comprehension of our less than profound treatment of studying behavior. You have a .0625 probability of making a perfect score on these items simply by virtue of chance. Throw in your natural intelligence and the probability becomes astronomical.

1. Attempts to modify studying behavior via operant procedures have been
   (a) Embarrassingly unsuccessful,
   (b) About as successful as attempts to modify other process behaviors,
   (c) The most successful of any operant applications,
   (d) Exercises in buffoonery.
2. If Ms. Wells developed a system for increasing studying behavior, she
   (a) Could be assured that academic performance would also improve,
   (b) Could have reasonable confidence ($p < .05$) that academic achievement would also improve,
   (c) Should not necessarily expect concomitant improvement in academic achievement,
   (d) Should be chastised by the Board of Education for attempting to manipulate students.

Scholastic Achievement

Now we are getting to the heart of the matter. At some point, operant methodology must demonstrate its utility in improving academic products. These products could include performance on teacher-made assignments and tests or performance on standardized achievement measures. Although there is more to school than academic achievement, you would certainly have difficulty justifying the use of a teaching strategy that has no effect on scholastic performance.

Do external payoffs enhance academic achievement? It would be redundant to say that a major criticism of behavior management is that it emphasizes extrinsic rather than intrinsic payoffs. Classified as extrinsic are teacher approval, tokens, free time, tangible items, and external success feedback. Since we have already dealt with the ethical and theoretical dimensions of this issue, we can now proceed to the more practical question of how these extrinsic payoffs affect students' academic productivity.

Contingent teacher attention (consisting mainly of approval) has been employed more extensively than any other operant technique in modifying classroom behavior. The effects of teacher approval are often contrasted with those of teacher disapproval. In 1964, Kennedy and Willcutt reviewed thirty-three articles (covering fifty years of research) dealing with the effects of praise and blame on academic performance. Their review indicates that praise generally facilitates performance and disapproval impedes performance. The superiority of praise seems to hold irrespective of most subject characteristics such as age, sex, ability, and personality (Kennedy and Willcutt, 1963; White, 1967).

The effect of teacher approval on academic performance is lucidly demonstrated in a study by Clark and Walberg (1968). The treatment conditions were administered in after-school remedial reading classes for ten to thirteen year olds considered to be potential dropouts. Students kept their own records of the number of times praise was received from the teacher. Teachers in the experimental classes were instructed to distribute their approval comments to all children and to approve the children as frequently as possible. Though the control children kept a record of the times the teacher approved them, the experimenters made no effort to increase the frequency of approval received by these students. The study was conducted over a period of approximately six weeks. The students who received a high rate of teacher approval scored significantly higher on a standardized reading test (post-test) than did controls.

Another type of environmental consequence which should affect the rate at which students learn is knowledge of success. Skinner has repeatedly contended that success feedback is the most effective type of reinforcement for acquisition of academic content. Frequent feedback does appear to increase the rate of acquisition in programmed instruction. But what about the effect of feedback in more conventional academic activities? Chansky's study (1960) of college-level students showed that continuous feedback following a series of academic tasks is more effective in promoting recall than intermittent feedback. Chansky also found that feedback in the form of the correct answer was superior to feedback in the form of grading (i.e., labeling each response as right or wrong).

One of the more important issues related to feedback is the comparative merits of positive and negative feedback. Programmed instruction has historically emphasized positive feedback (95 percent minimum), whereas conventional teaching approaches have made extensive use of negative feedback. Teachers generally spend a great deal of time going over items that students have missed and comparatively little time discussing items answered correctly. At least two studies (Hayes and Hawkins, 1970; Sajwaj and Knight, 1971) clearly demonstrate that the conventional strategy increases errors. We recommend that teachers make a big fuss over the successful features of a student's work and give relatively little attention to his errors.

Operant theory also emphasizes the immediacy of feedback. Does it really make much difference whether a student receives feedback as soon as he completes an activity or a few hours or even a few days after completion of the activity? We must confess that the research findings on this issue are not entirely consistent. For instance, one study (More, 1969) found that immediate feedback yielded poorer results for both acquisition and retention than feedback given one or two and one-half days later. In direct contrast, Hillman (1969) reports that students who received feedback after every problem on daily assignments performed significantly better than students who received feedback twenty-four hours after completing each assignment. Consistent with Hillman's results are Kirby and Shields' (1972) finding that immediate feedback and praise produced an increase in both arithmetic response rate and attending behavior. We would guess that the efficacy of immediate feedback is very much related to the concurrent presence of teacher approval and the difficulty level of the material being learned.

A third consequence that has been very useful in improving students' social behavior is contingent free time. What effect would free time have on students' academic productivity? It is pretty obvious that free time which is contingent upon completion of academic work will increase rate of working. Hopkins, Schutte, and Garton (1971) found that allowing first and second graders to go to a playroom as soon as their daily printing and writing assignments had been completed and scored led to an increase in the printing and writing rates. Accelerated work rates continued despite the fact that the amount of time that could be spent in the playroom was progressively reduced. One of the most encouraging features of the Hopkins et al. study was that increases in productivity were accompanied by fewer errors in printing and writing. This finding is a bit surprising since the experimenters made no attempt to reinforce good work differentially. The experimenters pointed out, however, that the increase in quality may have occurred as a result of teacher approval.

The best way to be certain that free time will increase the quality of work is to make free time contingent on quality. Evans and Oswalt (1971) made an early recess or story period contingent upon the correct responses (e.g., spelling a word correctly, solving an arithmetic problem) of four underachieving students in the fourth and sixth grades. These procedures produced a marked increase in the target students' academic performance. Campbell and Sulzer (1971) used tokens backed up by special privileges to increase not only reading and spelling rates but also accuracy of performance in a class of mentally handicapped students. In this case, tokens were contingent upon correct responses. Nolen, Kunzelmann, and Haring (1967) also produced significant academic gains in students who had previously exhibited learning and behavior disorders by making activities known to be highly reinforcing contingent upon academic performance.

Of all the external consequences which have been used to affect academic performance, tangible rewards have probably had the most decisive impact. Tangible rewards have been particularly effective with disadvantaged students and students with a history of educational failures. Clark, Lachowicz, and Wolf (1968) awarded points exchangeable for money to students in an urban neighborhood youth corps for reducing the amount of time required to complete their lessons. In only eight weeks, these students made substantial gains in their reading and arithmetic scores on the California Achievement Test, whereas an on-the-job control group which received a similar amount of money (but not contingent upon their academic performance) either regressed or remained at essentially the same achievement level. At least two other studies (Staats and Butterfield, 1965; Staats et al., 1967) support the contention that tokens exchangeable for money are very effective in increasing the reading skills of students with an extensive history of school failure and misbehavior.

A unique study by Alschuler (1969) indicated that play money can also be highly effective in upgrading academic achievement. In this study, the teacher negotiated a contract with each student as to the amount of play money the student would receive for successfully completing a specified amount of work in math. Students had to pay a fine for not turning in their work on time, for revising the contract before the stated deadline, or for not producing the percentage of correct answers agreed upon. The fifth grade students operating under the contract made significantly greater gains on the Stanford Achievement Test of Mathematics than a control group taught in the conventional manner.

As you might guess, there are tangibles other than money which can be used to increase academic achievement. Wolf, Giles, and Hall (1968) awarded field trips, snacks, money, items in a "store" and a shopping trip for reading gains achieved by fifth and sixth grade remedial readers. It is not surprising that these students made significantly greater improvement on standardized reading measures over a one-year period than a matched control group which received similar instructions but no tangible payoffs. In their research with blacks and Mexican-American students, Chadwick and Day (1970) used items such as the school lunch, candy, gum, clothes, and jewelry to upgrade both social behavior and academic achievement. Benowitz and Busse (1970) found that a simple box of crayons contingent on "doing well" in spelling for an entire week produced an improvement in spelling for fourth grade black children in urban ghetto schools.

Some studies have employed a combination of tangibles and free-time activities to encourage academic performance. One such investigation (Tyler and Brown, 1968) used canteen items like candy and gum and special privileges to increase performance on true–false tests over current events. The subjects were thirteen- to fifteen-year-old boys attending a state training school. Two features of the Tyler and Brown study are worth remembering: (1) contingent tangible rewards had a significantly greater impact on academic performance than the same rewards administered noncontingently; (2) the superiority of contingent rewards was maintained over a twelve-week interval.

Is there any evidence that attempts to make learning activities inherently reinforcing lead to improvement in academic achievement? No teaching objective is more commendable than attempting to make academic pursuits inherently reinforcing. We consider it entirely appropriate to use points, free time, tangible payoffs, and social approval to encourage students to engage in academic experiences. If your students have been turned off to the joy and benefits of learning, it may take a multiplicity of extrinsic rewards to get them to engage in academic activities. Notwithstanding, we consider it indefensible to employ extrinsic rewards as a substitute for inherently reinforcing academic activities. A notable goal is to make the learning activities so highly reinforcing that free time and extrinsic rewards will eventually become unnecessary.

We cannot tell you exactly what to do to ensure that your instructional activities will be inherently reinforcing for student X. What we can do is suggest procedures which will increase the probability of his finding the instructional activities reinforcing. Our first suggestion would be to give him some measure of responsibility for identifying what he wants to accomplish and the manner in which he will accomplish it. Now before you throw up your hands in holy horror, let us say that we are not advocating the "you students can do what you want to today" philosophy. Such total lack of direction and accountability will almost always produce distressing results. In contrast, when students are given definite alternatives and are then evaluated as to their use of these alternatives, more encouraging results can be expected. The literature (Davis, 1971; McEwen, 1972; Ryan, 1965) indicates that student choice of academic activities consistently produces higher achievement levels than teacher choice of activities.

At what age are students capable of making wise decisions about what they will study? Our opinion is that from kindergarten on children should be given the opportunity to make decisions about activities in which they wish to engage at school. Kindergarten teachers have a unique opportunity to rely primarily on the reinforcement value of academic activities rather than extrinsic rewards. This assertion is based on the assumption that kindergarten children have not yet built up an antipathy to academic activities which necessitates the use of extrinsic rewards. One way to increase the probability that academic activities will remain reinforcing for students is to let them exercise some control over what they do from the very beginning. Nothing would be more educationally catastrophic than to force a young child to engage in an academic activity which he finds inherently nonreinforcing or aversive.

Instead of leaving choice completely undefined, it would be advisable, at least initially, to present a set of definite alternatives to students. Your system of alternatives should be flexible enough to allow students to identify their own activities when they find nothing on your list acceptable. As to the number of alternatives provided, a choice between even two activities is superior to no choice. Beyond that, the greater the number of alternatives the higher the probability of the student's finding something which is highly reinforcing. We must admit that for young children and children with special difficulties such as brain damage, it would probably be better to present two or three alternatives at a time. Otherwise the child might have difficulty in choosing because of the sheer multiplicity of stimuli with which he must deal.

As to the type of alternatives which should be provided, a prime criterion is enjoyability. Not much is gained by forcing a student to engage in an activity which the teacher believes has profound educational value but which the student finds distasteful. His distaste for that activity may very well generalize to academic activities which might otherwise be very enjoyable. On the other hand, if a child is allowed to engage in activities which he finds highly reinforcing, but which have no obvious educational value, he is likely to generalize that affinity to other school activities which by themselves might not be too reinforcing.

Would students acquire useful ideas if they selected what they wanted to study? The ultimate value of an idea is very difficult to establish. Are the ideas presented in Plato's *Republic* more important than those in Vroman's *Harlem Summer*? If indeed they are, does requiring the child to read the classic work insure that he will assimilate those auspicious ideas? It is much more likely that a child will acquire ideas which are important and relevant to him if he is allowed to choose what he reads. If it's vital that a student read Shakespeare's *Macbeth*, then it's the teacher's responsibility to make *Macbeth* sound so exciting and germane that the student will explore it without teacher coercion. Certainly, a teacher can channel the student's reading into areas he (the teacher) feels are important, by previewing those materials in an informative and stimulating way. If a child knows nothing at all about a book, he would have difficulty making a prudent decision about reading the book. But if the teacher gives him some idea of the content of the book, what he has found to be worthwhile about the book, and what he thinks the student might find exciting about the book, the student will at least be sensitized to some of the possibilities which the book offers.

A most intriguing description of an instructional arrangement that emphasizes inherently reinforcing academic activities is provided by Steven Daniels in his book *How 2 Gerbils, 20 Goldfish, 200 Games, 2000 Books, and I Taught Them How to Read* (1971).[1] As the title implies, Daniels literally made about 2000 books available to his students. (His book describes the procedures he used to obtain the necessary funds to purchase all these books!) Daniels stocked his class-

---

[1] Summarized from pages 62–69 of *How 2 Gerbils, 20 Goldfish, 200 Games, 2,000 Books, and I Taught Them How to Read,* by Steven Daniels. Copyright © 1971, The Westminster Press. Used by permission.

room library by first purchasing two copies of books he thought his students would enjoy. He chose books dealing with race, gangs, sex, sports, fairy tales, and highly controversial issues. Student use dictated whether he purchased additional copies of a book. For example, he wound up with thirty-five copies of *Manchild in the Promised Land*. He divided his books into six levels of difficulty, with the cutoff between levels deliberately left somewhat fuzzy (i.e., some books at each level were as easy as most of the books at the preceding level). The rationale for the overlap in difficulty was to minimize the discomfort in moving from one level to the next. Furthermore, many of the same topics were treated at different levels, which allowed a student just beginning a new level to choose a topic with which he was already familiar.

Each book in Daniels' class was assigned a point value. Points earned for reading books could periodically be exchanged for edibles. Each student's progress was charted on a comprehensive wall chart containing all the students' names. In addition, each student had a card in a central file on which he noted the title of the book he had read, the number of points he earned for reading the book, and the date he finished the book. The date was listed in order to discourage students from making unrealistic claims about what they had read. A student was required to read a specified number of books at each level before moving on to the next level. If a student couldn't find enough books at a given level which he wanted to read, he was taken to the public library to select the necessary additional books.

Is there any evidence that Daniels' program was successful, except that his students ostensibly read a great many books? For the purists, who insist on measuring the attainments of inner-city students by standardized tests, is there anything to indicate that Daniels' program was succesful? Only that his students, many of whom were previously nonreaders, beat the national average for growth on the Stanford Reading Achievement Test by 30 percent! Daniels accomplished this feat by providing a wealth of academic materials dealing with all kinds of subjects, by letting students choose materials they wished to pursue, and by carefully monitoring student choices and achievement. It is impossible to determine how much each of these factors contributed to the success of his students. Free-school advocates would probably contend that the success of the program was largely a function of the freedom of choice provided the students. Educators who emphasize accountability might claim that the systematic monitoring of student choices and achievement was the factor that produced success. For the time being, we can only say that Daniels identified a combination of factors that produced remarkable increments in reading achievement.

It is probably obvious from our response to this question that we think the ability to read well is the most important competency that students acquire at school. If children were initially taught to read in a reinforcing fashion, few children would ever develop serious reading difficulties. Tragically, early experiences in reading prove to be excruciating for many children. As a consequence, we have thousands of students classified at the junior and senior high level who are reading at primary levels. If a ninth grade student is actually reading at the fourth grade level, a simplistic solution to his problem might be to encourage him to read fourth grade materials. Yet, conventional fourth grade books would deal with topics which would be quite unappealing to the typical ninth grader. What he really needs is a book of fourth grade difficulty written about things in which he is vitally interested. A comprehensive listing of such materials (commonly referred to as high interest, low readability materials) is provided in the book *Good Reading for Poor Readers*, written by George D. Spache (1970). This book is periodically revised to include the latest information.

What operantly based instructional systems would probably enhance academic achievement? This question deals with specific arrangements of academic stimuli which would accelerate the acquisition of knowledge and skills. The operantly based instructional systems which appear to have the greatest potential for improving academic attainment are programmed instruction, individualized learning packages, and task analysis.

Programmed instruction is probably the most direct application of operant theory to the instructional process. Overt responding, frequent reinforcement, and immediate reinforcement are the major operant concepts on which programmed instruction is based. Despite this sound operant base, programmed instruction has not consistently proven superior to conventional types of instruction. Schramm's (1964) annotated bibliography cited thirty-six studies in which programmed instruction was compared to traditional modes of instruction. Programmed teaching was superior to the conventional arrangement in seventeen studies; there was no difference between the two approaches in eighteen of the studies; and in only one study was conventional instruction superior to programmed instruction.

A major difficulty in determining the relative merits of programmed instruction and conventional instruction is the global nature of these concepts. A particular type of conventional instruction might be highly superior to a particular type of programmed instruction, but the opposite could be true for many other types. Analysis of related research has led us to conclude that the following characteristics contribute most to the success of programmed instruction: (1) material is presented in a question format—apparently questions heighten attention to subject matter (Sime and Boyce, 1969); (2) frequent feedback relative to the correctness of responses to questions is given—the more difficult the questions, the greater the importance of feedback (Geis and Chapman, 1971); (3) frames are not written redundantly—recent evidence suggests that the typical frame-to-frame repetition not only contributes to boredom but impedes achievement (Valverde and Morgan, 1970); (4) provisions are made for branching—the strictly linear program makes no provision for individual differences in ability to comprehend small, medium, or large chunks of information; (5) the program includes frames calling for problem-solving responses—too many frames requiring nothing but specific factual responses may produce a high degree of satiation with the program; (6) the program includes brief narratives covering the same information as presented in the frames—this arrangement allows students who become bored, tired, or disenchanted with answering questions to change response modes (reading narrative materials) without sacrificing coverage of the materials; (7) the program permits students to ask questions (the computer is the only mechanical device that can presently accomplish this feat); and (8) the program is accompanied by independent assessment tools such as a pretest, comprehension checks, and a post-test—these instruments help the teacher and student to determine the appropriateness of the program for the student, the amount of progress the student is making as he moves through the program, and the student's achievement as a result of completing the program.

More recent and potentially more effective than programmed instruction is a system known as individualized learning packages (ILPs). Several features of ILPs are highly consistent with the operant paradigm: (1) emphasis on behavioral objectives; (2) provision of alternative activities for reaching those objectives; (3) utilization of different sensory modalities (e.g., vision, hearing, touch) in the acquiring of information and skills; (4) emphasis on individualized instruction; and (5) provision of frequent success feedback. It is obvious that ILPs provide a more practical, versatile, and reinforcing instructional arrangement than has usually been the case with programmed instruction. Regarding the impact of ILPs on academic achievement, we can only say that ILPs appear to have great potential. The limited evidence currently available presents a mixed picture of their effectiveness

(Johnson, 1971; Lewy, 1969). Research which appraises the importance of specific features of ILPs as well as the over-all effectiveness of the system is desperately needed.

You may need additional clarification as to the nature of individualized learning packets. One of the more comprehensive descriptions of ILPs has been provided by Kapfer and Ovard (1971). They describe ILPs as organized around five major ingredients: (1) concepts, (2) learning objectives, (3) individualized learning materials and activities, (4) pre-, self-, and postassessment, and (5) quest activities. Except for some differences in terminology, most of the ILPs that we have examined include these five ingredients. Now for a brief description of each of these components.[2]

One of the first steps in developing an ILP is to differentiate the content to be learned into major ideas and then put these ideas into some type of logical sequence. Usually, an ILP is developed around each major idea, which is subsequently broken down into a number of secondary ideas. For example, an initial package in classroom behavior management might be built around the idea "Positive reinforcement is any stimulus which strengthens the behavior that immediately precedes it." This major idea could be broken down into a number of contributing ideas, *e.g.*, "Only by measuring the effect that a stimulus has on a behavior can one determine if it is a positive reinforcer for that behavior," "High probability activities may serve as reinforcers for low probability activities," "A stimulus which is reinforcing for one student may not be for another," "An event which is reinforcing for a student on one occasion may not be reinforcing on another," and "Self-report is often a poor indication of what events will be reinforcing for a student." Each of the secondary ideas would become the focus of a different section of the ILP.

Any good learning package includes instructional objectives which identify behaviors a student would emit to demonstrate mastery of the primary and secondary ideas. In our classroom behavior management example, the student might be required to do the following: (1) write a definition of positive reinforcement; (2) from empirical data indicating the effects that different stimuli have on behavior, identify which stimuli are serving as positive reinforcers; (3) from a list of activities, some of which are designated as high probability and others as low probability, indicate how the high probability activities could be used to reinforce participation in the low probability activities; (4) identify

---

[2] An extensive treatment of the ILP components discussed in pp. 172–74 of this book is provided in P. G. Kapfer and G. F. Ovard, *Preparing and Using Individualized Learning Packages for Ungraded, Continuous Progress Education*. Englewood Cliffs, N.J.: Educational Technology Publications, 1971.

three reasons why self-report may not accurately reflect true reinforcement preferences.

It is apparent that the instructional objectives will to a large degree dictate the nature of the learning activities and evaluation tasks which would be appropriate for your ILP. These activities should be self-directing and should provide alternate modes of acquiring the ideas contained in the packet. For that reason, it would not be sufficient simply to provide one book which discusses the ideas the ILP is designed to teach. For students who may find reading difficult, possible options would be to listen to a recording of the book, listen to an oral review of the book, view a film about the book, read an easier book dealing with similar ideas, or participate in a group discussion of the ideas presented in the book. The more diverse the materials and activities contained in the ILP, the higher the probability that each student will be able to acquire the designated ideas and find working through the package a reinforcing experience. ILPs are noted for their emphasis on audio-visual activities (filmstrips, slides, movies, tapes, records, cassettes), as opposed to more conventional reading and writing tasks.

Evaluation of a student's comprehension of the ideas in the ILP is indispensable. Evaluation typically includes pre-, self-, and postassessment. The purpose of preassessment is to determine which, if any, of the instructional activities the student needs to pursue. The purpose of postassessment is to determine what the student has learned as a result of engaging in the learning activities. If the student does not indicate mastery of the designated ideas on the post-test, the teacher doesn't assume the student has failed. Instead, the teacher might direct the student to activities in the package which he had not originally pursued, develop other activities for this student, adjust the instructional objectives in the package, or direct the student to another ILP. Normally, the pre- and postassessments are made by the teacher. But between these assessments, the student engages in a considerable amount of self-assessment. The self-assessment items should be built into the instructional activities, indicate when a student can meet one objective and move on to the next activity, and apprise the student of his readiness for the postassessment. The self-assessment items are very much like the pre- and postassessment items. Commonly teachers write one examination and use alternate items for the self-assessment and the pre- and postassessment.

In most ILPs, there is a component which goes beyond the ideas the package is designed to teach. These activities are variously called "quest," "depth," or "challenge" activities. They may either precede or follow successful completion of the postassessment. The emphasis in individualized learning packages on self-direction and self-responsibility is most clearly seen in the quest activities. Although the student works independently to a great extent in other phases of an ILP, he basically operates within a structure which has been defined by someone else (usually the teacher). That is, the ideas to be learned, the objectives to be met, the instructional activities from which the student can choose, and the pre-, self- and postassessment procedures are delineated by the teacher. In contrast, quest activities allow students to identify their own objectives and/or instructional activities. Although the problems identified for study may evolve from the content of the ILP, the student should be allowed to pursue the quest activities with a minimum of teacher-imposed directions. Quest activities may consist of reading additional materials, developing a theory, writing a short story, experimenting, painting a picture, developing a skit, producing a play, conducting a community survey, or who knows.

The implementation of an ILP system may sound like a gargantuan amount of work to you. The transition to ILP does require a tremendous expenditure of time and effort. It's not something you can prepare for over your mid-morning coffee break. But in this respect, does ILP differ from other productive teaching approaches? We have become fully convinced that there is no quick and easy route to successful teaching. Since an ILP system requires extensive reorganization of academic activities, we recommend that you avoid initiating a crash ILP program in your school. Widespread use of ILPs should be preceded by careful appraisal of commercially available ILP systems (see Table 4), visits to schools where ILPs are being used, and gradual introduction of ILPs into your own school. Most schools which have introduced ILPs have had summer workshops in which teachers were taught the mechanics of developing and using ILPs.

In the absence of programmed materials and ILPs, don't despair. We feel that major features of these approaches can still be incorporated into your teaching. One possibility is task analysis. Academic skills are often presented in such general terms that students really don't know where to begin in acquiring each skill. In contrast, task analysis includes specification of terminal objectives and delineation of the component objectives which lead to the accomplishment of each terminal objective. In teaching writing, Rayek and Nesselroad (1972) stated one of their terminal objectives as "write from dictation all of the upper and lower case letters of the manuscript alphabet." The component objectives were: (1) copy the letter from visual model; (2) write the letter from dictation; (3) recognize the letter; and (4) name the letter. They went further in their analysis to say that "holding a pencil" and "discriminating between well- and ill-formed letters" were necessary prerequisites for achieving these component objectives.

TABLE 4
Commercially Available ILPs

Name of ILP	Agency and source	Subject matter coverage	Major features of the system
UNIPAC	Teachers UNIPAC Exchange W. B. Field and Associates Box 332 Miami-Kendall, Fla. 33156	All areas of curriculum for K–12; vocational and staff development packages for teachers, administrators, and parents.	UNIPAC Exchange conducts UNIPAC Production Workshops for Teachers, who then prepare UNI-PACs. These packets are scrutinized by specialists and then field tested. Only those teachers who have attended a workshop and contributed at least one acceptable UNIPAC are eligible to borrow programs from the bank.
LAP Learning Activity Packages	Continuous Progress Program Hughson Union High School Box 98 Hughson, Calif. 95326	Academic and vocational subjects for high school grades.	The rationale for each package explains where that particular LAP fits into the over-all structure of an academic area. If a student does not meet the minimum competency level for one LAP, he is re-cycled into other activities of that LAP or into another LAP.
PLAN* Program for Learning in Accordance with Needs	Westinghouse Learning Corporation 2680 Hanover St. Palo Alto, Calif. 94304	Mathematics, Language Arts, Science, and Social Studies for grades 1 through 12.	This program has around 4500 behavioral objectives and teaching-learning units to accomplish the objectives and placement and evaluation tests. It uses a computer management system to select instructional objectives, schedule learning activities, and provide overnight feedback to each student. As students move through PLAN* they assume increasing responsibility for identifying activities and objectives they wish to pursue.

TABLE 4 *(continued)*

Name of ILP	Agency and source	Subject matter coverage	Major features of the system
OMAPAC	Omaha Public School System 3902 Davenport St. Omaha, Nebr. 68131	Language Arts, Mathematics, Science and Social Studies for grades 4, 5, and 6; Mathematics for grades 7, 8, and 9; Physical Education for K–12 (PHYPACS).	The core of the OMAPACs, which identifies the purpose of the packet and specifies resources for meeting the objectives, is called COMPAC. Optional to the students are the depth activities which the students may choose to satisfy their own interests.
IPI Individually Prescribed Instruction	University of Pittsburgh Learning Research and Development Center Pittsburgh, Pa.	Entire elementary school curriculum.	Four types of assessment–placement, pre-test, post-test, and curriculum-embedded test (to assess mastery of each specific objective within an IPI unit)–are included.

The differentiation of component objectives is facilitated by moving backwards from the terminal objective and repeatedly asking the question "What does the student have to be able to do before he can do this?"

Like programmed instruction and ILPs, task analysis entails considerable individualization of instruction. Students achieve component skills at different rates and need step-by-step feedback concerning attainment of those skills. To achieve optimal individualization, arrangements such as peer tutoring and group contingent reinforcement would become imperative. The tutor could demonstrate each component behavior to the target student and provide immediate feedback to the target concerning his attainment of that component. Group contingent reinforcement would, no doubt, facilitate this tutoring arrangement.

What is the one operantly based administrative–instructional scheme that offers the greatest promise for increasing academic productivity? With fear and trepidation, we whisper the words "performance contracting." Despite the political sensitivities connected with performance contracting, we contend that it utilizes more operant principles than any other administrative–instructional scheme of our time. Though this arrangement (notably in Texarkana) has already caused some very uncomfortable moments, we honestly believe that it could prove to be the salvation of American education. It would be nice if such a prophetic utterance could be based on hard data. Regrettably, performance contracting is too young and has experienced too many postnatal disorders to provide a clear picture of its effectiveness at this time. Early returns are mixed. In the famous (or infamous if you prefer) Texarkana project, the students had gained 2.2 grade levels in reading and 1.4 in math after sixty hours of instruction, which is about twenty hours less than the amount of time the school would normally devote to each subject during a school year (Lessinger, 1970). As you may already know, the validity of these gains has been questioned. A federal audit revealed that students were being taught specific answers to questions on the test which was used to evaluate the students' academic growth. However, in addition to achievement gains, marked decrements in absenteeism, dropouts, and vandalism suggest substantial improvement in attitudes toward school.

Since the inception of the Texarkana project in 1969, many other districts have negotiated performance contracting programs. Although most of the performance contracts have focused on disadvantaged students, the approach has now infiltrated suburban schools (Mecklenburger and Wilson, 1971). To date, more than forty firms of all shapes and sizes have contracted their services to school systems ("Customers pass the test," 1970). We suspect that these firms have entered the field of performance contracting because of monetary possibilities. Nevertheless, we like what they are offering for the price. Instead of talking in terms of materials, equipment, personnel, and facilities which they will provide for such-and-such fee, they speak in terms of guaranteed achievement gains. Performance contracting gets us closer to bona fide accountability than anything we've tried. The contracting firm puts its monetary rewards on the line. In essence, it says "Unless we can demonstrate that the specified students can reach an agreed-upon level of achievement in a specified period of time, you pay us nothing." Certainly, all firms don't operate on such an all-or-none basis, but in all performance contracts there's a direct correlation between what the firm is paid and the achievement levels it produces.

The most extensive evaluation of performance contracting thus far has been made by the Office of Economic Opportunity ("OEO performance contract," 1972). Their preliminary findings are not encouraging. OEO appraised the impact of performance contracting on the reading and math achievement of disadvantaged children in eighteen school systems, ranging from large metropolitan areas to small rural districts. The study compared the achievement of approximately 13,000 children who operated under performance contracting arrangements with that of 10,000 other children who were taught in traditional ways. Children were picked from grades 1, 2, 3, 7, 8, and 9. Most of the performance contracting schools made extensive use of ILPs and programmed instruction. Some relied heavily on tangible rewards and free time. Distressingly, no significant differences have thus far been shown between the groups. In fact, both groups are continuing to do poorly. We must point out that in a study of this magnitude an incredible number of variables get thrown into one pot. Performance contracting and traditional instruction both subsume a multitude of diverse methods. Consequently, it would be easy to lose sight of some very important features of performance contracting in such a massive analysis.

Despite OEO's nasty findings, we remain enthusiastic about the possibilities of performance contracting. First of all, it makes the monetary rewards of teaching contingent upon student achievement. In too many cases, teachers have been rewarded for simply "putting in time." When the amount of money that a teacher earns is directly tied to how well students achieve, he may take rather seriously the question of what he's doing to facilitate student learning. This possibility poses no threat to the effective teacher. Under performance contracting, he will get the merit pay that he deserves. Obviously, the incompetent teacher may not fare too well under a performance contracting arrangement.

A second encouraging feature of performance contracting programs is that they provide the kind of setting events and reinforcements which would encourage students to accelerate their individual rates of learning. Most of them make extensive use of programmed materials and individualized learning packages. Students work on a nongraded individualized basis toward the attainment of specific instructional objectives. Tangible incentives (e.g., trading stamps, candy, money, and transistor radios) and free-time activities (e.g., reading magazines, working puzzles, playing games, listening to rock music, and rapping with friends) are frequently used to reinforce student achievement. Apparently, when their own tangible payoffs are on the line, teachers lose some of their sensitivity about tangible rewards for students.

Another reason for optimism about performance contracting is that it provides a means of cutting through some of the ✱✱✱ political bureaucracy that has crippled education. This political bureaucracy has allowed Minnie Jones, who hasn't had an intelligent thought in three decades, to teach until she was 168 years old and at the same time has thwarted the efforts of countless teachers to improve instruction in their classroom. Since private enterprise seems to be a bit more concerned about making money than preserving the Minnie Joneses, performance contracting programs have generally utilized personnel who are willing and able to help students achieve.

We do have one or two reservations about performance contracting. No, it's not the cost. Behavioral Research Laboratories operated an entire elementary school in Gary, Indiana, for $800 a pupil per year (assuming the students' made the agreed-upon progress), which is about what it had been costing the school system. What does concern us very deeply is the criteria of accountability used in performance contracting. We do not question the contention that students should learn some basic reading and math skills and that the attainment of these skills should be assessed in the most direct fashion possible. Our question is whether the standardized achievement test represents the optimal means of assessing academic progress. The fact that the Texarkana personnel taught directly for the achievement tests is not too surprising. Actually, what was wrong in their doing that? They invalidated application of the test norms to the Texarkana sample but they did not invalidate the fact that their students could indeed answer the items on the test. Since identified instructional objectives, known to one and all, are employed extensively in performance contracting, why not use these objectives as the basis of evaluating a student's academic progress? It is encouraging to note that in the "classic"

Texarkana project, the 100 percent reliance on standardized tests was modified to permit 25 percent of the assessment to be based on criterion-referenced tests.

An even more distressing aspect of the accountability question is the almost exclusive emphasis on academic achievement. What about creative accomplishments? What about social skills? What about the child's vocational success once he leaves school? What about the child's contribution to society? We do not mean to disdain the ability to read, write, add, and subtract; but if the teacher's success is going to be judged exclusively in these areas, that's where the teacher will devote his time. We are depressed at that prospect. The criteria of accountability must be expanded to include dimensions such as creative accomplishments, social behaviors, and vocational success. If we fail to consider these dimensions, we may produce a group of literate youngsters who are no better prepared to solve the problems of our world than were their predecessors. We see the urgency of going beyond basic academic skills as the major challenge facing performance contractors, and we're encouraged to find that some performance contractors are moving in that direction ("Three reports of performance," 1971).

Another concern that we have about performance contracting is the big-business aspect of the movement. We fear that most of the financial earnings will somehow migrate to the bank accounts of a few corporation executives. We feel that the bulk of the financial benefits should be enjoyed by those most directly responsible for the achievement gains, namely the teachers and the students. Instead of blindly opposing performance contracting, teachers should learn as much as possible about the movement and then do their own contracting.[3] The ideal arrangement might be for a group of teachers and their students to contract directly with a school system. If students as well as teachers were deriving significant financial benefits from the students' academic progress, we bet the rate of academic growth would be awe-inspiring.

A few pages back, we made a rather wild prediction about the future of performance contracting. Ten years from now, when performance contracting has become extinct, we may regret that prediction. But for now our heart's in Texarkana, Gary, San Diego, Dallas, Detroit, Portland, Philadelphia, and all the other school systems which have been bold enough to try something revolutionary in American education. (We call it new in spite of the fact that the folks down in Georgia

---

[3] Lake County, Florida, is presently experimenting with accountability pay for principals. This arrangement is very much to our liking since, in our estimation, the principal is the one person most responsible for the teaching–learning atmosphere in a school.

seemed to have tried something like performance contracting way back in 1819.)

Somewhere in the distant past, concern was expressed about the effects of operant procedures on scholastic achievement. Perhaps our responses to this concern were more than you bargained for. Since a majority of operant studies have not dealt with the dimension of academic achievement, we felt an irresistible compulsion to alert you to those studies which had. Your answering the following questions will indicate that you've fully comprehended our insights and are ready to proceed to the next section.

1. Research concerning the effect of teacher approval on academic achievement indicates that
   (a) Approval is most effective with underachievers,
   (b) Approval must be delivered contingently to facilitate student achievement,
   (c) Approval generally increases academic achievement and disapproval impedes performance,
   (d) There is a significant interaction between approval–disapproval and student characteristics (e.g., sex, age, ability, socioeconomic level, and personality).

2. Contingent free time has proven effective in increasing
   (a) Quantity of work, but not quality,
   (b) Quality of work, but not quantity,
   (c) Both quantity and quality,
   (d) Appropriate social behaviors, but not academic achievement.

3. To increase the probability that instructional activities will be reinforcing to students, the authors suggest
   (a) Giving each student some measure of responsibility for identifying what he wants to accomplish and how he will accomplish it,
   (b) Requiring students to read the great classics of the ages,
   (c) Using the "you students can do what you want to today" approach,
   (d) The elimination of tangible rewards from public education.

4. Williams and Anandam were very impressed with the approach described in Steven Daniels' *How 2 Gerbils, 20 Goldfish, 200 Games, 2000 Books, and I Taught Them How to Read* (1971) probably because Daniels
   (a) Allowed students to choose what they wanted to read,
   (b) Refused to use points and tangibles in rewarding students,
   (c) Didn't bother to check his students' growth on standardized achievement tests,

    (d) Concentrated on vocational skills rather than reading skills in working with inner-city students.

5. Research concerning the effects of programmed instruction on academic achievement indicates that
    (a) It is consistently superior to conventional instruction,
    (b) It is usually as effective as conventional instruction and in many cases better,
    (c) Conventional instruction is generally superior to programmed instruction,
    (d) Conventional instruction and programmed instruction are equally effective.

6. Which of the following characteristics contributes to the effectiveness of programmed instruction?
    (a) Material is presented in a question format;
    (b) Frequent feedback is given relative to the correctness of the student's responses;
    (c) Frames are not written redundantly;
    (d) All of the above. (Don't you just hate those "All of the above" alternatives!)

7. A first step in developing an ILP is to
    (a) Identify a major idea which will be the focus of the package,
    (b) Identify appropriate learning activities,
    (c) Develop quest activities,
    (d) Go to the john.

8. If a student fails to demonstrate mastery of an ILP on the post-assessment,
    (a) He should be given a failing grade,
    (b) The teacher should suggest other activities for acquiring the designated objectives,
    (c) The teacher should ask the principal to talk to the student,
    (d) He should be put back into a conventional academic setting.

9. When a teacher does not have access to programmed materials or individualized learning packages, he
    (a) Should submit his resignation effective the following Monday,
    (b) Can utilize major features of these approaches via an arrangement such as task analysis,
    (c) Can still individualize instruction without much effort,
    (d) Should denounce teachers who are favored with the availability of these materials.

10. In performance contracting, the contracting firm (organization, group, teacher) is paid on the basis of
    (a) Increments in student achievement,

(b) How much new equipment it provides for the school,

(c) Textbooks granted to the school,

(d) How well the superintendent knows the head of the contracting firm.

11. Williams and Anandam endorse performance contracting because it

(a) Provides contingent monetary rewards to teachers for increments in student achievement,

(b) Makes extensive use of programmed materials and ILPs,

(c) Utilizes tangible rewards to facilitate student performance,

(d) All of the above.

12. The authors' major reservation about performance contracting is

(a) The expense involved,

(b) The use of too many instructional objectives,

(c) Its current lack of emphasis on creative accomplishments, social skills, and vocational success,

(d) Its deemphasis on norm-referenced measurement.

Creative Behavior

Many educators feel that the primary objective of education ought to be the facilitation of creative thinking. Many of these same educators contend that the typical ways of measuring academic achievement are quite insensitive to creative responses. Although behavior modification techniques have proven valuable in improving social conduct, studying behavior, and academic achievement, the possibility still remains that they are ineffective in enhancing creative thinking. In fact, many critics of behavior modification have vociferously claimed that operant procedures produce conforming rather than creative behaviors. We disagree with that analysis and will "unequivocally" prove that operant techniques can be used to facilitate creative thinking. (By now you should know that we always make such bold claims when we're totally confused.)

Our first difficulty in appraising the impact of operant procedures on creativity is defining what is meant by "creative thinking" and "creative behavior." Since you are already well aware of our affinity for behavioral descriptions, we will henceforth speak only of creative behavior. Although several tests (for example, Guilford's Unusual Uses Test, Torrance's Ask-and-Guess Test) have been developed to measure creative behavior, we prefer to think of creativity more in the context of day-to-day classroom happenings. Stated differently, what kinds of in-class student responses could be considered creative? Two major criteria are usually employed in judging the creativeness of a student's response: novelty and appropriateness. Unfortunately, judging what is creative may be one of those cases where beauty is in the eye of the beholder. What Williams construes as original and appropriate, Anandam may not. (At least, that's the way it goes with most of our discussions.) So the major issue is, "Can *I* use behavior modification procedures to increase what *I* consider to be unusual and appropriate student responses?"

What setting events should facilitate creative responses? We would, first of all, recommend that you pose many problems and questions which have no *one* correct answer. It would be difficult to provide an unusual and yet appropriate response to a question such as "Is Knoxville the capital of Tennessee?" In contrast, a question like "In what ways might Knoxville have made an appropriate capital of Tennessee?" would be considerably more conducive to creative responses. Our recommendation is that instead of posing questions or problems which call for specific factual information (e.g., names, dates, formulas, and definitions), you pose questions which could be answered in a variety of ways (e.g., questions calling for comparisons, statements of cause and effect, speculations, predictions, preferences, proposals, and examples which illustrate a point).

Secondly, we recommend that you instruct students to be as flexible and original as possible in their responses. Because most students have had so many school experiences in which they were expected to conform or to give the "right" answer, it may be difficult for them to perceive that it's really okay to give wild answers. Informing your students that unusual responses are not only permissible but desirable should pave the way for increased originality in the classroom. This is one of those cases where being told the reinforcement contingencies seems to facilitate the emission of the selected response (Maltzman, Bogartz, and Breger, 1958).

Another instructional arrangement that could enhance creative responding is programmed instruction. There is some evidence that production of original responses is related to the amount of information possessed by students (Williams, 1965). It would seem, therefore, that an instructional system which increases the rate at which students acquire information would indirectly enhance creative behavior. So, in this respect, programmed instruction sounds like it has possibilities. On the other hand, there are features of programmed instruction which appear to be incompatible with creative responding. The major difficulty is in the type of response which programmed materials require (i.e., giving the correct answer to each question). Extensive use of such programmed materials might create a response set that would undermine creative responding. To this point, efforts to increase creative behavior through conventional programmed materials have generally been unproductive (Ripple and Dacey, 1967; Treffinger and Ripple, 1971).

The ineffectiveness of conventional programs in facilitating creative responding does not rule out the possibility of developing programs specifically for the purpose of teaching creative behavior. Crutchfield and Covington (1966) have suggested that such a program might consist of a series of problems to be solved, starting with relatively simple problems and progressing to those which are quite difficult. The problems would be accompanied by step-by-step instruction in problem-solving strategies. The program would include considerable provision for branching, much larger steps than the conventional programs, and feedback in terms of illustrative answers. Research data (Reese and Parnes, 1970) indicate that programs of this nature can yield substantial gains on standard measures of creativity.

What types of consequences would serve as reinforcers for creative behavior? The literature on creativity invariably suggests that creative behavior is most likely to occur in a permissive and nonpunishing atmosphere. That being the case, the use of positively reinforcing consequences should be far more facilitative of creative responding than the use of aversive stimulation. Teacher approval ought to be particularly potent in increasing creative behavior. Goetz and Baer (1971) used that approval to increase diversity, then repetition, and finally diversity in the block-building behaviors of a group of three and four year olds. The content of the approval often indicated the type of behavior being approved, e.g., "How nice, that's different," or "I like that—another . . ." A postcheck of one child's behavior indicated that she continued at a high level of form diversity after the systematic approval had been eliminated. Goetz and Salmonson (1972) also demonstrated that the number of different forms used in easel painting could be altered through teacher approval. Form diversity was greater when children were given descriptive approval (e.g., "That's a new kind of line") than when they were given general approval (e.g., "That's beautiful") or were simply watched.

In working with young children, other researchers (Savoca, 1965; Torrance, 1965) have attempted to increase creative behaviors by making tangible rewards contingent upon creative responses. In the Torrance study, some students received money for exhibiting original behavior and others for exhibiting conforming behaviors. The students performed according to the reward contingencies. In Savoca's study, a small toy was awarded for emitting uncommon responses. This method proved quite effective in increasing original responses. A tangible payoff that may have more potential for increasing the creative responses of young children than either toys or money is some edible such as candy or cereal. Two noted behavior modifiers, Bijou and Baer (1967), suggest that candy is probably the most durable and universal type of reinforcement that can be used with children. Blase and Hopkins (1972) have shown that a combination of free time and candy can increase the diversity of sentence structures employed even by students in the fourth through sixth grades. These experimenters also suggest that compositions are more likely to be judged as creative if they employ greater diversity of sentence structures (particularly verbs).

You're needing an opportunity to satisfy your own creative impulses. Answer the following uncreative multiple choice questions and then give us your ideas on this issue: Can a person reach the point where reinforcement for creative activity is largely internal? Or is creative effort always sustained through some type of external consequence?

1. It is clear from Williams and Anandam's treatment of creative behavior that they
   (a) Know nothing about creativity (Don't you dare choose this alternative!),
   (b) Believe creativity is an innate quality which cannot be altered through environmental stimulation,
   (c) Believe programmed instruction is the best way to increase creativity,
   (d) Believe teachers should pose many open-response questions.
2. Which of the following would probably be the most effective type of teacher approval for increasing creative play?
   (a) "That's a different game you're playing,"
   (b) "I like the way you play,"
   (c) "You're a nice child,"
   (d) "You certainly come from a fine family."
3. Research on the use of tangibles to increase creative responses indicates that
   (a) Tangibles are completely ineffective in increasing original responses,
   (b) Candy is a much more effective reinforcer for creative responses than either toys or money,
   (c) Money and toys can be used to increase unusual responses,
   (d) Children object to money and toys on ethical grounds.

Chapter VII

IN PURSUIT
OF HAPPINESS
Contributions of Classroom Behavior
Management to Social Progress

The ultimate aim of education ought to be the enhancement of human life. That being the case, we must concern ourselves with what happens to people once they complete their formal education. Do they have the skills, attitudes, and behaviors necessary to successfully engage in that "pursuit of happiness" promised by our founding fathers? Do they have the wherewithal to deal with those ominous problems which threaten the foundations of our society? In this final chapter, we shall address ourselves to these exceedingly vital issues.

You may immediately question the propriety of treating social issues in a text on classroom behavior management. Our logic is very simple: (1) a major purpose of education is to improve society; (2) a major purpose of behavior modification is to improve education; (3) therefore, classroom behavior management ought to have something to contribute to the long-range improvement of society. In exploring proposition three, we will have to go far beyond existing data. For example, the behavior modification study has not yet appeared which tells us how to solve the problem of war. However, there may be a number of operant principles derived from other types of experimentation which could be applied in the sphere of international relations.

What you will find in this chapter is primarily a compilation of our personal views as to how operant strategies could be used in the classroom to facilitate social progress. Undoubtedly, you will question the logic and the utility of some of these ideas. We make no pretense of having the "truth" in any area and would certainly expect you to examine all of our postulations critically. However, we believe that one assumption is definitely valid—you are concerned about upgrading the quality of human life on this planet and so are we. No one's honor, patriotism, or integrity is at stake. We invite you now to consider some specific possibilities for accomplishing our mutual goals.

Since our various social problems have many common components, we shall attempt to provide an over-all model which can be applied to each of these problems. Our analysis is based on the assumption that the classroom is a microcosm of the larger society. Dealing with social problems at the classroom level could ultimately be the most powerful means of solving problems at the societal level.

Reinforcing incompatible behavior. A fundamental strategy for weakening an undesirable behavior is to reinforce a behavior which is incompatible with that response. So if we could identify those behaviors which are contributing to social problems, our task in the classroom would then be to reinforce the opposite of those behaviors. To illustrate, you can't listen to a political discussion of war without identifying "aggression" as a key word. Admittedly, a great many behaviors subsumed under the concept of war could legitimately be labeled as aggression or counteraggression. A primary objective of the teacher, then, should be the strengthening of nonaggressive behaviors. When students are willing to talk about their differences instead of fighting about them, that talking should be reinforced. This could hardly be considered a profound insight, but students are not going to be turned on to nonaggressive reactions unless you frequently approve those responses. An example might be, "I'm glad you were able to talk about your problems and be friends again. You're a great example for the rest of us."

A second behavior that seems particularly incompatible with the usual response to international conflict is the admission of fault. Discussions between nations often degenerate into a debate of who is right and who is wrong. The highest moral virtue is typically assigned to being "right" and the most ignominious shame to being "wrong." Given those contingencies, it's kind of difficult to admit fault or to understand the other's viewpoint. We wonder how quickly international conflicts could be resolved if each nation would readily admit blame and accept the validity of the other's contentions. On a personal level, admission of blame by one or more parties in a conflict usually hastens the resolution of that conflict. Could the same be true at an international level? Assuming that it might, we believe you should reinforce students for admitting error and for confessing that others are right. Instead of praising students for defending their positions come what may, you should praise them for their ability to see the validity of others' opinions. Your personal approval can be the vehicle for making admission of fault an act of honor and strength among your students.

This idea of reinforcing incompatible behaviors could also be applied in the area of race relations. Despite the dearth of biracial interaction in most classrooms, some interaction between races does occur. It may be little more than sitting near each other, exchanging smiles, or asking to borrow something from each other, but it's worth shaping into a higher level of interaction. In reinforcing such behavior, you should primarily direct your approval toward the students' feelings of satisfaction in these relationships. By helping students to perceive the interaction as a source of reinforcement, you increase the probability of their seeking biracial experiences on their own initiative. One way to exhibit this type of approval is to write your comments on students' group reports (e.g., "I bet you had lots of fun working together"; "Your report reflects honest sharing of feelings").

Currently there is much emphasis on eliminating the sexual stereotypes in our society. Society has generally conditioned females to behave in a dependent, submissive, and cautious manner. On the other hand, males have been conditioned to conceal emotion, to be tough, and to dominate females. We generally feel that sexual identity should not be used as a criterion of appropriate behavior. It's desirable for *people* to behave independently, compassionately, and competently. However, the sexual stereotypes aren't going to disappear magically unless you make a deliberate, ambitious attempt to reinforce students for behaviors which are antithetical to these stereotypes. Girls in particular should be reinforced for taking leadership roles, for choosing unconventional academic activities, and for accepting new challenges. It thrills our souls to hear teachers saying, "Debbie, I'm really excited about your taking auto mechanics," "Sharon, I'm glad you're thinking about a career in law," "Joyce, I like the way you provide leadership in a situation," "Bronco, you have a wonderful ability to show compassion for others."

Another avenue for reinforcing atypical sex role behavior is role play. Suppose you want to reinforce students for unconventional behaviors in the vocational sphere. You could simulate different types of vocational situations and have students assume nonstereotypic roles in those situations (for instance, a female department head interviewing a male for a secretarial position; a female doctor working with a male nurse in diagnosing a male's difficulty). You could use these occasions to recognize unconventional, yet entirely appropriate, vocational behaviors exhibited by the students.

A general category of behavior that is incompatible with socially debilitating responses is helping behavior. Yes, we want to reinforce students for behaving independently, but we also want to reinforce them for helping others. What society desperately needs is not more competitive activity but more cooperative behaviors. When you employ group contingent reinforcement, when you use reinforcement sharing, and when you reward students for peer tutoring, you are bound to strengthen cooperative activity in the classroom. The principal message that should be conveyed through your reinforcement is that much more can be accomplished, personally and collectively, by working with other human beings than by working against them.

In sum, the task of the classroom teacher is to identify those behaviors which are incompatible with socially destructive activity and then directly reinforce these incompatible responses in the classroom. Although the teacher will be the prime reinforcer, selected peers can also be trained to systematically reinforce biracial interaction, unconventional sex role behaviors, and helping responses.

Using appropriate role models. There is probably no behavior mod strategy that has more general application to social problems than role modeling. If the desired behaviors are simply not in the repertoire of your students, you can usually find role models who exemplify those behaviors. For example, in changing sexual stereotypes, we would depend heavily upon role models whose behaviors and vocational commitments are at variance with traditional sex role expectations. You need not worry about providing conventional models for most students. Their homes and communities are replete with such models. In contrast, individuals who are functioning in atypical roles are still a bit difficult to find. If such people are available within your community, they should certainly be invited to your classroom. During these visits, students should be given the opportunity of finding out why these persons selected the unconventional roles, the fulfillment they have found in those roles, and the obstacles which they have had to overcome to be successful in their present roles.

Considerable role modeling can also occur through exposure to literature. Deplorably, most of children's literature is male-dominated (Meade, 1971; Pogrebin, 1972). There are many more males than females (even among animals) presented in children's stories. Boys are also portrayed as having a much more exciting time than girls. About the most exciting thing that a girl can do is to keep her dress clean in the midst of all the dust kicked up by the boys. Little Miss Muffett epitomizes the docile, helpless female to whom children are frequently exposed in literature.

It is encouraging to note that lists of nonsexist writings are now beginning to appear. In the March, 1971, issue of *Woman's Day*, Meade describes a number of picture books for girls under age eight and fiction books for girls age eight to fifteen which portray females engaging in the same types of fascinating activities as boys. Another useful source of information about nonsexist literature for children is *Ms.* magazine. The initial issue (Spring, 1972) includes a list of nonsexist books at the preschool, elementary, and junior high levels, and a listing of biographies and autobiographies of famous women such as Mary McLeod Bethune, Elizabeth Blackwell, Nellie Bly, Amelia Earhart, Edna St. Vincent Millay, and Eleanor Roosevelt.[1] We've been hearing about George, Tom, and Abe for a long time; let's devote some time to discussing Mary, Liz, and Nell.

Your behavior as a teacher can also contribute to the demise of conventional male–female role expectations. If you describe personal experiences which run counter to the traditional stereotypes, you will become a liberated model with whom many of your students can readily identify. So, men, describe those good meals you've been cooking at home and how much you enjoy taking care of the children. And women, go ahead and admit the work you did on the car and the excitement you derive from playing football. In the classroom, you will have many opportunities for demonstrating personal and professional qualities which transcend sex role expectations.

A second area where appropriate role models are desperately needed is in the biracial domain. Let's begin with your potential as a role model. Students will often respond to a member of another race as they see you responding to that person. It is thus imperative for you to respond consistently and positively to members of all ethnic groups. Many teachers have a tendency to be more paternalistic, protective, defensive, or reinforcing in their responses to one race than the other. Something as innocuous as shortening students' names, calling students by nicknames, and touching students may be looked upon as quite paternalistic or discriminatory if confined primarily to one racial group. By now, you know that we believe very strongly in the efficacy of teacher approval. Your approval is a major means of demonstrating that a student is acceptable to you. For that reason, one racial group should not enjoy a greater measure of your approval than does another.

---

[1] The complete bibliography can be ordered from *Ms.* magazine, 370 Lexington Avenue, New York 10017.

A facet of the racial scene that is extremely difficult to manage is the role modeling that takes place among peers. In many classrooms, finding peers who could serve as models of biracial interaction for other students is like hunting for the proverbial "needle in a haystack." In one of our studies (Williams et al., 1971), we attempted to use peer role models to alter interracial behaviors. The intent was to put racial isolates into group situations in which they would be exposed to black and white peers who interacted very positively with each other. Biracial triads (problem-solving groups) composed of an isolate, a role model of the isolate's race, and a high status model of the opposite race were the major vehicles of treatment implementation. Triad sessions were devoted to a variety of tasks including working on assigned subject matter, constructing model cars, playing word games, conducting experiments in science, working on class reports, and discussing problems in school. Although this role modeling treatment did result in modest improvement in biracial interaction, its effectiveness was severely limited by the scarcity of positive role models in the class.

Failure to find effective biracial models within your own class does not give you license to join the KKK or the Weathermen. Students can still be exposed to positive models via visitors to the class, the public media, and literature. We are not claiming students should be shielded from black and white separatists. To do so might intensify the attractiveness of those groups. What we are saying is that students should also be exposed to blacks and whites who are interacting positively with each other in a variety of vocational and social settings. A poignant example of a black–white friendship is the relationship between professional football star Gale Sayers (black) and the late Brian Piccolo (white). We believe this kind of story holds a significant message for students in this era of racial estrangement.

International conflict is a third sphere in which alternative role models could be extremely valuable. Earlier we mentioned the need to reinforce students for nonaggressive reactions to human conflicts. A primary means of teaching nonaggressive behaviors is for you to respond to stress nonaggressively. The antithesis of what we're saying is the use of corporal punishment to reduce physical aggression. Though the teacher may temporarily subdue a child's aggressive behavior by whipping that child, the long-range effect would probably be the strengthening of the child's aggressive tendencies. The teacher would indicate that he also deals with interpersonal stress by resorting to physical aggression. As a consequence, the child may later seek to control other people and even other nations by corporal force. Responding to aggressive acts in the classroom by administering calm disapproval or precise penalties provides a far better example for students.

In our previous discussion of incompatible behaviors which might weaken our proclivity toward war, we identified admission of blame as a possibility. What kind of role model are you in this respect? Traditionally students have viewed the teacher as an authority figure who portrays an "I know it all; Do as I say; Don't you dare question me" image. How often do we admit that we're wrong on a point, that we have made a mistake, that we have dealt with a student or class unfairly, or that we're willing to make some specific changes in our teaching procedures? It's not surprising that a majority of students attempt to impose their wills on others when it comes their turn to be authority figures. If that student who will either elect or be tomorrow's president is going to be able to admit the deficiencies of this nation and see the value of other political systems, then he must have opportunity to see you admit mistakes. When you confess to your students that you've goofed, it calls for an international celebration.

The application of role modeling to societal problems is almost endless. Role modeling could play a principal role in our dealing with dilemmas such as drug abuse and population control. In drug education, an optimal model for the student who is not yet committed to drugs is someone who is functioning quite well without drugs. For the adolescent who is already heavily committed to drug use, an appropriate model would be a person who used drugs but has subsequently found more satisfying modes of behavior. If you wish to employ negative role models to discourage drug use, get a model who is still experiencing all the pangs of drug addiction. The worst type of model is the former drug addict who has later achieved fame and fortune. The use of this kind of model tends to sensationalize drug use and may even leave the impression that drugs are a part of the prescription for success. Don't forget that even in this area *you* will be serving as a role model for students. If you claim that people can find meaning through experiences other than drugs and yet you manifest all the signs of boredom, anxiety, and pessimism, don't expect students to be too overwhelmed by your verbal exhortations.

Some sociologists contend that overpopulation is the problem that will ultimately paralyze society. As it stands now, society provides considerable reinforcement for procreative behavior. Grandparents want to know when they're going to have a grandchild, friends have baby showers for expectant mothers, and the government provides tax deductions for additional children. To change these values, we must provide role models who are finding satisfaction in life through avenues other than bearing children. We propose, therefore, that exposing students to vocationally successful, well-adjusted role models who have remained unmarried, or who are married but have had either none or few children, should contribute to the deceleration of the birth rate.

By this time, our model for dealing with social problems should be becoming quite clear: (1) for a given social problem, identify behaviors which are antithetical to the responses contributing to the problem; (2) directly reinforce these incompatible responses in the classroom; (3) provide successful role models who exemplify the incompatible behaviors. Of these role models, you are the "chiefest."

Increasing the reinforcement value of others. Friendship probably boils down to the amount of reinforcement we are receiving from another person or group. If A and B are estranged, one way to break this estrangement is to make A a significant reinforcer for B or vice versa. We have used this exact strategy in promoting biracial interaction during classroom free-time activities (Williams et al., 1971). A sociometric test was first administered to the students to determine patterns of likes and dislikes in the class. The three black and three white students who gave and received the highest number of biracial choices in the class, who received a high number of choices from within their own race, and who gave and received few biracial rejections served as peer reinforcers for racial isolates. Children designated as peer reinforcers were trained via video-taped demonstrations and role play to attend to (praise, smile, touch, talk, listen) appropriate behaviors exhibited by the isolates and to ignore their inappropriate behaviors. The class in which the peer reinforcement treatment was implemented was together for four periods during the day. Each reinforcer was asked to work with a particular isolate each period. Assignments to isolates were rotated so that each reinforcer worked with every isolate several times during the course of the treatment. In order to prevent the reinforcers from acquiring such stigmas as "Uncle Tom" or "Nigger Lover," they were intermittently paired with isolates of both races.

The major rationale behind this peer reinforcement treatment was that students would come to interact more frequently with peers who were sources of positive reinforcement for them. In essence, the giving of positive attention was expected to increase the reinforcement value of the giver. It would follow from this assumption that the more occasions whites can experience reinforcement (e.g., approval, attention, privileges) from blacks and vice versa, the higher the reinforcement value the races will have for each other.

Would this strategy work when it comes to relationships among people who are separated by oceans and continents? There is probably no classroom event that could have a more profound impact on your students' respect for other nations than inviting someone from another country to visit your class. If you teach near a university, you can work through the international organization on campus in identifying foreign students who would be willing to meet with your class. If these visits prove to be reinforcing to your students, you will have made it a little more difficult for those students to disdain the value of human life in other societies.

Increasing self-respect through positive reinforcement. If you would permit us to be a bit nonbehavioral for a moment, we would like to point out that low self-esteem is often associated with socially destructive behaviors. A simple means of counteracting these injurious behaviors might be the upgrading of self-respect. In other words, how you respond to another person is not only a function of the perceived reinforcement value of that person but also of your own self-perception. You remember from our declarations in the chapter on ethics that we believe social approval is a principal means of improving self-esteem. It follows that increasing the amount of social approval received by a person should lead to enhancement of his social relationships.

We tested the previously specified hypothesis in the area of race relations (Williams et al., 1971). Teachers were trained to provide consistent approval for appropriate behaviors exhibited by black and white racial isolates. The appropriate behaviors related to academic achievement and general classroom conduct, not biracial interaction. Despite the fact the teachers never made any attempt to reinforce interaction across racial lines, the isolates made greater advances (to a modest degree) in biracial interaction than control students who were not generally reinforced for desirable behavior. In increasing the frequency of your approval, particularly across racial lines, you must be very cautious about the perceived sincerity of that approval. Too many smiles, back slaps, and "good boys" are not likely to enhance students' self-respect dramatically. In contrast, approval administered according to the guidelines described in Chapter III should convey genuine positive regard for students.

The ideal arrangement for increasing self-esteem through social approval is to teach students how to elicit approval from others. Analysis of drug research indicates that peer approval is a frequent contributing factor in drug abuse. The student's task is to acquire behaviors other than taking drugs for eliciting peer approval. It would be easy to recommend that instead of succumbing to drugs, students should excell in some activity (music, drama, athletics) which their peers would admire and approve. It is quite improbable, though, that all students have the capacity for developing laudatory skills. To compensate for lack of special competences, some students seek to win peer approval through material payoffs. The artificiality of this approval makes its contribution to self-esteem very tenuous.

As we see it, the basic challenge facing the student is whether he can become the type of person that peers will approve even if he chooses not to take drugs, develops no unusual skills, and has limited money. Since behavior modification is very much a reciprocal process, a primary means for the student to elicit approval from his peers is by giving approval. That students can be trained to behave in ways which would evoke approval from others has been substantiated by Graubard, Rosenberg, and Miller (1971). In fact, they trained students in a special education class to modify both teachers' and peers' reactions to them. The children were taught to reinforce their teachers' appropriate behavior by establishing eye contact with the teachers, sitting up straight in their seats, nodding agreement to the teachers, asking for extra help, and making approval comments such as "It makes me feel good when you praise me" and "I like the way you teach." With respect to peers, the children were trained to ignore inappropriate behavior (hostile physical contacts and teasing) and approve instances of positive interaction. This study is unique in that it not only demonstrates that students can be trained to exhibit behavior which will obtain reinforcement from others, but it reverses the usual direction of behavior modification, i.e., from teacher and peers to deviant children.

Solving social problems through productive class discussion. From time immemorial educators have felt that the way to solve human problems is by talking about them. Talking is certainly better than fighting, but we have seen an awful lot of talk lead nowhere. What should happen in a discussion before we label it as productive? An initial benefit ought to be personal catharsis. (We know we aren't supposed to use that word—just a Freudian slip!) Students frequently report relief when they are able to express deeply hidden anxieties, hostilities, and aspirations. A second benefit should be the critical reappraisal of one's own attitudes and opinions. Discussion should allow each student to examine what he believes and why he believes it. Changes in attitudes and opinions often follow such penetrating self-examination. A third benefit should be increased awareness of what others believe and their reasons for their beliefs. In many instances, we are able to accept a person more fully once we come to understand why he feels as he does about a particular issue.

What types of setting events and reinforcement procedures are required to achieve these benefits from class discussion? Since most students have experienced few classroom settings in which they could risk being honest, they may initially feel gravely insecure about divulging their feelings. Some teachers break the ice by letting students see others discussing sensitive social questions. Films or tapes of such discussions may make students much more aware of the discussion atmosphere you are attempting to establish and considerably more secure about expressing their own feelings on volatile issues. In other words, we are postulating a role-modeling effect from the films and tapes. In the same vein, it would be extremely helpful to have in the class discussion leaders of different ethnic backgrounds, sexes, and viewpoints. Discussion might be initiated by the leaders' simply interacting with each other. Under this arrangement, all students would have a live model after whom to pattern their discussion.

A teacher can indicate that it's okay to discuss certain problems by bringing up these problems himself. In an area such as interracial conflicts, students may not initially be ready to volunteer questions such as "Should we play Dixie at our basketball games?" "How do you feel about interracial dating?" "What meaning do you associate with the labels 'black,' 'Negro,' 'Negra,' 'Afro-American,' 'colored,' and 'nigger'?" "What connotations are associated with labels like 'honkie,' 'whitie,' 'red neck,' and 'caucasian'?" "Why don't we have more blacks (or whites) in the school band?" "Why is it that our black and white students sit on different sides of the room?" "Why do blacks and whites generally not eat together in the cafeteria?" "What do you fear most in your interaction with a black (white) person?" Your asking probing questions does not ensure student response; it simply says that you view these issues as legitimate areas for discussion. Most likely, you will have to do a great deal of shaping to get students to deal with the really controversial dimensions of social problems. Questions such as "What could students do to make others feel accepted?" or "What kinds of social functions should we have in the school?" may provide a better starting point.

When students start reacting fast and furiously to your questions, besides praying for deliverance, what should you do? What types of behaviors do you then want to reinforce? One behavior that should be reinforced is simply the expressing of attitudes and opinions. Your function is not to label opinions as good or bad, right or wrong. Such pronouncements would unquestionably prevent many opinions from being expressed. If a student holds an opinion which is personally distasteful to you or to other students, isn't it better to treat his opinion with respect, help him examine the basis of his opinion, and explore the consequences of his holding that opinion than to create a discussion atmosphere which would prevent him from speaking up? Periodic approval of the honesty being manifested in the class, of students' willingness to express very personal feelings, and of their abilities to express opinions with which others may strongly disagree should serve to reinforce the process of candid discussion.

When students begin expressing opinions which may be distasteful to you and to other members of the class, it is imperative that you be at your nondirective best. For instance, Roy states, "If niggers don't like our playing Dixie, they should go to another school." This statement may elicit considerable hissing, hooting, or cheering from other members of the class, but your primary responsibility is to respond to Roy's statement. "Okay, Roy has very honestly indicated that he feels Dixie should be played at our athletic contests and that if black students don't like it they should just go to another school. Now, I know that some of you violently disagree and are anxious to let us know how you feel. But first let's find out why Roy feels as he does." What would follow would be a series of questions designed to help you, Roy, and other class members understand why Roy holds his present opinion, the viability of that opinion, and the impact of that opinion on others. "Roy, how do you feel you personally benefit from the playing of Dixie?" "Why do you feel that blacks are offended by this song?" "Why do you feel that you have more of a right to determine what happens within our school than do blacks?" "Do you think a person should do something which he likes if it's offensive to someone else?" Often, questioning students concerning their reasons for holding particular views will help them see that their views are *not* based on factual information. Conversely, questioning a student's reasons may produce a logical basis for what otherwise seems an outlandish opinion. When you have thoroughly examined the rationale and ramifications of Roy's opinion, you can then treat other students' opinions with the same consideration and care. Just as you attempt to reinforce students for stating their opinions, you should be even more supportive of students' willingness to examine why they hold those opinions and the interpersonal consequences of espousing those opinions.

The discussion strategy we have just proposed has probably made you quite apprehensive. We know what's bothering you. You can't imagine a classroom situation in which prejudiced and militant students would allow each other the prerogative of expressing deep anxieties and hostilities about problems such as biracial disharmonies.

Quite frankly, we're doing a little sweating ourselves. It is exceedingly difficult to get students to listen to each other in this type of discussion. They are extremely anxious to put somebody else down or to make sure that so-and-so doesn't get away with saying such-and-such. Many times they attempt to cut each other off and literally disallow certain opinions from being expressed or certain people from expressing their views.

Now that we've all just wallowed in anxiety, let's pull ourselves together and discuss this point rationally. You may establish a conducive atmosphere for listening by assuring students that everyone will be given the right to express his opinions and that listening does not mean endorsement of what is being said. Once discussion starts, the major factor which will affect the way students listen is the way you listen. If students are going to listen to each other, you must listen to them. So as the side comments begin to mount, keep your attention focused on the student initially granted the privilege to speak. You must demonstrate that you're going to listen to that student come hell or high water. When students do listen to others, even to the smallest degree, that behavior should be recognized and approved. "I'm really pleased that you've given Bette the chance to express how she feels about this problem." "I know that it's painful to listen to views with which you strongly disagree, but your willingness to do that has really enhanced our discussion." Occasionally, you find students who not only sit quietly while others express their views but who get so caught up in the spirit of things that they begin responding nondirectively and approvingly toward others. You're a real dodo if you fail to reinforce that behavior. The ability to listen will be the most difficult skill to establish in your students. Being the great "shaper" that you are, you undoubtedly recognize that skillful listening (like Rome) cannot be developed in a day.

You may have been getting rather perturbed at the nondirective, nonjudgmental role described for the teacher. When does the teacher lay down the law and tell students the "right" position to take on the critical issues? We're not sure that you should ever do that. The teacher certainly has the right to express his own opinion (preferably late in the discussion) and present his rationale for holding that opinion. If an atmosphere of exploration rather than of agreement–disagreement has been established, the students will feel little more compelled to concur with your opinion than anyone else's.

We feel that the discussion format just delineated could be applied to any type of social problem, including military conflict, sex roles, overpopulation, environmental pollution, or drug usage. We would even include in the discussable category the students' perceptions of *you*. Unless you're a teacher the likes of whom we've never seen, some of your students will have negative reactions to you and your teaching approaches. In a biracial classroom, you may be accused of being prejudiced, of favoring one group over the other (it is not uncommon to find that black and white students both perceive the teacher as favoring the other group), of being condescending in your treatment of minority students, and of many other offenses of which you feel you're not guilty. In responding to these criticisms, you must make a special effort to be nondefensive and reinforce the expression of student feelings. As much as you would like to, lodging a counterattack on students or declaring your virtue probably won't dispel the negative perceptions.

Operant analysis of society. We would assume that the classroom application of our social progress model would make students acutely aware of contingencies which affect social problems. We would hope that by the time these students complete their formal education they would have the behavior mod expertise necessary to redesign social contingencies. This expectation is much more likely to be fulfilled if a substantial portion of a student's education is devoted to an operant analysis of society's problems.

No educational endeavor is more imperative than designing operant strategies applicable at a societal level. We have historically used some very ill-fated techniques in dealing with our problems. For example, we have basically tried to meet the problem of aggression with counter-aggression. As a result, we have perpetuated the aggression–counter-aggression cycle and have been a role model of aggression for other nations. The continuation of military conflicts is proof positive that we haven't yet found the contingencies that will solve the problem of war.

To illustrate the kinds of designs that students might formulate, let's talk briefly about the problem of overpopulation. In analyzing this problem, students might come up with a set of contingencies similar to what Kangas (1970) has recommended. According to Kangas, the government could provide direct monetary payments for delaying marriage, accepting contraceptives or sterilization, not having children, and limiting family size. These incentives could be provided on either an individual or group basis. If communities were receiving group benefits, e.g., parks, roads, schools, and money, in relation to family size, over-all birth rate, use of contraceptives, and participation in family planning programs, the intra-group pressures and reinforcement might become even more decisive than the external payoffs. For social agencies concerned with birth control, government payments could be contingent upon the number of contraceptives and vasectomies administered, number of clients who practice contraception successfully, and number of people enrolled in formal family planning. Like all good behavior modifiers, Kangas emphasizes the *immediacy* of these incentives. Social security benefits at age 65 are much less likely to be effective than monthly, semi-annual, or even annual payments during the procreative years.

Perhaps we're dreaming too much, but what would be the ultimate impact on society if students formulated operant analyses of our social problems and came up with models indicating the incompatible behaviors to be strengthened, the optimal setting events and reinforcement procedures for strengthening those behaviors, the most appropriate use of role models for producing desired social responses, programs for making our nation more reinforcing to other nations, reinforcers that society could use to enhance individual self-respect, and techniques for conducting constructive dialogue between nations, ethnic groups, and, in general, people of different cultures and viewpoints?

Epilogue

Throughout this book, we have emphasized the use of positive reinforcement procedures in dealing with students. Ideally, the use of these procedures should be based on a deep philosophical commitment. That commitment, as we see it, is to emphasize what is positive, good, and wholesome about children. We endorse a classroom atmosphere in which children regularly experience genuine approval and success. This kind of atmosphere can best be achieved through cooperation among teachers, students, counselors, administrators, and parents. We believe that a child who has extensive exposure to cooperative classroom management stands to gain in the following ways: (1) increased self-esteem; (2) increased academic achievement; (3) increased concern for other human beings; (4) increased ability to actually help other human beings; (5) increased ability to make positive changes in society; (6) increased ability to think creatively; (7) increased ability to explore ideas which are different from his own; and (8) increased ability to accept people who in culture, language, color, and political ideology are different from himself. However, in none of these areas does classroom behavior management represent the final word.

Bibliography

A. *Books and Sections of Books*

*Ackerman, J. M. *Operant Conditioning Techniques for the Classroom Teachers.* Glenview, Ill.: Scott, Foresman and Company, 1972.

Babkin, B. P. *Pavlov—A Biography.* Chicago: The University of Chicago Press, 1949.

*Baer, D. M. Behavior modification: You shouldn't. In E. A. Ramp and B. L. Hopkins (eds.), *A New Direction for Education: Behavior Analysis 1971.* The University of Kansas: Support and Development Center for Follow Through, 1971. pp. 358–67.

Bandura, A. and R. H. Walters. *Social Learning and Personality Development.* New York: Holt, Rinehart, & Winston, Inc., 1963.

Behavioral Objectives: A Guide to Individualized Learning. Palo Alto, Calif.: Westinghouse Learning Press, 1971.

Bijou, S. W. and D. M. Baer. Operant methods in child behavior and development. In S. W. Bijou and D. M. Baer (eds.), *Child Development: Readings in Experimental Analysis.* New York: Appleton-Century-Crofts, 1967. pp. 333–404.

Bronfenbrenner, U. *Two Worlds of Childhood: U.S. and U.S.S.R.* New York: Russell Sage Foundation, 1970.

*Cohen, S. I., J. M. Keyworth, R. I. Kleiner, and J. M. Libert. The support of school behaviors by home-based reinforcement via parent–child contingency contracts. In E. A. Ramp and B. L. Hopkins (eds.), *A New Direction for Education: Behavior Analysis 1971.* The University of Kansas: Support and Development Center for Follow Through, 1971. pp. 282–306.

*Daniels, S. *How 2 Gerbils, 20 Goldfish, 200 Games, 2,000 Books, and I Taught Them How to Read.* Philadelphia: The Westminister Press, 1971.

Deibert, A. N. and A. J. Harmon. *New Tools for Changing Behavior.* Champaign, Ill.: Research Press, 1970.

*Evans, G. W. and G. L. Oswalt. Acceleration of academic progress through the manipulation of peer influence. In C. E. Pitts (ed.), *Operant Conditioning in the Classroom.* New York: Thomas Y. Crowell Company, 1971. pp. 184–93.

*Goetz, E. M. and D. M. Baer. Descriptive social reinforcement of "creative" block building by young children. In E. A. Ramp and B. L. Hopkins (eds.), *A New Direction for Education: Behavior Analysis 1971.* The University of Kansas: Support and Development Center for Follow Through, 1971. pp. 72–79.

*Graubard, P. S., H. Rosenberg, and M. B. Miller. Student applications of behavior modification to teachers and environments or ecological approaches to social deviancy. In E. A. Ramp and B. L. Hopkins (eds.), *A New Direction for Education: Behavior Analysis 1971.* The University

---

* Though all bibliographic entrees provide useful information, those with an asterisk should be particularly useful.

of Kansas: Support and Development Center for Follow Through, 1971. pp. 80–101.

*Hamblin, R. I., C. Hathaway, and J. Wodarski. Group contingencies, peer tutoring and accelerating academic achievement. In E. A. Ramp and B. L. Hopkins (eds.), *A New Direction for Education: Behavior Analysis 1971*. The University of Kansas: Support and Development Center for Follow Through, 1971. pp. 41–53.

*Hanley, E. M. and P. F. Perelman. Research resulting from a model cities program designed to train paraprofessionals to aid teachers in elementary school classrooms. In E. A. Ramp and B. L. Hopkins (eds.), *A New Direction for Education: Behavior Analysis 1971*. The University of Kansas: Support and Development Center for Follow Through, 1971. pp. 158–63.

*Kapfer, P. G. and G. F. Ovard. *Preparing and Using Individualized Learning Packages for Ungraded Continuous Progress Education*. Englewood Cliffs, N.J.: Educational Technology Publications, 1971.

*Kibler, R. J., L. L. Barker, and D. T. Miles. *Behavioral Objectives and Instruction*. Boston: Allyn & Bacon, Inc., 1970.

*Madsen, C. H., Jr., W. C. Becker, D. R. Thomas, L. Koser, and E. Plazer. An analysis of the reinforcing function of "sit down" commands. In R. K. Parker (ed.), *Readings in Educational Psychology*. Boston: Allyn & Bacon, Inc., 1968. pp. 265–78.

*Mager, R. F. *Preparing Instructional Objectives*. Palo Alto, Calif.: Fearon Publishers, 1962.

McAshan, H. H. *Writing Behavioral Objectives*. New York: Harper & Row, Publishers, 1970.

McNeil, J. *ABC Learning Activities*. New York: American Book Company, 1966.

Patterson, G. R. and J. B. Reid. Reciprocity and coercion: Two facets of social systems. In C. Neurenger and J. L. Michael (eds.), *Behavior Modification in Clinical Psychology*. New York: Appleton-Century-Crofts, 1970. pp. 133–77.

*Reese, E. P. *The Analysis of Human Operant Behavior*. Dubuque, Iowa: William C. Brown Company, Publishers, 1966.

Rosenthal, R. *Experimenter Effects in Behavior Research*. New York: Appleton-Century-Crofts, 1966.

*Sajwaj, T. and P. Knight. The detrimental effects of a correction procedure for errors in a tutoring program for a young retarded boy. In E. A. Ramp and B. L. Hopkins (eds.), *A New Direction for Education: Behavior Analysis 1971*. The University of Kansas: Support and Development Center for Follow Through, 1971. pp. 115–23.

Sidman, M. *Tactics of Scientific Research*. New York: Basic Books, Inc., Publishers, 1960.

Sidman, M. and L. T. Stoddard. Programming perception and learning for retarded children. In N. R. Ellis (ed.), *International Review of Research in Mental Retardation*, Vol. 2. New York: Academic Press, Inc., 1966. pp. 151–208.

Skinner, B. F. *The Behavior of Organisms*. New York: Appleton-Century-Crofts, 1938.

*Skinner, B. F. *Walden Two*. New York: The Macmillan Company, 1948.

Skinner, B. F. *The Technology of Teaching*. New York: Appleton-Century-Crofts, 1968.

*Skinner, B. F. *Beyond Freedom and Dignity*. New York: Alfred A. Knopf, 1971.

*Spache, G. D. *Good Reading for Poor Readers*. Champaign, Ill.: Garrard Publishing Co., 1970.

*Sulzer, B., S. Hunt, E. Ashby, C. Koniarski, and M. Krams. Increasing rate and percentage correct in reading and spelling in a fifth grade public school class of slow readers by means of a token system. In E. A. Ramp and B. L. Hopkins (eds.), *A New Direction for Education: Behavior Analysis 1971*. The University of Kansas: Support and Development Center for Follow Through, 1971. pp. 5–28.

Torrance, E. P. *Rewarding Creative Behavior*. Englewood Cliffs, N.J.: Prentice-Hall, Inc., 1965.

Zigler, E. Rigidity in the feeble minded. In E. P. Trapp and P. Himelstein (eds.), *Readings on the Exceptional Child*. New York: Appleton-Century-Crofts, 1962. pp. 141–62.

B. Journal Articles

Adams, R. S. Duration and incident frequencies as observation indices. *Educational and Psychological Measurement*, 1970, *30*, 669–74.

*Alschuler, A. S. The effects of classroom structure on achievement motivation and academic performance. *Educational Technology*, August 1969, *9*, 19–24.

*Anandam, K., M. Davis, and W. A. Poppen. Feelings . . . To fear or to free? *Elementary School Guidance and Counseling*, 1971, *5*, 181–89.

*Anandam, K. and R. L. Williams. A model for consultation with classroom teachers on behavior management. *The School Counselor*, 1971, *18*, 253–59.

Atkins, J. W. and R. L. Williams. The utility of self-report in determining reinforcement priorities of primary school children. *Journal of Educational Research*, 1972, *65*, 324–28.

*Baker, E. L. The instructional objectives exchange: Assistance in goal-referenced evaluation. *Journal of Secondary Education*, 1970, *45*, 158–66.

Behaviorally Speaking. Dayton: Society of Behaviorists, June 1971.

Benowitz, M. L. and T. V. Busse. Material incentives and the learning of spelling words in a typical school situation. *Journal of Educational Psychology*, 1970, *61*, 24–26.

*Berberich, J. P. Do the child's responses shape the teaching behavior of adults? *Journal of Experimental Research in Personality*, 1971, *5*, 92–97.

*Birnbrauer, J. S. Generalization of punishment effects—A case study. *Journal of Applied Behavior Analysis*, 1968, *1*, 201–12.

*Birnbrauer, J. S. Contingency management research. *Educational Technology*, April 1971, *11*, 71–77.

Birnbrauer, J. S., M. M. Wolf, J. D. Kidder, and C. E. Tague. Classroom behavior of retarded pupils with token reinforcement. *Journal of Experimental Child Psychology*, 1965, *2*, 219–35.

*Broden, M., C. Bruce, M. A. Mitchell, V. Carter, and R. V. Hall. Effects of teacher attention on attending behavior of two boys at adjacent desks. *Journal of Applied Behavior Analysis*, 1970, *3*, 199–204.

*Brown, R. E., R. Copeland, and R. V. Hall. The school principal as a behavior modifier. *The Journal of Educational Research,* 1972, *66,* 175–80.

Buell, J., P. Stoddard, F. R. Harris, and D. M. Baer. Collateral social development accompanying reinforcement of outdoor play in a preschool child. *Journal of Applied Behavior Analysis,* 1968, *1,* 167–73.

*Bushell, D., Jr., P. A. Wrobel, and M. L. Michaelis. Applying "group" contingencies to the classroom study behavior of preschool children. *Journal of Applied Behavior Analysis,* 1968, *1,* 55–61.

*Cantrell, R. P., M. L. Cantrell, C. M. Huddleston, and R. L. Wooldridge. Contingency contracting with school problems. *Journal of Applied Behavior Analysis,* 1969, *2,* 215–20.

Chansky, N. M. Learning: A function of schedule and type of feedback. *Psychological Reports,* 1960, *7,* 362.

Clark, M., J. Lachowicz, and M. Wolf. A pilot basic education program for school dropouts incorporating a token reinforcement system. *Behaviour Research and Therapy,* 1968, *6,* 183–88.

Clark, C. A. and H. J. Walberg. The influence of massive rewards on reading achievement in potential urban school dropouts. *American Education Research Journal,* 1968, *5,* 305–10.

Coleman, R. A conditioning technique applicable to elementary school classrooms. *Journal of Applied Behavior Analysis,* 1970, *3,* 293–97.

Crutchfield, R. S. and M. V. Covington. Programmed instruction and creativity. *Theory into Practice,* 1966, *5,* 179–83.

Cunningham, L. L. Hey, man, you our principal? Urban education as I saw it. *Phi Delta Kappan,* November 1969, *51,* 123–28.

Customers pass the test, or else: Discussion of performance contracting. *Education Digest,* 1970, *36,* 5–7.

Davis, W. K. Student choice of means and ends. *NSPI Journal,* 1971, *10,* 12–13, 21.

*Deci, E. L. Intrinsic motivation, extrinsic reinforcement, and inequity. *Journal of Personality and Social Psychology,* 1972, *22,* 113–20.

Douvan, E. Social status and success strivings. *Journal of Abnormal and Social Psychology,* 1956, *52,* 219–23.

*Duncan, A. D. Self-application of behavior modification techniques by teenagers. *Adolescence,* 1969, *4,* 541–56.

*Ferritor, D. E., D. Buckholdt, R. L. Hamblin, and L. Smith. The noneffects of contingent reinforcement for attending behavior on work accomplished. *Journal of Applied Behavior Analysis,* 1972, *5,* 7–17.

Feshbach, N. D. Effects of teacher's reinforcement style upon children's imitation and preferences. *Proceedings of the 75th Annual Convention of the American Psychological Association,* 1967, *2,* 281–82.

Fleming, J. C. Pupil tutors and tutees learn together. *Today's Education,* October 1969, *58,* 22–24.

*Frager, S. and C. Stern. Learning by teaching. *The Reading Teacher,* 1970, *23,* 403–5, 417.

Geis, G. L. and R. Chapman. Knowledge of results and other possible reinforcers in self-instructional systems. *Educational Technology,* April 1971, *11,* 38–51.

*Glynn, E. L. Classroom applications of self-determined reinforcement. *Journal of Applied Behavior Analysis,* 1970, *3,* 123–32.

*Goldiamond, I. Self-control procedures in personal behavior problems. *Psychological Reports*, 1965, *17*, 851–68.

*Hall, R. V., C. Cristler, S. S. Cranston, and B. Tucker. Teachers and parents as researchers using multiple baseline designs. *Journal of Applied Behavior Analysis*, 1970, *3*, 247–55.

*Hall, R. V., R. Fox, D. Willard, L. Goldsmith, M. Emerson, M. Owen, F. Davis, and E. Porcia. The teacher as observer and experimenter in the modification of disputing and talking-out behaviors. *Journal of Applied Behavior Analysis*, 1971, *4*, 141–49.

Hall, R. V., D. Lund, and D. Jackson. Effects of teacher attention on study behavior. *Journal of Applied Behavior Analysis*, 1968, *1*, 1–12.

*Herman, S. H. and J. Tramontana. Instructions and group versus individual reinforcement in modifying disruptive group behavior. *Journal of Applied Behavior Analysis*, 1971, *4*, 113–19.

Hewett, F. M., F. D. Taylor, and A. A. Artuso. The Santa Monica project: Evaluation of an engineered classroom design with emotionally disturbed children. *Exceptional Children*, 1969, *35*, 523–29.

Higgins, M. J. A comparison of the effects of extrinsic reward on the test performance of sixth-grade students of two socioeconomic groups. *Dissertation Abstracts*, 1967, *28*, 940-A.

Hillman, B. W. Two methods of facilitating classroom learning: Implications for the counselor–consultant. *The School Counselor*, 1969, *17*, 131–37.

Hirsch, J. Learning without awareness and extinction following awareness as a function of reinforcement. *Journal of Experimental Psychology*, 1957, *54*, 218–24.

Homme, L. Contingency management. *Newsletter*, American Psychological Association, Division of Clinical Psychology, 1966, *5*: 4.

*Hopkins, B. L., R. C. Schutte, and K. L. Garton. The effects of access to a playroom on the rate and quality of printing and writing of first and second grade students. *Journal of Applied Behavior Analysis*, 1971, *4*, 77–87.

Hurlock, E. The value of praise and reproof as incentives for children. *Archives of Psychology*, 1924, *9*: 71, 1–79.

Jens, K. G. and R. E. Shores. Behavioral graphs as reinforcers for work behavior of mentally retarded adolescents. *Education and Training of the Mentally Retarded*, 1969, *4*, 21–27.

Johnson, R. B. Self-instructional packages: Good or bad. *Junior College Journal*, 1971, *42*, 18–20.

*Johnston, J. M. and H. S. Pennypacker. A behavioral approach to college teaching. *American Psychologist*, 1971, *26*, 219–44.

Kanfer, F. H. and A. R. Marston. The effect of task-relevant information on verbal conditioning. *Journal of Psychology*, 1962, *53*, 29–36.

Kangas, L. W. Integrated incentives for fertility control. *Science*, 1970, *169*, 1278–83.

Kaufman, B. Going back up the down staircase. *McCall's*, February 1972, 101 ff.

*Keller, F. S. "Good-bye, teacher . . ." *Journal of Applied Behavior Analysis*, 1968, *1*, 79–89.

Kennedy, W. A. and H. C. Willcutt. Praise and blame as incentives. *Psychological Bulletin*, 1964, *62*, 323–32.

*Kirby, F. D. and F. Shields. Modification of arithmetic response rate and attending behavior in a seventh grade student. *Journal of Applied Behavior Analysis,* 1972, *5,* 79–84.

*Klein, S. S. Student influence on teacher behavior. *American Educational Research Journal,* 1971, *8,* 403–21.

Kounin, J. S., P. V. Gump, and J. J. Ryan, III. Explorations in classroom management. *The Journal of Teacher Education,* 1961, *12,* 235–46.

*Krech, D. The chemistry of learning. *Saturday Review.* January 20, 1968, 48–50, 68.

Kuypers, D. S., W. C. Becker, and K. D. O'Leary. How to make a token system fail. *Exceptional Children,* 1968, *35,* 101–9.

*Lessinger, L. M. Accountability in public education. *Today's Education,* May 1970, *59,* 52–53.

Lloyd, K. E. Contingency management in university courses. *Educational Technology,* April 1971, *11,* 18–23.

Lloyd, K. E. and N. J. Knutzen. A self-paced programmed undergraduate course in the experimental analysis of behavior. *Journal of Applied Analysis,* 1969, *2,* 125–33.

Lovaas, O. I., B. Schaeffer, and J. Q. Simmons. Building social behavior in autistic children by use of electric shock. *Journal of Experimental Research in Personality,* 1965, *1,* 99–109.

Lovaas, O. I. and J. Q. Simmons. Manipulation of self-destruction in three retarded children. *Journal of Applied Behavior Analysis,* 1969, *2,* 143–57.

*Lovitt, T. C. and K. A. Curtiss. Academic response as a function of teacher and self-imposed contingencies. *Journal of Applied Behavior Analysis,* 1969, *2,* 49–53.

*McAllister, L. W., J. G. Stachowiak, D. M. Baer, and L. Conderman. The application of operant conditioning techniques in a secondary school classroom. *Journal of Applied Behavior Analysis,* 1969, *2,* 277–85.

*MacDonald, W. S., R. Gallimore, and G. MacDonald. Contingency counseling by school personnel: An economical model of intervention. *Journal of Applied Behavior Analysis,* 1970, *3,* 175–82.

McIntire, R., G. Davis, and D. Pumroy. Improved classroom performance by reinforcement outside of the classroom. *Proceedings of the 78th Annual Convention of the American Psychological Association,* 1970, *5,* 747–48.

McMichael, J. S. and J. R. Corey. Contingency management in an introductory psychology course produces better learning. *Journal of Applied Behavior Analysis,* 1969, *2,* 79–83.

*Madsen, C. H., Jr., W. C. Becker, and D. C. Thomas. Rules, praise, and ignoring: Elements of elementary classroom control. *Journal of Applied Behavior Analysis,* 1968, *1,* 139–50.

Maltzman, I., W. Bogartz, and L. Breger. A procedure for increasing word association originality and its transfer effects. *Journal of Experimental Psychology,* 1958, *56,* 392–98.

*Meade, M. Miss Muffet must go. *Woman's Day,* March 1971, 64 ff.

Mecklenburger, J. A. and J. A. Wilson. Performance contracting in Cherry Creek. *Phi Delta Kappan,* September 1971, *53,* 51–54.

Meichenbaum, D. H., K. S. Bowers, and R. R. Ross. Modification of classroom behavior of institutionalized female adolescent offenders. *Behaviour Research and Therapy,* 1968, *6,* 343–53.

More, A. J. Delay of feedback and the acquisition and retention of verbal materials in the classroom. *Journal of Educational Psychology*, 1969, 60, 339–42.

Myers, W. A. Operant learning principles applied to teaching introductory statistics. *Journal of Applied Behavior Analysis*, 1970, 3, 191–97.

Myrick, R. Growth groups: Implications for teachers and counselors. *Elementary School Guidance and Counseling*, 1969, 4, 35–42.

National Association of Secondary School Principals. Administrative internship project. *The Bulletin of NASSP*, 1969, 53, 3–18.

*Neidermeyer, F. C. Effects of training on the instructional behaviors of student tutors. *Journal of Educational Research*, 1970, 64, 119–23.

Nolen, P. A., H. P. Kunzelmann, and N. G. Haring. Behavioral modification in a junior high learning disabilities classroom. *Exceptional Children*, 1967, 34, 163–68.

*OEO performance contract results hide no successes. *Education Daily*, 1972, 5, 1–3.

O'Leary, K. D. and W. C. Becker. Behavior modification of an adjustment class: A token reinforcement program. *Exceptional Children*, 1967, 33, 637–42.

*O'Leary, K. D., W. C. Becker, M. B. Evans, and R. A. Saudargas. A token reinforcement program in a public school: A replication and systematic analysis. *Journal of Applied Behavior Analysis*, 1969, 2, 3–13.

*O'Leary, K. D. and R. Drabman. Token reinforcement programs in the classroom: A review. *Psychological Bulletin*, 1971, 75, 379–98.

*Packard, R. G. The control of "classroom attention": A group contingency for complex behavior. *Journal of Applied Behavior Analysis*, 1970, 3, 13–28.

Peterson, H. W. To look and look again. *The Journal of Teacher Education*, 1967, 18, 206–10.

Philbrick, E. B. and L. Postman. A further analysis of "learning without awareness." *American Journal of Psychology*, 1955, 68, 417–24.

*Popham, W. J. The instructional objectives exchange: New support for criterion-referenced instruction. *Phi Delta Kappan*, November 1970, 52, 174–75.

*Premack, D. Toward empirical behavior laws: I. Positive reinforcement. *Psychological Review*, 1959, 66, 219–33.

*Probing the brain. *Newsweek*, June 21, 1971, 60–67.

*Pogrebin, L. C. Down with sexist upbringing. *Ms.* magazine, Spring 1972, 1, 18 ff.

*Reese, H. W. and S. J. Parnes. Programming creative behavior. *Child Development*, 1970, 41, 413–23.

Reynolds, N. J. and T. R. Risley. The role of social and material reinforcers in increasing talking of a disadvantaged preschool child. *Journal of Applied Behavior Analysis*, 1968, 1, 253–62.

*Ripple, R. E. and J. Dacey. The facilitation of problem solving and verbal creativity by exposure to programmed instruction. *Psychology in the Schools*, 1967, 4, 240–45.

Risley, T. R. The effects and side-effects of punishing the autistic behaviors of a deviant child. *Journal of Applied Behavior Analysis*, 1968, 1, 21–34.

Ryan, T. A. Testing instructional approaches for increased learning. *Phi Delta Kappan*, 1965, 46, 534–36.

Sassenrath, J. M. Transfer of learning without awareness. *Psychological Reports,* 1962, *10,* 411–20.

Savoca, A. F. The effects of reward, race, I. Q. and socioeconomic status on creative production of preschool children. *Dissertation Abstracts,* 1965, *26,* 2327.

*Schmidt, G. W. and R. E. Ulrich. Effects of group contingent events upon classroom noise. *Journal of Applied Behavior Analysis,* 1969, *2,* 171–79.

Schwitzebel, R. and D. A. Kolb. Inducing behaviour change in adolescent delinquents. *Behaviour Research and Therapy,* 1964, *1,* 297–304.

Siegel, G. M., J. Lenske, and P. Broen. Suppression of normal speech disfluencies through response cost. *Journal of Applied Behavior Analysis,* 1969, *2,* 265–76.

Sime, M. and G. Boyce. Overt responses, knowledge of results, and learning. *Programmed Learning and Educational Technology,* 1969, *6,* 12–19.

Sopina, M. V. Self-concept changes in adolescents following behavior modification. *Dissertation Abstracts International,* 1971, *31,* 6268–69.

*Staats, A. W. and W. H. Butterfield. Treatment of non-reading in a culturally deprived juvenile delinquent: An application of reinforcement principles. *Child Development,* 1965, *36,* 925–42.

Staats, A., K. A. Minke, W. Goodwin, and J. Landeen. Cognitive behavior modification: "Motivated learning" reading treatment with subprofessional therapy-technicians. *Behaviour Research and Therapy,* 1967, *5,* 283–99.

Stillwell, C., J. W. Harris, and R. V. Hall. Effects of provision for individual differences and teacher attention upon study behavior and assignments completed. *Child Study Journal,* 1972, *2,* 75–81.

*Sulzbacher, S. I. Psychotropic medication with children: An evaluation of procedural biases in results of reported studies. *Pediatrics,* 1972 (in press).

Sulzbacher, S. I. and J. E. Houser. A tactic to eliminate disruptive behaviors in the classroom: Group contingent consequences. *American Journal of Mental Deficiency,* 1968, *73,* 88–90.

*Surrat, P. R., R. E. Ulrich, and R. P. Hawkins. An elementary student as a behavioral engineer. *Journal of Applied Behavior Analysis,* 1969, *2,* 85–92.

Terrell, G., Jr., K. Durkin, and M. Wiesley. Social class and the nature of the incentive in discrimination learning. *Journal of Abnormal and Social Psychology,* 1959, *59,* 270–72.

*Thelen, H. A. Tutoring by students. *The School Review,* 1969, *77,* 229–44.

*Thomas, D. R., W. C. Becker, and M. Armstrong. Production and elimination of disruptive classroom behavior by systematically varying teacher's behavior. *Journal of Applied Behavior Analysis,* 1968, *1,* 35–45.

Three reports of performance contracting now in action. *Instructor,* June/July 1971, *80,* 23–26.

*Treffinger, D. J. and R. E. Ripple. Programmed instruction in creative problem solving. *Educational Leadership,* 1971, *28,* 667–75.

Tyler, V. O. and G. D. Brown. Token reinforcement of academic performance with institutionalized delinquent boys. *Journal of Educational Psychology,* 1968, *59,* 164–68.

Valverde, H. H. and R. L. Morgan. Influence on student achievement of redundancy in self-instructional materials. *Programmed Learning and Educational Technology,* 1970, *7,* 194–99.

*Wahler, R. G. and H. R. Pollio. Behavior and insight: A case study in behavior therapy. *Journal of Experimental Research in Personality,* 1968, *3,* 45–56.

*Wahler, R. G., K. A. Sperling, M. R. Thomas, N. C. Teeter, and H. L. Luper. The modification of childhood stuttering: Some response–response relationships. *Journal of Experimental Psychology,* 1970, *9,* 411–28.

Webb, J. N. and B. B. Brown. The effects of training observers of classroom behavior. *The Journal of Teacher Education,* 1970, *21,* 197–202.

White, W. F. Personality determinants of the effects of praise and reproof in classroom achievement. *Proceedings of the 75th Annual Convention of the American Psychological Association,* 1967, *2,* 323–24.

Williams, R. L. and K. Anandam. The effect of behavior contracting on grades. *Journal of Educational Research* (in press).

*Williams, R. L., W. H. Cormier, G. L. Sapp, and H. B. Andrews. The utility of behavior management techniques in changing interracial behaviors. *The Journal of Psychology,* 1971, *77,* 127–38.

*Williams, R. L., J. D. Long, and R. W. Yoakley. The utility of behavior contracts and behavior proclamations with advantaged senior high school students. *Journal of School Psychology,* 1972, *10* (in press).

Wolf, M. M., D. K. Giles, and R. V. Hall. Experiments with token reinforcement in a remedial classroom. *Behaviour Research and Therapy,* 1968, *6,* 51–64.

C. Government Reports

*Cormier, W. H. *Effects of Approving Teaching Behaviors on Classroom Behaviors of Disadvantaged Adolescents.* Washington: U.S. Department of Health, Education and Welfare, 1970.

Kennedy, W. A. and H. C. Willcutt. *Motivation of School Children.* Washington: U.S. Department of Health, Education and Welfare, 1963.

Lewy, R. A. *Individually Prescribed Instruction and Academic Achievement.* 1969. ERIC:SP003210.

Prince, A. J. *Conditioning Children for School.* 1967. ERIC:ED019802.

Schramm, W. *The Research on Programmed Instruction.* Washington: U.S. Department of Health, Education and Welfare, 1964.

Spence, J. T. *A Study of Certain Factors Affecting Children's School Performance.* 1966. ERIC:ED011086.

D. Unpublished Documents

*Allen, K. E. Integration of normal and handicapped children in a behavior modification preschool: A case study. Paper presented at the 3rd Annual Kansas Conference on Behavior Analysis in Education, Lawrence, May 1972.

*Andrews, H. B. The effects of group contingent reinforcement on student behavior. Paper presented at the meeting of the American Personnel and Guidance Association, Atlantic City, N.J., March 1971.

Arwood, B., J. Long, and R. L. Williams. A systematic comparison of behavior contracts and behavior proclamations in a suburban high school. MS., The University of Tennessee, 1972.

Blase, K. A. and B. L. Hopkins. The modification of sentence structure and its relationship to subjective judgments of creativity in writing. Paper presented at the 3rd Annual Kansas Conference on Behavior Analysis in Education, Lawrence, May 1972.

Campbell, A. and B. Sulzer. Naturally available reinforcers as motivators towards reading and spelling achievement by educable mentally handicapped students. Paper presented at the meeting of the American Educational Research Association, New York, February 1971.

Chadwick, B. A. and R. C. Day. Systematic reinforcement: Academic performance of Mexican–American and black students. MS., University of Washington, 1970.

*Conlon, M. F., C. Hall, and E. M. Hanley. The effects of a peer correction procedure on the arithmetic accuracy for two elementary school children. Paper presented at the 3rd Annual Kansas Conference on Behavior Analysis in Education, Lawrence, May 1972.

*Copeland, R. E., R. Brown, and R. V. Hall. The school principal and behavior analysis. Paper presented at the 3rd Annual Kansas Conference on Behavior Analysis in Education, Lawrence, May 1972.

*Davis, M. Some effects of having one remedial student tutor another remedial student. Paper presented at the 3rd Annual Kansas Conference on Behavior Analysis in Education, Lawrence, May 1972.

Finkler, J. B. Rate of acquisition and level of retention of a verbal operant behavior as a function of contingency instructions. Ed.D. diss., The University of Tennessee, 1971.

Goetz, E. M. and M. M. Salmonson. The effect of general and descriptive reinforcement on "creativity" in easel painting. Paper presented at the 3rd Annual Kansas Conference on Behavior Analysis in Education, Lawrence, May 1972.

*Harris, V. W., J. A. Sherman, and D. G. Henderson. The effect of a tutoring procedure on the spelling performance of elementary classroom students. Paper presented at the 3rd Annual Kansas Conference on Behavior Analysis in Education, Lawrence, May 1972.

Hayes, J. E. and R. P. Hawkins. An analysis of instruction duration as a consequence for correct and incorrect answers. Paper presented at the meeting of the American Psychological Association, Miami Beach, September 1970.

Jessee, R. E. The effects of points and backup reinforcers on appropriate classroom behavior. M.S. thesis, The University of Tennessee, 1971.

*Long, J. D. The comparative utility of structured lessons, group and individually contingent events, and conditioned reinforcers in modifying classroom behaviors. Ed.D. diss., The University of Tennessee, 1972a.

Long, J. D. The comparative utility of three levels of token reinforcement in a class of behaviorally retarded students. MS., The University of Tennessee, 1972b.

Malott, R. W. Contingency management in an introductory psychology course for 1000 students. Paper presented at meeting of the American Psychological Association, San Francisco, 1968.

McEwen, J. H. An examination of the effects of manipulating setting events on the behavior and academic achievement of secondary school students. Ed.D. diss., The University of Tennessee, 1972.

*Nedelman, D. and S. I. Sulzbacher. Dicky at 13 years of age: A long-term success following early application of operant conditioning procedures. Paper presented at the 3rd Annual Kansas Conference on Behavior Analysis in Education, Lawrence, May 1972.

Patterson, G. R. and A. Harris. Some methodological considerations for observation procedures. Paper presented at meeting of the American Psychological Association, San Francisco, 1968.

Rayek, E. and E. Nesselroad. Application of behavior principles to the teaching of writing, spelling, and composition. Paper presented at the 3rd Annual Kansas Conference on Behavior Analysis in Education, Lawrence, May 1972.

Sajwaj, T., S. Twardosz, N. Kanter, and M. Burke. Side effects of extinction procedures in a remedial preschool. Paper presented at the meeting of the Southeastern Psychological Association, Louisville, 1970.

*Salzberg, C. The development of freedom and responsibility in elementary school. Paper presented at the 3rd Annual Kansas Conference on Behavior Analysis in Education, Lawrence, May 1972.

*Sapp, G. L. The application of contingency management systems to the classroom behavior of Negro adolescents. Paper presented at the meeting of the American Personnel and Guidance Association, Atlantic City, N.J., 1971.

Sears, P. and D. H. Feldman. Changes in young children's classroom behavior after a year of computer-assisted instruction: An exploratory study. Research Memorandum No. 31, Stanford Center for Research and Development in Teaching, 1968.

*Sherman, T. M. An examination of the relationship between student behavior change and teacher mode of response. Ed.D. diss., The University of Tennessee, 1971.

*Stephens, I. L. B. The role of the principal in modifying teachers' in-class behavior. Ed.D. diss., The University of Tennessee, 1972.

Sulzer, B. Match to sample performance by normals and institutionalized retardates under different reinforcing conditions. Doctoral diss., University of Minnesota, 1966.

Walker, H. M., R. H. Mattson, and N. K. Buckley. Special class placement as a treatment alternative for deviant behavior in children. University of Oregon, Monograph No. 1, 1969.

Williams, F. E. Practice and reinforcement as training factors in creative performance. Doctoral diss., University of Utah, 1965.

*Willis, J., J. Crowder, and B. Morris. A behavioral approach to remedial reading using students as behavioral engineers. Paper presented at the 3rd Annual Kansas Conference on Behavior Analysis in Education, Lawrence, May 1972.

Wilson, A. W. Aversive properties of an auditory stimulus as a function of association with removal of group contingent reinforcement. Ed.D. diss., The University of Tennessee, 1971.

Wilson, S. The use of group contingent free time in a first grade class. MS., The University of Tennessee, 1972.

Index